HAROLD SHIPMAN
MIND SET ON MURDER

Why Shipman Killed and Killed Again
The True Story

Carole Peters

CARLTON
BOOKS

First published in 2005 by
Carlton Books Limited
An imprint of the
Carlton Publishing Group
20 Mortimer Street
London W1T 3JW

ISBN 184442 587 8

Typeset by E-Type, Liverpool
Printed and bound in Great Britain by Mackays

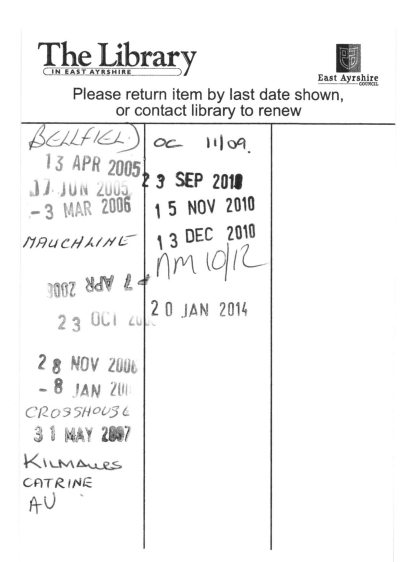

CONTENTS

ACKNOWLEDGEMENTS

My grateful thanks to Brian Lapping for his support and encouragement.

To Beth, Anna, Tina, Tim, Mark and Safi who are not only a very talented documentary team, but also my mates.

I am eternally grateful also to Brian Whittle for his detailed research into Fred Shipman's early life. The information he amassed not only formed the basis for the section on Shipman's childhood in my ITV documentary but provided the research material for much of an analysis carried out by the criminal profilers I consulted.

To all the contributors, on and off the record, thank you for having us in your homes. But for revisiting some of the saddest moments of your lives for me, no thanks will ever be enough here.

And finally to DC and DD – without either I could not have got through to the end.

FOREWORD

Do you expect Santa Claus to come and steal your Christmas presents? Of course you don't. Do you expect your GP to be the person who's coming to kill you? Why on Earth would he come to kill little old Aunt Mary? Isn't he looking after us all? Isn't he happily married? Isn't he a pillar of the community, doesn't he have children and all of the rest of it? Of course there's nothing wrong with him, I'd trust him with my life. You'd be wrong.

Paul Britton, criminal and forensic psychologist

At the beginning of 1998 I wrote a proposal for a television documentary that attempted to use forensic psychology to look at Britain's most infamous serial killers. As an opening line I used as a quote from Bill Waddell, the former curator of Scotland Yard's Black Museum.

'*Somewhere out there, there's a serial killer at work. Now. We just haven't discovered him.*'

Those words seem all too prophetic now.

Within weeks of the proposal being accepted by ITV, the newspaper headlines proclaimed the discovery of a new serial killer, possibly the most prolific this country had known; worse still a family GP.

I filmed the series *To Kill and Kill Again*, in 2000, just after the doctor's conviction for the murder of 15 of his patients. It seemed only right that we should look at the case and we carried out a number of interviews with key people involved in the police investigation. However, it was clear to me that any forensic psychology would have to wait until the whole story of Shipman's crimes was revealed.

But, while I waited, a high-profile drama documentary starring James Bolam appeared to remove the need for an old-fashioned in-depth forensic documentary. But never one to give up, in 2003, I once again approached ITV with a proposal to make a 90-minute special on D. Harold Frederick Shipman and his crimes. The Final Report of the Shipman Public Inquiry was due to be published in the summer of 2004. It was an ideal time to screen a documentary.

Then, just two days into our research, yet again my documentary subject matter collided head on with current affairs – Shipman committed suicide in prison.

It now seemed, in every way, the relatives of his victims could at last have closure.

While I am well aware that these relatives and friends wish to put the past behind them and I hope that with the publishing of the final stage of the Inquiry Report, they can. But many felt it important to take part in a final definitive documentary that would become a lasting memorial to their loved ones; others merely felt it was important that we are all made aware of the whole shocking history of Shipman and his crimes.

Still, it seems, they all had two key questions left unanswered by Shipman's death – how and why did Harold Frederick Shipman kill and kill again?

As with the ITV Documentary, this book is an attempt to answer these two questions and in the pages that follow, I have hopefully been able to add a greater depth and understanding than was possible in 90 minutes of television. And I thank all those who took part in the documentary for allowing me to use their words here. I hope it helps.

The recollections of the relatives and friends helped me to personalise the narrative of this tragic case, but I could not have told the whole story without the help of those who were involved in the case professionally, from the police officers, especially Bernard Postles and Chris Gregg, through to those like Brian Whittle who recorded the events as they unfolded, and of course all those involved in the Public Inquiry. Dame Janet Smith's Reports are as insightful they are compassionate.

It is important to point out that in both the documentary and this book the understanding of how and why Shipman killed comes not from me, but from the criminal and forensic psychologists who have provided me with an amazing guide to the workings of the minds of serial killers. They are first to point out that this is not an exact science, it relies on interpretation, but I feel I am dealing with the best interpreters there are and I'm sure you will agree. So I thank them for their time and perceptions.

Serial killers pick their victims from the vulnerable, from the exposed. It is no coincidence that the victims of serial killers are mainly prostitutes or the homeless. Serial killings are also known as stranger killings and as one senior police office once said to me, who else but prostitutes, runaways and the desperate would get in the car, open the door or go somewhere alone with a stranger?

But Dr Shipman wasn't a stranger to his victims. They were vulnerable, often elderly, living alone, but they would certainly never have opened their door to a stranger.

They trusted him because he was their doctor and he preyed on that trust.

The mother of one of Fred and Rosemary West's victims once asked me why serial murders are always known by the killer's or killers' names, not the victims'. 'It makes them seem more important than those they killed, that's not true and it's not fair.' She said.

I agree, so I hope in some way this book will be a memorial to the victims, it is their stories that fill this book as much as his. His story is here only to help their loved ones find answers.

Finally in way of explanation, the figures relating to the numbers of possible murder victims combine those deaths that Dame Janet Smith believed were unlawful killings with those that were suspected of being unlawful killings, I am well aware that this may be seen by some as an attempt to achieving the most sensational of totals, but this is not the reason.

It is simply the fact that the relatives in the cases, where the evidence allows Dame Janet only to suspect unlawful killings, feel strongly the deaths should be included in any final figures.

THE MAYORESS AND THE TYPEWRITER

I think it did need something as bizarre as my mum's will, because you trust a doctor, don't you. That's what it's all about. Everybody trusts their doctor and you don't look back and think has he killed them.

Angela Woodruff

Wednesday in Hyde is a busy day. Like most of the small industrial towns on the south-west fringe of Manchester, at its centre is a large gothic town hall overlooking an outdoor market. In Hyde's heyday, when a number of imposing red-brick mills produced cotton for the rest of the world, the home of the town's municipal leaders reflected its wealth and status.

But time has not been kind to Hyde. The mills have long since been demolished or the interiors that were once packed with noisy looms have been divided up into small, cheap-rent industrial units – at best, home to pine furniture sellers, at worst, left empty, windows smashed and walls vandalised. Nowadays, the only cotton found for sale here will be cheap foreign imports spread out on the stalls in the market.

Hyde, like many of its population, is now in its twilight years and living on a lower income than it did when it was younger. But that doesn't mean it is tired of life. The market has recently had a makeover with brightly coloured canopies and there's plenty of new building and renovation work going on. In other words, Hyde, like its elderly population, still has plenty of energy and a future to look forward to.

Old traditions die hard here. The midweek shop is an institution here. It ensures that the market is always bustling on a Wednesday, while the pensioners' luncheon club at Werneth House is an ideal stopping-off point on the way to or from a town-centre shop.

But on Wednesday, June 24, 1998 the club had a problem – there was no lunch. It seemed that the Club's organiser, who shopped for the food, and helped prepare and serve it, hadn't turned up. At 81, Kathleen Grundy was a good twenty years older than the other volunteers and even some of the club members, but that didn't seem to make a difference to her.

From the descriptions given to me of Kathleen Grundy, I can picture a very elegant, vibrant and enthusiastic person. It seems she was always busy; friends describe her as dashing everywhere, someone who couldn't sit still for a moment. 'She was a 25-year-old in an 80-year-old body. That's my summing up of Kathleen,' John Shaw, her friend and regular taxi driver, told me during our interview.

Illness seemed an unlikely reason for her absence. She had seemed fine the night before when she'd been round at a friend's house having coffee, but had left early so she could be home in time to watch the World Cup highlights on the television. Anyway, she would have telephoned if she had been unwell.

When they called her, there was no answer from her home phone. Concerned that the phone wasn't working, or that she had been the victim of an accident, two friends from the luncheon club decided to go round to check.

Kathleen Grundy lived in Gee Cross, about half a mile away from Werneth House. Still referred to as 'the village', Gee Cross is one of the oldest parts of Hyde. On the hill overlooking Hyde's industrial centre is Werneth Low, a ridge of land that separates the Peak District hills and Lancashire moors from the flood plain of the River Mersey, home to the urban sprawl of Manchester and Liverpool. You descend into Hyde from Werneth Low via the steep narrow Joel Lane. It's a journey that gives you a potted architectural history of the industrial revolution. At the top of the Lane is a cluster of ancient rural cottages; at the bottom are rows of Victorian red-brick terraces and 1930s urban semis.

Halfway down is Loughrigg Cottage. The 17th-century stone façade has been darkened by the years of industrial pollution, but it is a picture-perfect cottage and had been Kathleen Grundy's home for longer than most people could remember. She had certainly lived there while her husband John had been Mayor of Hyde – he had died of a heart attack while climbing a mountain in the Lake District in 1968. Most people expected Kathleen would also go suddenly, probably in the middle of one of her many volunteer activities.

So when her two friends arrived at Loughrigg Cottage, just before noon on that Wednesday morning, they were prepared for the worst. Even so, they were more than a little shocked to find her front door open.

It was normally kept secure with two mortise locks and rarely used. Even when John Shaw picked her up in his taxi, he used the side gate and the back door.

'When I went for Kathleen, I didn't stand at the front door blowing my horn. I just simply went and tapped on her back door and saw that she negotiated those slippery slabs outside the cottage before she got in the car. Again, any time I took Kathleen to the station or took her back home again, I always took her cases into the kitchen; I made sure that everything was okay, that there'd been no intruders.'

As a former Mayoress and local councillor Kathleen Grundy was still invited to a number of civic functions. John Shaw explained to me that he would be called on to take her home after a Saturday night event. Kathleen would go into the house then give him a little signal. She had an old gas street lamp in her front garden with an electric bulb fitted. Kathleen used to flash the light on and off two or three times to let him know that she was okay.

But on the Wednesday morning things were not okay. Inside the cottage Kathleen Grundy was lying on her settee. She was fully clothed and curled up as if she was asleep. The only clue that she was dead was her colour. Her complexion was grey and her lips blue. It was 11.55 am.

Kathleen Grundy had one child, a daughter Angela. Like many of her generation Angela had moved away from Hyde. A successful solicitor, she now lived with her husband, David Woodruff, more than a hundred miles away in Warwickshire. That didn't mean mother and daughter weren't in regular contact. John Shaw's services would be called on three or four times a year to take Kathleen to the station. Although she had a car, she always made the trip to Warwickshire by train. They also talked a lot on the phone.

Angela Woodruff learned of her mother's sudden death from Hyde police. 'I knew that if it was the police at Hyde, it was something awful. And I was very shocked because I had spoken to her a few days before on the phone, and she was always very well.'

Angela explained that her first thought was to ring her mother's doctor. 'I phoned up Dr Shipman's surgery because I knew that he'd been to see her after she'd died. And he told me that he had in fact seen her that morning. I got the impression that she'd called him out because she'd been ill, from the way he'd said it, and he said that she hadn't been too well.'

Shipman explained that he had seen her mother the day before her death, just for a 'routine thing'. He was vague and mentioned chest pains, possibly due to indigestion. He said he had arranged to collect a blood sample the next morning. Later, during a police interview, he said that Kathleen Grundy had been to see him the previous day because she'd got wax in her ears and needed them syringing. He felt that she looked 'in poor

3

health' and he had decided to take a blood sample to check for diabetes and anaemia, but that the sample had to be taken first thing in the morning.

As the sample had to be available for collection at 11 am, Shipman visited Kathleen Grundy at 8.30 am. He said that when he called she was still in her housecoat and looked old and moved slowly.

His story seems improbable to Angela Woodruff. She believes that if her mother was well enough to answer the door she would have been dressed, especially as she expecting the doctor to call, and it is clear that she was expecting Dr Shipman to call the next day. The night before, Kathleen Grundy had told her friend that the doctor was coming first thing in the morning to take a blood sample. It was only much later that the friend recalled that Kathleen had also given a second reason for his visit – he had wanted her to sign some papers.

Interestingly, Dr Shipman did not mention the blood sample to either of the friends who discovered Kathleen Grundy's body and had called him out. In court, when questioned about the blood sample, he said he had been so busy that morning that he had forgotten to send the sample for testing. He threw it away, thinking he would have to obtain another. Previously, in his interview with the police, he had told them that he had sent it off, but that the sample had been lost by the laboratory.

There was no record of a blood sample being received at the pathology lab and they were at pains to point out to the police when contacted that they had never, ever lost a sample that had been sent to them.

Shipman was also less than consistent when it came to the cause of death. On his second visit to Loughrigg Cottage that Wednesday, Kathleen Grundy's two friends noted that the GP hardly examined the body of his former patient. He quickly announced Kathleen Grundy had been dead for two hours and had died from cardiac arrest. But, after a brief telephone discussion with the Registrar, it was agreed that 'old age' would be the cause on the death certificate.

The Registrar cannot register a death and has to report it to the coroner if the doctor who certified the cause the death has not seen the deceased for more than 14 days, or if the doctor was not called to examine the body just after they have died. He can also report the death if he believes, or someone else believes, it to be suspicious.

Dr Shipman had attended Kathleen Grundy just before she died and examined her body after death. As no one voiced any suspicions, the death was registered. The cause of death given by Dr Shipman was not questioned.

Angela Woodruff says, 'We met him at the surgery the following day and he gave us the death certificate and explained to us that he'd put on it "old age". I knew this wasn't right but I got the impression from him that she might have had a heart attack. And he said something about her being nominated for a prize. It was all very strange. I couldn't understand how she died. It just didn't make any sense to me.'

On the telephone the night before Dr Shipman had few words of comfort for Kathleen's grieving daughter. His voice had taken the slightly superior lecturing tone he used whenever he discussed medical matters with fellow professionals as he explained that some old people complain of feeling unwell a few days before they die then, as he put it, 'they just die'.

When Angela and her husband finally got to Loughrigg Cottage, things made even less sense. If her mother had been unwell, Angela would have expected to find evidence of it at her home. But the house was perfectly neat and tidy. Kathleen Grundy did all her own cleaning and the garden, her pride and joy, looked as if it had been tended that morning.

'All her geraniums were in the garden. It looked absolutely beautiful. The lawn was cut. I began to have theories like, perhaps she had been ill and he'd helped her to die, or perhaps she'd committed suicide for some reason I couldn't think of. It just didn't seem right.'

Angela put her initial concerns down to grief and shock, partly because she had a good reason for not wanting a post mortem to be carried out on her mother's body. 'When my father died, climbing in the Lake District, he had to have a post mortem and I had to identify his body after the post mortem. I was twenty-three and I still have the picture in my mind. I really didn't want to imagine that happening to my mother.'

So Angela busied herself organising the funeral and sorting out her mother's estate. Kathleen Grundy had been a relatively wealthy woman. Loughrigg Cottage was prime real estate in Hyde terms and she also owned a second cottage in the town and a flat in the Lakes. On top of this, she had a few well-chosen investments. The former Mayoress had always entrusted her legal affairs to her solicitor daughter, so Angela was well aware that her mother's will, written years earlier, left most of her estate to her close family.

But a second unexpected phone call from Hyde was about to bring Angela yet more shocking news. 'About three weeks after she died, I had a phone call from a solicitor in Hyde saying that he had a will, which had been sent to him on the day my mum died, and it was apparently a will that she'd made. He didn't know my mum at all and I didn't know him.'

The will appeared to have been signed and dated on June 9, 1998. It had arrived at the offices of the Hyde solicitors Hamilton Ward along with a typed letter signed 'K. Grundy'. The letter asked the solicitors to be execu-tors of the will and said that she intended to make an appointment to discuss this in the near future. The staff filed the will away and awaited further contact.

Six days later, another letter arrived in the post. This had no address but was dated June 28 and was also typed. The letter read:

> *Mrs K. Grundy of 79, Joel Lane, Hyde, died last week. I understand that she lodged a will with you as I, a friend, typed it out for her. Her daughter is at the address and you can contact her there.*

It was signed *S or F Smith*.

S/F Smith has never come forward, nor do any of Kathleen Grundy's family or friends recall her knowing anyone of that name. However, when, several weeks later, Hamilton Ward's probate manager, Brian Burgess, finally tracked Angela Woodruff down, the mysterious friend was the least of her concerns. 'I couldn't understand it at all, because I'd made her will years and years before and I had it, so he said he would fax it through to me, and he did.'

When Angela saw the will she was even more concerned. 'I knew it was nothing to do with my mother. It was typed on a typewriter, very badly typed, and she would never have typed anything. She had immaculate handwriting.' The typed will lacked all but the occasional full stop as punctuation. It was mainly typed in capital letters which were sometimes hard to distinguish. The E, W and A keys seemed not to have struck the ribbon, leaving gaps in the lettering on words like 'family' and 'reward'. Occasionally, lower-case letters were inappropriately used, as in the 'I' in the post code 'SKi4', which should have read 'SK14'.

'She would never have made a will like that because she was a professional sort of person. If she hadn't liked the will that I made for her, she would have gone to another solicitor and had it done properly. And my name wasn't even mentioned, it was just my daughter. The wording wasn't hers, and the signature wasn't hers either.'

However, the real shock was the fact that Kathleen Grundy appeared to have disinherited her daughter and her beloved grandchildren. Instead, she had left her entire estate to her doctor. The wording was simple and to the point. Next to the section marked specific gifts and legacies and after the words 'I give' was typed in the pale capitals:

… ALL MY ESTATE, MONEY AND HOUSE TO MY DOCTOR. MY FAMILY ARE NOT IN NEED AND I WANT TO REWARD HIM FOR ALL THE CARE HE HAS GIVEN ME AND THE PEOPLE OF HYDE. HE IS SENSIBLE ENOUGH TO HANDLE ANY PROBLEMS THIS MAY GIVE HIM.

The criminal and forensic psychologist Paul Britton says that, even at first glance, the wording of the legacy is interesting, that the author is giving this doctor a reference to the world, recognition of the great goodwill, the great work that he did for the people of Hyde.

Leaving everything to her doctor was not a completely bizarre thing for Kathleen Grundy to do. She had been a loyal patient of his for many years and she was not alone. His regular home visits and keen interest in the health of his older patients had encouraged the elderly of Hyde to register with Dr Harold Shipman in their hundreds. He was adored by most of them, who saw him as by far the best doctor in the area.

But what was bizarre was that the beloved doctor was not only the sole beneficiary of Kathleen Grundy's estate but also appeared, apart from the mysterious S/F Smith who had written to the solicitors, to be her sole confidant when it came to her plans to revise the will.

When he was asked by the two friends who had found Kathleen Grundy's body what they should do next, Dr Shipman had suggested they make contact with local solicitors Hamilton Ward as they would handle everything. Shipman had also commented to another GP in Hyde, only days after Kathleen Grundy's death and before the will was discovered, that he was about to come into an inheritance and was planning to move to France, to retire, 'very soon'.

Later, when the police visited him to question him about the will and its contents, he provided Detective Superintendent Bernard Postles, the man in charge of the investigation, with yet another exclusive fact about Kathleen Grundy. 'He was at the surgery, locking up, and when the officers arrived and showed him the warrant to search his premises he immediately indicated a cupboard that held a typewriter. He also told us that on occasions Kathleen Grundy had borrowed the typewriter, but he was unable to tell us when she returned it to him.'

The portable Brother typewriter had misaligned E, A and W keys, which meant that they often failed to strike the ribbon properly. This made anything typed on it distinctive and instantly recognisable. It was clear that the will and the letter that accompanied it had been typed out on this electric portable. A fingerprint expert would later find no prints from Kathleen Grundy on the typewriter, but he found the prints of both Dr Shipman and his wife, Primrose.

Angela Woodruff knew nothing of this at the time, but still had strong suspicions that Shipman had forged her mother's will. As a lawyer she was also well aware of the legal implications of accusing a doctor of forgery.

Angela knew that they needed hard evidence and that required some detective work. The first thing they needed to do was verify the signatures on the will. When compared with her normal handwriting and signature, Kathleen Grundy's name on the will looked as if it might have been traced. So what about the signatures of the witnesses?

David Woodruff spent the next few days in Hyde Library and managed to find out that both the names of the witnesses were real people. The next stage was to find out if they had actually witnessed the will. The first to be tracked down was Claire Hutchinson. 'Her husband came to the door and we said to him, "We understand that your wife's witnessed a will." That was our mistake because we weren't very good detectives. We shouldn't have said a will, but anyway we did. And Claire was there and she said she had witnessed a will, at Dr Shipman's surgery.'

It took another three days for the amateur sleuths to find the second witness, Paul Spencer. This time, Angela deliberately did not use the word 'will'. She just asked Paul if he had signed something in the surgery. He said he had but, when the couple showed him a copy of the will, he shook his head and said, 'That's not my signature.'

On June 10 Paul Spencer had been in the surgery waiting to see the doctor. The only other patient waiting was young mum Claire. Both remember Dr Shipman sticking his head round his consulting room door and asking them if they minded being witnesses to a signature. He beckoned them into his room and sitting inside on the patients' chair next to Shipman's desk was an elderly lady. Paul Spencer recalls Shipman asking the elderly woman: 'Are you sure this is OK, Kath?' He then produced a document that had been folded in such a way that neither Paul Spencer nor Claire Hutchinson could see anything but the name Kathleen Grundy and a signature.

The two were told to print their names and addresses and sign where indicated. Unwittingly, they had just signed Kathleen Grundy's death warrant.

After meeting the witnesses, Angela Woodruff felt that she had the missing pieces to the puzzle of the will. About two weeks before her death, Dr Shipman had asked Kathleen Grundy to participate in a survey on ageing and had told her that one of his colleagues at Manchester University was involved in the research. Dr Shipman told her that, as she was an extremely healthy person, they wanted to know what her secret was.

There was no colleague and no survey, but the flattery worked. Kathleen Grundy agreed to take part in the survey and Dr Shipman explained that she'd have to give a blood sample. He then told her that she needed to sign a consent form for the survey. It was probably this form that Paul Spencer and Claire Hutchinson witnessed. Detective Superintendent Bernard Postles believes Shipman had thought the whole process through.

'He had been very clever in obtaining signatures of genuine individuals. If somebody made some cursory checks they would see those individuals existed. He thought that tracing over the genuine signature might enable him to pass off any enquiries that were made in relation to it. But he was very poorly informed about the process of criminal investigation.'

Bernard Postles believes that Shipman later traced the signatures of Kathleen Grundy and Claire Hutchinson onto a copy of the will. But for some reason he chose to rewrite Paul Spencer's signature instead of tracing over it as he had done the others.

At this stage, Dr Shipman was facing a much larger complication to his plan, as Angela Woodruff explained. 'He said the results of the tests would go to my mum, to her doctor, Dr Shipman, and to her solicitor. So my mum said, "Well that's my daughter." So he said, "Oh that's OK, that's fine."'

Clearly it was not fine.

The news that Kathleen Grundy's daughter was her solicitor was not good. For Shipman's plan to work the will had to go to someone who would not check back with Kathleen Grundy. His solution was to send it to different solicitors. Hamilton Ward were probably chosen because their offices were just round the corner from Shipman's surgery.

With hindsight, this seems reckless behaviour but, according to criminal psychologist Julian Boon, this all made perfect sense to Shipman. After all, he could not conceive of anyone suspecting him, a doctor, of forging the will. 'This obviously forged document is something that he wouldn't even dream he would be questioned about. It is a perfect illustration of how he sees other people seeing him, as this solid, good doctor and also the idea that, if he presented this document, it would be taken as credible. It shows terrific delusions of grandeur and a complete sense of omnipotence over everybody else – "No one would dare question me!"'

Julian Boon is one of a number of real-life Crackers, psychologists who work regularly with the National Crime Faculty at Bramshill, building up profiles on killers and advising the police on interviewing techniques. The police asked him for a psychological perspective on the case. They looked at the will and Boon explained that the wording was extremely revealing. It gave a clear impression of how Shipman saw himself, in a very elevated, egocentric sort of way. This explains something of the confidence with which he was able to commit his crimes.

To start with Shipman had been right to believe he would not be suspected, as Angela Woodruff points out: 'It was so ridiculous to think that a doctor could have killed anybody. To actually believe that, I had to go through a lot of thought processes, but then to convince someone else that that had happened seemed almost impossible to do.'

But she was determined to try. Angela drafted a report of her investigations and showed it to one of her legal partners, who was a criminal lawyer. It took him just 30 minutes to read it and tell Angela that she needed to report Shipman to the police straight away. He spoke to his contacts at Warwickshire Police and within hours they had referred it on to Greater Manchester Police. They called Angela the following day and arranged to visit her two days later.

Detective Inspector Stan Egerton was sent to see Angela and she told him her suspicions, that the doctor had forged her mother's will and then killed her.

At the time of her first interview with Greater Manchester Police Officers, Detective Inspector Egerton had been more than impressed by Angela Woodruff and on his return to Hyde he immediately rang his boss Detective Superintendent Postles:

'I was brought in, a senior officer, at an early stage, because Stan realised the potential of it and realised that there might be something more to this than a forgery. The most logical explanation was that Harold Shipman forged that will and murdered Kathleen Grundy.'

Sixteen months later, just after the jury had found Shipman guilty of Kathleen Grundy's murder, Detective Superintendent Bernard Postles paid heartfelt tribute to Angela's determination and detective work. Standing outside Preston Crown Court, shortly after the verdict was announced, the senior detective admitted simply: 'Without Mrs Woodruff we would not be here today.'

Angela Woodruff had given the police the equivalent of a smoking gun but Bernard Postles needed to find the bullet. 'As far as I was concerned the very important piece of evidence that I needed was the cause of death of Kathleen Grundy. According to Harold Shipman she had died of old age. I found that incredible, given the description that had been given to me by her daughter and by other people who had been interviewed about her condition in the few days before her death, when she'd been fit and healthy.

'The only way that I saw that we were going to resolve this was actually to exhume the body and have a post mortem carried out.'

Dr Shipman thought he had made sure this could not happen. On the bottom of the will is a section marked 'funeral wishes'. The box marked 'cremated' had been ticked and in case there was any doubt, the box marked 'buried' obscured with four Xs.

However, throughout her life Kathleen Grundy had made it clear she wanted to be buried and, as the new will didn't surface until after the funeral had taken place, it was her wishes, not those of her murderer, that had been carried out. The headstone on her grave simply reads: *Died*

Unexpectedly After A Lifetime Of Helping Others. It is fitting that even after death she continued to help.

The exhumation of a body is not undertaken lightly. There are procedures to follow and rules that are designed to bring minimum distress to the family. Only a coroner can give permission for a grave to be re-opened and a body removed for post mortem examination and he needs a very good reason to give that permission.

When John Pollard, the coroner for South Manchester, received the formal application for the exhumation of Kathleen Grundy's body he had to balance the potential evidence that might be obtained from the body against the obvious upset to the family.

'The decision was made a little bit easier for me because I was aware that Angela Woodruff was a solicitor and I felt sure that she must have contemplated the likely outcome of the complaint she was making. My feelings at that time were obviously feelings of despair. You don't want to think that doctors are killing their patients. It's a horrendous thought.'

However, after hearing the evidence, John Pollard granted the police request and arrangements were then made for the exhumation to take place three or four days later.

In the early hours of the morning, Stan Egerton was joined by a detective constable, three scene-of-crime officers, three specialist workers from UK Exhumations, the unique company that is normally brought in to oversee the re-opening of graves, and a police photographer. Kathleen Grundy's grave was re-opened exactly one month after her mourners had stood at her graveside on 1 August.

The funeral directors who had buried Kathleen Grundy that day also attended the exhumation. Alan Massey is the third generation of his family to run Hyde's oldest-established firm of undertakers. He still finds the events of that morning upsetting. 'It felt all wrong, the exhumation. You see, we bury people, we don't dig them up, and that's what we were doing.'

For the process, the grave is covered with a white tent, which is supposed to ensure privacy, but good light is also vital so arc lights are used to illuminate the work. Unfortunately, they also make the sides of the tent transparent. Add to this the humming of the generators that power the lights and the noise of the mini-digger used to open the grave and the operation can hardly be described as discreet.

It wasn't long before the local residents were woken by the strange goings-on in the small graveyard and by morning it seemed that the whole town knew that Kathleen Grundy was being 'dug up because Dr Shipman had eased her passing'.

11

Dr Shipman seemed untroubled by the police investigation. Dr Wally Ashworth, Shipman's personal GP, remembers a visit he had from his patient that day. 'Shipman came to me and said that he was in trouble mainly because the police had taken his typewriter away as they were accusing him of forging a will. Then we heard it was a murder and a forged will. We thought the police had gone mad.'

Shipman even held a small press conference outside the back of his Market Street surgery. Among the first to arrive were a reporter and a photographer from a local news agency that fed the national papers, as well as local TV and radio.

The agency was run by Brian Whittle, a brusque northerner with years of sound journalistic experience and a nose for news. He was intrigued by the police interest in a forged will and a possible mercy killing. 'There was a story in the local paper about this doctor who was being investigated over the death of an old lady and the fact that he'd left been left a great deal of money in her will. A police investigation started. It was covered by the *Manchester Evening News* but not really picked up by the national press. I thought there was potentially a really good story in it and sent out a reporter and a photographer to see Dr Shipman. He was quite gruff and said a few words, posed for a picture and back he went into his surgery and that was more or less the end of it for a few days.'

When, for the documentary, I projected and slowed the news footage taken that day, I began to view Shipman in the same microscopic light as the criminal psychologists. In those few frames of video are clear clues to his personality, clues readily, if unwittingly, provided by his defiant stance, the folded arms and his arrogant dismissal of the assembled press.

Although the national papers didn't catch up until the end of the month, the local papers carried the story that night, mainly due to Brian Whittle's perseverance. He and his team stuck with the story for the next two years and it was his agency's picture of Shipman that provided the world with the unforgettable image of the bearded, bespectacled, serial-killing GP.

Back inside the surgery, Dr Shipman was greeted by a group of patients who had come down to offer their support. They were led by a former detective and the administrator of Shipman's Patient Fund, Len Fellows: 'I just said, "By heck, Fred, this will business is causing you a lot of grief", and he said, "Oh, don't, tell me about it" and that was the end of the conversation because I didn't think he'd done it.'

Peter Wagstaff had also called in to offer his support to the man who had been his family doctor for twenty years. Shipman confided in his patient that he was just hoping after the exhumation that the post mortem didn't reveal, in his words, 'as much as an aspirin'.

*

But they did find much more than an aspirin.

Julie Evans, the toxicologist from the Forensic Science Unit at Chorley, couldn't believe her luck when she found morphine quite soon. In some ways Shipman's choice of drug was fortunate as morphine is relatively stable and it remains in the tissues of the body for a significant time after death.

The unit had been sent samples of Kathleen Grundy's muscle tissue and liver and Julie Evans had been assigned to the case. The test produces a graph showing the various levels of different chemicals in the sample. The morphine peak was sizeable.

Detective Superintendent Bernard Postles also feels he owes a great deal to good fortune: 'We were lucky that he picked something detectable. My discussions with the toxicologist Julie Evans and the pathologist Dr John Rutherford shortly after the post mortem revolved around what the drug was that had been utilised. They had talked about drugs that occur naturally in the body and would be difficult to identify as being at a level indicating they been administered for a purpose other than therapeutic.'

Bernard Postles felt it important to warn Angela Woodruff that this might be the case.

'He told me that if Shipman had used insulin then we'd never be able to find it and so would never know, and that to me was a kind of nightmare. I needed desperately to know how she'd died.'

But the FBI's most senior profiler believes the choice was logical from Shipman's point of view. Colonel Robert Ressler, who interviewed most of America's serial killers during his long career with the Federal Bureau of Investigation, looked at the Shipman case for the documentary.

'A medical doctor who has access to various forms of drugs will utilise more sophisticated ways of killing rather than strangling or stabbing. They'll use poisons or injections and things of that nature to stop life scientifically. He had a ready supply of it; it would be fairly easy for him to get fairly large amounts of diamorphine or morphine.'

Just as with the forged will, there is a contradiction. As a doctor, Shipman's medical training would have made him aware that morphine could be detected in the body after death and, as Julie Evans and Dr John Rutherford pointed out to Bernard Postles, Shipman could have chosen a wide variety of drugs that would not have been detected. As the investigation continued, Bernard Postles discovered that Harold Frederick Shipman simply believed that the morphine would never be found, because he believed it would never be looked for.

But it had been found and it had confirmed Angela Woodruff's suspicions: her mother's doctor had murdered his adoring patient. 'I believe that on the day she died, Dr Shipman said to her that he needed another blood sample, which had to be taken early in the morning for this survey of the ageing. He told us that he had gone to take a blood sample from her, although he'd said it was because she hadn't been feeling very well.

'So he went to her house before surgery and he told us that she wasn't dressed, but I know that she would be dressed, because she'd be all smart and waiting for the doctor. And of course he said he was taking a blood sample, but he injected her with diamorphine and left her.'

We can only guess at the amount of diamorphine Shipman injected into Kathleen Grundy, but the levels were high enough to rule out any chance of it coming from an over-the-counter medical preparation. She would have had to take in the order of a litre of kaolin and morphine to get to the levels found.

Angela has one consolation. 'I've been told that she'd be dead within about five minutes, probably unconscious within two.' The pathologist Dr John Rutherford explained that one of the advantages of morphine is that it is a depressor of brain activity as well as respiratory activity or breathing, so people become calm and relaxed and this leads to a very peaceful death.

It may have been peaceful, but it was still murder and the police needed to make arrangements to arrest Dr Shipman and interview him. However, that wasn't something that they were going to rush into. Shipman had a very good reputation in the area and what the police didn't want to do was arrest him with the blaze of the media spotlight upon them, only to have to release him again.

'We needed to consolidate the evidence that we had, the intelligence that we had and to utilise that wisely when he was interviewed,' Bernard Postles explained to me as he talked me through the police strategy.

'We decided to search both the surgery and his home on the same day and almost at the same time. This was because of this idea about the destruction of evidence. While we were uncovering evidence at one site further evidence might have been destroyed at the other. This was a possibility we had to guard against.'

Dr Shipman might have still believed he was above suspicion, but one of his patients knew differently. A former detective sergeant, Len Fellows was a good friend of Detective Inspector Stan Egerton. 'Stan and I were Masons and I had got another fellow Mason who was a patient of Shipman's to organise a hot pot supper at the Masonic Hall to raise money for the Patient Fund.

'Anyway, Stan whispered in my ear, "Please don't tell anybody but Mrs Grundy is full of morphine. I'm making an appointment for him to come to the police station and I'm going to be arresting him for murder." So he said that the social had better be cancelled.'

The hot pot supper was cancelled and the police chose that Saturday morning to arrive unannounced at Shipman's house and surgery. The Shipman family home is a modest semi situated in the leafy Roe Cross Green in Mottram, a few miles outside Hyde. There the police first realised that all was not as it seemed with Dr Shipman. The officers who arrived that morning were shocked to find the family home filthy. One of them later commented that it was the sort of house where you wiped your feet on the way out, not in.

Len Fellows confirmed this: 'Once, I'd arranged to collect Sam, Shipman's youngest son, to go and watch rugby and I went into the house and was taken aback by the state of it. It wasn't what I expected a doctor's house to look like. It was untidy and it was unclean. The carpet looked as though they'd had a scrum on it on a muddy winter's day.'

In the middle of all the mess the police found a large cardboard box in the house and in a carrier bag in the garage between them they contained the medical records of 150 of his former patients. Some were labelled with the word 'dead' written with a red pen.

They found Dr Shipman at his Market Street surgery. His manner was arrogant and supercilious and, as Bernard Postles explained, although he wasn't necessarily expecting the police, he seemed prepared. When they showed him their search warrant he immediately took them to the Brother typewriter.

'The warrant of course outlined the fact that we were looking for a typewriter among other things so it was hardly surprising, but he volunteered that it was in a cupboard. He was co-operative and gave Kathleen Grundy's medical records to the officers who went along to search, so he did not attempt to be obstructive at that stage.

'My view is that at that stage he believed he was going to bluff his way out of this, that he was above the people who had come along to search his surgery and it wouldn't be very difficult for him to give a coherent explanation about why Kathleen Grundy had died in the circumstances she did.'

Paul Britton believes he knows why Shipman was so confident. 'One of the things that separates out people like Shipman is they tell the big lie. Most people don't expect to murder someone and then simply say, they just died on me, and say it without a trace of concern. When people are in the presence of someone telling a lie they expect to see signs of stress. They expect to see little give-away signs.

'But doctors normally give none of those signs. They develop ways of communicating that are part of the job. Even when they give a patient bad news there tends to be no hesitation, no pauses, no inconsistencies. So, all of these things will help him to tell lies convincingly.'

Shipman would bring all his training into play two weeks later when the police made arrangements for the GP to go to the police station with his solicitor for an interview about Kathleen Grundy's death. Len Fellows remembers his friend Stan Egerton telling him how arrogant the GP had been. He apparently didn't think that a mere detective inspector should interview him – it should be a Chief Constable, no less!

The transcripts of his interview tapes reveal an arrogant manipulator. He clearly believes that he would not be kept behind bars for long. His word as a doctor would not be challenged.

Police and Criminal Evidence Tape Recording 7th September 1998

DS Walker: This interview is being tape-recorded and may be given in evidence if your case is brought to court. For the purpose of the tape could you tell me your full name, please?
Shipman: Harold Frederick Shipman

At the start of the interview, unaware of the results of the post mortem on Kathleen Grundy, Shipman still believed he was being questioned about the will and by this time he knew that the police had spoken to the two witnesses. His voice is firm and precise and his manner confident.

Shipman: Can I clarify something first? I've had a chance to mull over the questions this morning and I didn't make clear what happened when Mrs Grundy asked me to witness the will … at that point I stood up walked outside and got the two witnesses. That obviously didn't come out in this morning's interview and now I've clarified the situation.

Bernard Postles did not attend the interview but monitored it from an adjoining room. He did not expect to hear what followed:

'He was very different from other murderers I have interviewed. Many people who face murder allegations are either totally co-operative because they want to get it off their chests or they will hardly answer any questions at all and just put a barrier up.

'What Harold Shipman seemed to be trying to do was to verbally fence, in that he seemed to be thinking, "What answers I am going to give here? You will believe those answers and I will walk out of here."

'I believe he came to the police station that morning believing that by about five o'clock that afternoon he would have explained things away and gone back to the surgery and home to have his evening meal.'

Paul Britton has worked on a number of high-profile serial killing cases, including those of Fred and Rosemary West and Dennis Nilsen. He says Shipman's attempt to end the interview before it had even begun is to be expected:

'He clearly thought, "They can't touch me; they cannot connect this to me. I've been interviewed, I've been over all these different things. The very worst they can do to me is catch me with some administrative issues."

'Remember, this is a person who has always felt that the system owed him deference. The characteristics that we would think of as bravado are much deeper in him – arrogance, conceit, the belief that there is a huge distinction between his ability and that of those around him.'

Paul Britton believes the fact that Shipman couldn't control the situation came as a complete shock to the confident GP who had held a press call only days before. 'He's used to being able to deflect things by simple inter-personal stature. These are fairly well rehearsed but very narrow little routines. He's now discovering that he's in a much, much bigger arena and it's one that he's probably not well prepared for.'

Bernard Postles saw this at first hand. 'I think at the time when he realised that he wasn't going to leave he was incredulous. He was a doctor, he didn't actually say this, but it was almost written in his face. "I'm a doctor. I've given my explanation, you should be accepting it and I should be going home now."

'The next thing that he found difficult to come to terms with was that he was kept in custody overnight and was to go before the court the next morning. I think that he believed that, even if he was charged, as an upright member of the community he wouldn't abscond and consequently he would get bail.'

Getting bail meant getting surety. A crisis meeting was held at the Shipman family home to try to raise the bail money. Among those they asked to contribute was Shipman's own GP, Dr Wally Ashworth.

'I think they said at this stage they needed something like a hundred and fifty thousand pound bail. I believe they were hoping that I could provide something like eighteen thousand pounds.' A similar amount was offered by a loyal patient who ran his own carpet-fitting business, while Jane Stokes, who ran a sandwich shop business with Primrose Shipman, put up over twenty thousand pounds in bail money.

Wally Ashworth is a semi-retired GP. Like the other two, he has a comfortable home but nobody would describe him as rich, yet he was happy to act as surety for his patient. 'One doesn't suspect a colleague of murder and although he'd been a little bit aggressive at times – it's not unusual for doctors when they're working under stress to become this way – nobody in their right mind would ever at that stage have suspected him of murder.

'It made one think when they ask for that much bail, but still we expected it to be granted and so it came as quite a shock when the judge threw out the application. He did it most vigorously and this left us to wonder what all this was about and could he be guilty.'

During his police interview Detective Sergeant John Walker and Detective Constable Mark Denham made it very clear they believed the man sitting opposite them at Ashton Police Station was guilty:

DS Walker: I'd suggest to you that you injected Mrs Grundy with a fatal overdose of morphine that brought about her death.
Shipman: No. And you tell me that people in Hyde don't have access to drugs. I think you should talk to your drugs squad.

Shipman had assumed that Kathleen Grundy's body would be cremated and it must have come as a huge annoyance to him that his plans had been disrupted. His reply displayed an arrogance towards the officers, scoffing at their lack of medical knowledge.

Paul Britton believes Shipman assumed that all he had to do now was provide a medical explanation of why Kathleen Grundy's body contained high traces of an opiate drug. Shipman was, in his own eyes, the only expert in the health and lack of health of people around him. It was something he thought that he would be believed about.

During the interview he referred DS Walker and DC Denham to three particular entries in Kathleen Grundy's written medical records.

Shipman: You go back to the entry of 12th of 10th, 96 – here I've commented IBS [irritable bowel syndrome] again, odd pupils, small pupils, constipated, query drug abuse?
So then in July I deliberately have made the comment that she's having these IBS attacks every day. Pupils small, dry mouth, possible drug abuse again. Now I'm sure you're well aware that drugs like morphine, heroin, pethidine all cause constipation and small pupils.

According to the hand-written medical notes, Dr Shipman had written that he suspected that Kathleen Grundy's irritable bowel syndrome (IBS) had been caused by misuse of an opiate. The references to addiction were written in the margins or at the end of other notes and were clearly written much later than the original notes.

The police found no evidence of morphine-based drugs or syringes that would suggest drug abuse at Kathleen Grundy's home, and when they checked Dr Shipman's credit-card statements they discovered that he hadn't even been working on one of the days he claimed to be treating her 'addiction'.

It seems most likely that Shipman added these notes when news of the exhumation reached him. He would have realised that the morphine would be detected and had come up with a medical reason for its presence. He was accusing the 81-year-old former Mayoress of being a heroin addict.

No one who knew Kathleen Grundy could ever have believed that. She certainly could never be described as liberal-minded as far as drugs were concerned. The mere mention of drug addiction brought condemnation. Yet, despite this, Shipman assumed he would be believed.

Julian Boon sees it as yet another example of Shipman's ego and vision of himself as god-like, one more illustration, as with the will itself, of his supreme arrogance that, if he said something, he believed it would be accepted. His grossly inflated ego and completely distorted reality made him think that he was simply beyond question.

DS Walker could not disguise his incredulity at Shipman's claim:

DS Walker: Are you seriously suggesting that Mrs Grundy, a well-respected lady, who led a hard decent life, inflicted a fatal overdose upon herself? Are you really suggesting that to us?
Shipman: I'm not suggesting anything. I'm just telling you my worries about this lady at this time. I've said that I had my suspicions that she was actually abusing a narcotic of some sort or at least taking a narcotic of some sort over a period of a year.

Paul Britton believes that by now Shipman was finding it tougher going than he had thought it would be. 'I think that when you look at him giving what we now decide are preposterous accounts of the Mayoress as a heroin addict, it may not have seemed preposterous to him at the time.

'Firstly, remember he is having to respond on the hoof. He's now being asked very specific questions; they're not questions he expected to be asked. He is not used to being approached by people who are coming at him in a dedicated, continuous fashion.'

By the end of the day the police had charged Dr Harold Frederick Shipman with the murder of Kathleen Grundy. Shipman had murdered his former patient and forged her will to inherit her wealth. But the police never really considered greed as the motive – by now they were well aware that Kathleen Grundy had not been Shipman's only victim.

When we were originally contacted we were only aware of Kathleen Grundy's death being investigated. Having come back with the original indications of morphine we were quickly informed that we could be looking at numerous exhumations but the exact figure was always unknown.

Julie Evans, toxicologist

PSYCHOPATHS AND SOFTWARE

I think it's fair to say that within a fortnight we had come to the conclusion that this was bigger than anything that any of us had ever been come across in our careers or would in the future.

Detective Superintendent Bernard Postles

When, on August 20, the early morning delivery van dropped off the bundles of daily papers at the newsagent's on Market Street in Hyde it was already light, so anyone passing could have read the headlines …

DOCTOR IN PROBE ON 20 DEATHS – PATIENT KATH LEAVES HIM HOME ran a huge banner in the *Sun*. *WIDOW EXHUMED AS FAMILY CONTEST WILL* was the more subtle approach of the *Daily Telegraph*, while *The Times* kept to the facts: *POLICE EXAMINE 19 DEATHS AFTER WIDOW CHANGES WILL FOR DOCTOR.*

The copy underneath the headlines had been supplied by Brian Whittle and his team. They had been on the case since that first press conference outside the surgery. 'We got into the story early and then I had a stroke of good fortune in that I befriended Stan Egerton. From the contact with him it became apparent to us that before the Christmas of that year, the police had over a hundred names on a list.'

Although that information was still 'off the record', Hyde woke up to headline news proclaiming that their local GP had murdered at least one of his elderly female patients.

The news seemed improbable to most of those who opened their papers that morning. Dr Harold Frederick Shipman had a reputation as the best doctor in the area. Even those who didn't have him as their GP knew of him or knew someone who was registered with him. The bearded, bespectacled, fifty-something-year-old doctor was a well-known sight around the town.

He had been a GP in Hyde since the 1970s, but in 1992 he set up his own single-handed practice on Market Street in the centre of the town. In middle of a row of 1970s shops he was sandwiched between Hyde's two main medical centres, the Brook and Donneybrook. Most GPs would have struggled in that position, but not Dr Shipman. With over three thousand patients, he had the biggest patient list in Hyde and there was a queue of still more people, mainly elderly ladies, waiting for a vacancy so he could be their GP.

Len Fellows explains that the doctor was known as Fred. 'When I first joined his practice I knew him as Harold Shipman. Then one day he said that his relatives and close friends called him Fred. So from that day on I called him Fred.'

Fred Shipman had a reputation as an old-fashioned GP and particularly appealed to the elderly. Dr Jeremy Dirckze, who worked across the road at the rival Brook Practice, said this reputation was well earned. 'I did actually respect his medical practice at the time. He'd won plenty of awards for his practice for asthma care and heart care and he had a reputation of going beyond the norm for a GP. Patients would often talk about the way he would go out of his way to help them, and they still do.

'And I think that's what has made it so hard for people who knew him to accept and understand what had exactly been going on. There was never any inkling in his behaviour that he was this different character who would act in that way.'

It is true the age of his patients had led to him being given what would turn out to be an ironic nickname. As Brian Whittle told me: 'There was a joke made to a local reporter initially looking at the story – "Oh, you mean Doctor Death", because so many old ladies in the area seemed to be popping their clogs.'

But that was all it was, a joke, and it certainly didn't put people off wanting him as their GP.

Father Dennis Maher is the local Catholic priest and a great many of his elderly female parishioners were patients of Dr Shipman. 'From the day I arrived here everybody told me what a wonderful doctor we had in the town. I knew about him from the day I arrived in the parish. The priest who was here before me had left a little note for me, informing me that he had got me as a patient on Dr Shipman's panel and how fortunate I was that he was able to do this for me, because, he put in a little note at the end, he is the best doctor in the town.'

On the surface Father Dennis Maher is everything you would expect from an Irish Catholic priest down to the lilting brogue, but he is full of surprises. On the day he met me at Hyde's main cemetery he pulled up in a flashy BMW, sporting a very fashionable suede coat and cashmere scarf – presents from parishioners. I didn't dare ask about the car. Having seen him in this light, I wasn't surprised when he told me he had declined the honour of having Dr Shipman as his GP. He put it down to his Irish pride – he didn't like the old priest telling him which doctor he should to go to.

But Len Fellows, who ran Shipman's Patient Fund for six years, believes the father missed out. 'You couldn't, you really couldn't, find a more dedicated, conscientious GP. When my daughter was pregnant, she was going to go into hospital to have her second child, Andrew, but the baby arrived very suddenly abut eight o'clock one morning when she was still at home. They rang Shipman and within about twenty minutes he was at my daughter's house in Gee Cross. It didn't matter what time you rang him up. I had his home phone number and didn't have to wait for the surgery. I have asthma and once had an asthma attack at seven o'clock in the morning and he was here in twenty minutes.'

Len believes the Patient Fund was proof of just how popular Dr Shipman was. 'When he decided to go solo and moved to the Market Street surgery, I was quite taken with the surgery. It was like going into a BUPA waiting-room as opposed to going to the Donneybrook surgery, which was more like a railway station waiting room. I offered to buy him a piece of equipment or a picture for the surgery. And he said, "I've had a number of offers like that, Len, and I've been thinking of setting up a medical equipment fund for the surgery. And I was thinking that there was only one person I would like to do it for me – will you do it?"

'I got a pig and we put him on the counter, put a notice up in the waiting room saying what the aims were – to raise money to buy medical equipment. I thought if we raised a hundred or two hundred quid in a year we might be doing well. Anyway, he was obviously very, very popular with his patients because in the six years that the Patients Fund ran I raised nineteen thousand, two hundred and ninety-six pounds. Now in Hyde that's a considerable sum. But it showed what the patients thought of Shipman.'

Five years after his conviction, most people were at pains to tell me that, despite his horrendous crimes, Dr Shipman had also been a caring and dedicated GP. Even those who are relatives of his victims have stories to tell about what a good doctor he was.

Peter Wagstaff was one of his patients. 'One of the reasons that we thought so highly of him was that he just seemed to do the extra things other doctors might not. My dad died very suddenly when our youngest daughter Louise was only six days old. Obviously I was very upset but I didn't contact him at all, never thought to, and he just turned up in the evening to see if I was all right and needed anything, which I thought was amazingly kind and considerate. Throughout the twenty years he looked after us we had so much respect for him. In fact, we used to say what a pity Dr Shipman won't be able to look after us in our old age.'

Like many of his patients, Peter and Angela Wagstaff simply could not believe Shipman could be guilty of murder. Angela, a quiet, well-spoken, primary teacher, was so incensed at the newspaper reports that she rang up one of the news desks. 'I rarely phone people up to complain but I just could not believe it, the person they were implicating was not the Dr Shipman I knew. I said you know there are all these claims and there is nothing substantiated and I just think it's not fair. I felt it was a witch hunt.'

Within a few weeks of making the call a shocked Angela discovered that the doctor she had defended so vehemently was not only guilty of the newspaper accusations, but that he had also murdered her own mother-in-law. Unaware of their own personal connection to the case, Angela and Peter wrote a letter of support and took flowers down to the surgery.

They weren't the only ones.

'The surgery walls were covered in cards of support,' recalls Len Fellows. 'It was like going into the surgery at Christmas. These cards were pasted all over the waiting-room walls.'

Among the cards was one from Ann Smith, who worked in the local pharmacy and visited Dr Shipman's Market Street surgery every day to pick up repeat prescriptions. Two years later, Ann would discover that she too had a personal connection to the case. Dr Shipman had murdered her aunt.

While the national newspaper coverage had prompted a show of support from some of Shipman's patients, others had a strange sense of *déjà vu*.

Joe Kitchen is a local Labour councillor and familiar face in Hyde. His brother Mick, who is a lot shyer than his younger brother, is a taxi driver. The brothers had both been patients of Dr Shipman's since they were teenagers.

'I've known him since he came to Hyde,' Joe explained to me. 'He always came across as a very caring GP. He always had time for his patients; he did most of his visits himself and he did have a sense of humour at times – I can remember going to see him when I was in my early twenties. I had injured my back at work. I'd only taken my coat off but I'd obviously slipped a disc and I was in absolutely agony when I walked into his surgery. I couldn't stand upright and he just burst out laughing and said, "If you could see the way you look now."'

Joe had known Kathleen Grundy through their local council connections. 'I worked with her on the local council and a charity committee.

When I heard about Kathleen Grundy's death I was quite shocked because I knew her and she was always so healthy and full of life. Then it was in the papers that the police were investigating Kathleen Grundy's death and six other deaths. That's when Mick phoned me up and asked me if I knew whether they were investigating my mother's death.'

Alice Kitchen was 70 when she died, suddenly, at home in the afternoon. Her gravestone, like many in Hyde's main cemetery, contains a small picture of her set in an oval frame. It comes from a larger picture of the tiny Alice Kitchen standing between her two older sisters in their nun's habits. In her youth I am sure Alice Kitchen would have been described as pretty. Even in the photograph taken shortly before her death, you are aware of her beautiful and fine bone structure. But her delicate features and tiny frame disguised her undoubted strength of character. She had overcome a lot in her life. She had been sent to England from Ireland as a teenager. Neither Alice nor her two sisters would reveal the reason for her exile, but Joe says she once talked about him having an older brother he did not know about.

Joe's late father suffered from severe mental problems and Alice herself had a long history of mental problems that had meant the boys had spent time in care. But she fought hard to get her family back round her and lived with her sons Mick and Bernard, who was also a taxi driver, in a smart council semi on the outskirts of Hyde. She had eight children in all and when she died she had 21 grandchildren. After the troubles in her early married life, Joe Kitchen knew that keeping her family close to her was very important. She would often say these were the best years of her life, with her children all settled and lots of grandchildren to make a real fuss of.

Her neighbours in Kirkstone Road all knew and liked the little Irish lady who smoked like a chimney. She was always very welcoming and used to sit in the house facing the window so if anybody came down the path she'd drag them in and give them a cup of tea.

These habits, the sitting facing the window and the constant smoking, would highlight inconsistencies in Dr Shipman's story and made the boys suspicious about her sudden death. Alice Kitchen had died at her home on Friday, June 17, 1994. It was only when she died that her family discovered that she had celebrated her birthday on the wrong day each year and thought she was 66. The fact that she could pass for a woman four years younger was a testimony to her character and good health.

However, on that Friday lunchtime when Mick Kitchen left for work his mother was lying down on the bed. Five weeks before her death Alice Kitchen had been into hospital to have a hysterectomy. She had recovered well, but liked a have a little nap in the afternoon. Mick spoke to his mum through the bedroom door. 'Mick actually left the house round about one o'clock or just after. He spoke to my mother although he didn't see her because she was lying down at the time. She was obviously well because she offered to make him a brew before he went to work and he said he'd see her at teatime.'

Mick has gone over and over that last conversation in his head but he still believes there was nothing in her voice or manner to make him at all concerned, in fact they had discussed what she would cook him for tea. But on his return home from work at 6 pm, instead of finding his tea cooked and waiting for him, Mick Kitchen found his mother was dead. She was sitting on the sofa, dressed, her head slumped to one side, and she appeared to be asleep. She looked peaceful, although she had been sick. Her glasses were near her hand. There was a half-drunk cup of tea on a tray at the edge of the sofa and nearby was an ashtray with a half-smoked cigarette in it.

On the mantelpiece above the gas fire was a piece of paper that appeared to be torn from a notepad. It was from Dr Shipman and said that he had visited Alice and that she had had a mild stroke but had refused to go to hospital. The note asked Mick to take Alice to hospital or contact Shipman when he got in from work.

Mick called the doctor but he also called an ambulance. The paramedics who arrived were surprised by the note – one even commented to Mick that he had never seen anything like that written by a doctor before.

'I think it was while we were discussing that that Shipman actually arrived at the house. My brother had phoned him so he came and he explained to us the circumstances surrounding Mum's death. He told us that she had phoned the surgery saying that she'd got a cold and would he call round.

'Shipman said he arrived at the house round about four o'clock. She let him in but it was obvious to him that she'd had a stroke – she was dragging her foot and holding her arm and slurring her speech but she refused to go into hospital. I asked him why he didn't actually make her or let any of us know and he said that Alice insisted she'd wait for Mick coming home for his tea,' Joe explained.

A Post-it note written by a surgery receptionist requesting a home visit to Alice Kitchen was found at the surgery and a neighbour saw Dr Shipman leave the house about 4 pm. But these seem to be the only elements of truth in Shipman's story.

When I spoke to Dr Dirckze at the Brook Surgery, he told me that another doctor would have immediately questioned Dr Shipman's story. 'If a person has had a significant stroke it wouldn't really be possible for them to get up and answer the door to let somebody in.'

He also believes that it is unlikely that any medical practitioner would have left a patient alone in that condition. 'I think you have to respect the patient's wishes but if somebody was as seriously ill as that and totally unable to cope, I don't think a doctor would have left them by themselves. I personally would call an ambulance, regardless. I certainly wouldn't feel somebody could or should be left by themselves in that situation.'

But without access to a second medical opinion, Shipman knew his version of events would be believed, as Paul Britton puts it: 'He tended to focus on people who were surrounded by people who were manageable. One of the characteristics of the elderly people who were his prey is that the folks around them were ordinary people who could be guaranteed to trust and respect their GP.'

The Kitchens may have been 'ordinary people' who trusted Dr. Shipman but Alice's family no longer respected him. The fact that the doctor had left their mother on her own to die had angered Joe Kitchen. 'I didn't disbelieve him; I was more annoyed that he'd left her to die. I thought he would have done more as my brother's a taxi driver and their office is practically opposite the surgery. He knew that, so I just couldn't understand why he didn't do more to contact one of us.

'I did challenge him and his response was that if he had got her to hospital and she had had another stoke – and that's what's obviously killed her, the second stroke – she could've ended up paralysed in a wheelchair. So he said basically that it was in her interests to die at home where she'd want to be rather than in hospital and not suffering.'

Paul Britton gave me a psychologist's insight into Shipman's abrupt manner. 'I think that, when you look at his behaviour after death and with the bereaved, there are a number of things that you shouldn't lose track of. You have to understand that by now the value of the death for the killer is largely gone and that, in dealing with the family, it would be important firstly to give no inkling at all that this deceased person might have any particular value to him. I would expect, after the killing, to see some change in demeanour, even in a practised killer, some release of tension that may be expressed in the inter-personal behaviour to the family.'

At the time the family thought Dr Shipman had been incompetent, but when the newspapers carried the details of Kathleen Grundy's death Mick and Joe Kitchen began to suspect him of something far worse. 'The circumstances of Kathleen Grundy's death exactly mirrored my mother's case. Then there was the fact she was on the settee – she never sat on the settee as her back would have been to the window. She always sat in the chair looking out of the window. The cigarette was another thing. Mum smoked them down to the butt; she would never have stubbed it out.

'Then the next-door neighbour, who we'd known for about thirty years, told us something she hadn't mentioned before. On the day Mum died the neighbour came home round about four o'clock and actually saw Dr Shipman leaving the house and he never told her to keep an eye on Mum.'

Joe Kitchen rang the police and told them of his suspicions, but he wasn't the only relative to do this. In Warwickshire, Angela Woodruff had started remembering her mother telling her about the deaths of other patients of Dr Shipman. 'My mum had actually found a couple of her neighbours in Joel Lane. She used to do the shopping for one of them and one day she went round and found her dead in her chair. She was one of Dr Shipman's patients and so was another old lady that my mum had found, in her chair, fully clothed, apparently nothing wrong with her.'

But it wasn't just the deaths of two of Kathleen Grundy's neighbours that now seemed to Angela Woodruff to be remarkably similar to the sudden death of her mother. 'My auntie died four years before my mum, at home, sitting in her chair, with her newspaper on her lap and her glasses on. She was a patient of Dr Shipman and he had been round after she'd died. My mum was called immediately, and she was there when Dr Shipman came round. So we just thought, "Oh what a nice way to die." It's really strange, because I know old people don't die like that.'

Seventy-three-year-old Joan Melia had also died like that. She had been found dead in her sitting room just 12 days before Kathleen Grundy's body was discovered. A divorcée with no children, she lived on her own but had been having an on-off affair with Derek Steele for over ten years. He had taken her to see Dr Shipman that morning as she was suffering from a minor chest problem.

Joan Melia had been diagnosed with emphysema years before and always made sure she kept it under control, so any chest infection meant a trip to the doctor. She told Derek Steele that Dr Shipman had diagnosed pleurisy and pneumonia and that she had to pick up some antibiotics from the local chemist. At the same time she picked up some throat pastilles for her sore throat and then called in at the market to get a birthday card for a friend. Derek Steele then drove her home and, as she seemed tired, he suggested she should have a rest.

At 5 pm, he called round to her flat in Commercial Street to see why she wasn't answering the phone. When she didn't come to the door he let himself in, and found her looking as if she had just fallen asleep sitting in a chair with her glasses on and a crossword puzzle on her knees. She was dead and her body was cold. Derek Steele called Dr Shipman. When he arrived he simply looked at Joan Melia and commented that the tablets had not had time to work. He did not touch her and left the flat after just five minutes, saying he would make out a death certificate.

Joan Melia had thought very highly of her GP, but her niece Jean found the doctor rude and abrupt when she rang him to discuss her aunt's sudden death. In a blunt, insensitive and short conversation Dr Shipman said that her aunt had been very poorly when he saw her in the surgery the previous morning. He had told her to go home to bed. There was no point in taking her to hospital, as she might have died on the way there. He gave the cause of death as lobar pneumonia of two or three days' duration, with emphysema as an unrelated contributory condition.

Derek Steele and Joan Melia's relatives didn't know about the other sudden deaths or that Dr Shipman had given Alice Kitchen's relatives a similarly insensitive reason for what appeared to be a total lack of care by her GP.

But as Dr Jeffery Moysey from the Donneybrook Practice in Hyde pointed out, 'It is not a subject that relatives usually talk about to each other. Nobody had an overview of what was going on. So, while it would be unlikely to find every single one of them had died in relatively peaceful conditions, it was only Shipman who knew about them all.'

Maybe if the families had met and talked to each other alarm bells would have rung earlier. But luckily they did ring when the news of Kathleen Grundy's death hit the headlines. Joan Melia's niece rang the police.

All over the country it seemed that relatives and friends of patients of Dr Shipman who had died suddenly and unexpectedly were having similar thoughts. Within twenty-four hours of it becoming national news people started to ring the police incident room wanting to know whether the death of their loved one was one of the deaths that the police were investigating. Others claimed to have harboured suspicions in relation to a loved one's death for years, so they were added to the list.

But before the police could launch a serial murder investigation they had to rule out other possibilities. It was one of the areas that forensic and criminal psychologist Julian Boon was concerned with. 'My involvement initially was to try to see whether there was any possible rational explanation without a sinister connotation.

'So we looked very carefully at the cases to see if there was a possibility of any euthanasia angle. Shipman never claimed that, but it's possible that he might have been practising euthanasia and, because it wasn't above board, denying it later. But there was absolutely nothing to indicate euthanasia.

'We also looked to see whether there was any suggestion of malpractice, as in medical negligence, but there were simply too many for this to be the case. It would just be inconceivable that somebody could make that number of mistakes.'

Bernard Postles and the rest of his team now had no other option open to them. They had to face the fact that they had a serial killer in custody and a body count of victims that just kept rising. 'I found it incredible that we were virtually doubling the list that we had at that stage and starting to ask ourselves when it was all going to end.'

The incident room had received over a hundred calls and Postles and his team now had more than sixty deaths to investigate. This was a problem. A single murder inquiry can take weeks or months and complete and absorb the full attention of a whole team. The team worked in twos; they were given five or six names from the list to check out. If they found themselves dealing with one that was potentially a murder case then the others were passed back to be re-assigned. The problem was they just kept finding that they were dealing with a potential murder.

The team had to find a way of prioritising the cases. They came up with a scoring system that would prioritise the cases by the number of points they were given and decide the order in which they would be investigated.

Written on a wipe board in the incident room were four basic criteria that would allow the police to compile the strongest case for murder. A point would be given for each of these and a fifth point would be awarded if the case scored in all four areas. That case would then go to the top of the pile and become a top priority.

A point was awarded if the victim had been buried, not cremated. Cremation would have destroyed any evidence of morphine. The toxicology results on Kathleen Grundy had proved that post mortems on exhumed bodies could give the police hard evidence. A point was given to the case if the family had harboured suspicions over the years about the circumstances surrounding the death, as this meant circumstantial evidence could be added to the forensic evidence.

A third point was added if the evidence so far gathered by the investigating team had made them suspicious about the death, for example, if the cause of death on the death certificate was different from the explanation given by Shipman to the family at the time.

Finally, a point was awarded if the patient's medical records had been altered. This would show that Shipman had either planned the murder in advance or tried to cover it up after the event, linking him directly to the crime.

Dr Shipman prided himself on running a modern, efficient practice with all the latest technology at his disposal. This included an expensive computer system that held all the patient records on one database. Dr Shipman considered himself some sort of expert when it came to computers. At his previous surgery he had persuaded the doctors to computerise their system and, within a year of moving to his own practice, he had starting keeping a set of computerised medical records for each patient as well as his paper Lloyd George Notes (a record system for GPs first established in 1914).

'We didn't know what we could find from the records. It is almost an instinctive thing; you start looking round for evidence and you look in every place that you can and one of the places that we were likely to find it was in the medical records, the computerised medical records because we already had the paper-based ones, they'd been given to us by Shipman on the day of the exhumation.'

Once again Bernard Postles believed that luck played a huge role in the case. Greater Manchester Police had a dedicated criminal computer forensic unit. 'The thing that I hoped for was that some alteration had been made to the records and that was exactly what we did find. Alterations had been made. But even in my wildest dreams I couldn't ever have envisaged that we would get what we did get from the computerised records.'

Bernard Postles asked the head of the computer forensic unit, Detective Sergeant John Ashley, to examine the records of the 63 patients on his list and see what he could find. John Ashley left the force shortly after the case and moved to Virginia where he is a director of a company that specialises in investigating computer fraud. But, back in 1998, he had no idea how significant his findings would prove for the case and for his future career.

When he examined the computer's server he found it was protected with a high-level security password. In October 1998 Dr Shipman had updated the special medical software he used. Among the various additions to the new Medi Doc system was a security program.

It protected the records, only allowing access to those with security passwords. But, on the back-up on the main server, the programme also recorded the date and time of every entry. The information was encoded but John knew how to access it.

He contacted the manufactures of the software to get a super-user password that not only gave him access to the server but also allowed him to decode the hidden information recorded with each entry.

'I started to focus on the first 12 names I'd been given by Bernard, the ones who had scored three points. I printed off the full medical histories and then I started to dig deeper. Over a number of hours, into the following day, I started to see disparities between the dates on which records had actually been created and the dates of the entries on the notes.

'So I saw a pattern developing where maybe five or six records would be created on a given day within a number of minutes, out of sequence and historically going back two or three years. These records all related to the same medical condition for each person. So, on the face of it, the entry might be made in August 1997, or June 1977, or March 1998, but all three were actually typed in on the same date some time later, say, May 1998.'

The significance of the date and time that all these additions were made was lost on Ashley. He wasn't working in the incident room where the names and pictures of all the possible victims had started to go up on the wipe boards. Next to each name was the date they had died.

'I started to report my findings to Bernard Postles, Stan Egerton and the rest of the murder investigation team on the Wednesday afternoon. I had created a portfolio for each of the 12 victims to show my findings. I started with Kathleen Grundy and I detailed the dates and the times when the various alterations had been made to her records, backdated to make it look as if she had a heart condition.

'Right away, people round the room started to whisper. This date obviously meant something to them and I think it was Bernard who turned to me and said, "That was the date when Kathleen Grundy was murdered." We went through the other 11 records and on each of them the alterations I had found related to the date when the person had been murdered and normally prior to the body being discovered.'

Once the software timings were revealed, Dr Shipman's medical records acted just like a diary. The computer would be switched on some time before 8 am when he arrived at the surgery, entries would be made in patient records from 9 am and the computer would go quiet about 11.30. This tied in with the appointments system operated at the Market Street surgery. Appointments would start just before nine and end at 10.30 am then Shipman held an open surgery and would see patients without pre-booked appointments. This was scheduled to finish at about 11.15 am, but it always overran.

Shipman appeared to make no entries in his computer for several hours after that. This tied in with his habit of having a short and early lunch break with his staff and then going out to make home visits. He would return for evening surgery at about 4 pm. On Tuesdays an ante-natal clinic meant he didn't start home visits till after 1 pm and on Wednesdays and Fridays he scheduled them before and after his 2 pm till 3 pm clinics. The computer showed entries from about 4 pm, when he came in from his rounds and started entering notes. That was also the time when he created a false medical history for a patient he had just killed.

There was no premeditation. He hadn't altered the notes the day before or the week before. Paul Britton believes this is significant in working out a motive for Shipman's crimes. 'I think you have all of those possibilities of victim selection open to you. Some would have been earmarked for quite a little time; some would have been spontaneous; some might have been determined by the nature of the weather, where the parking was, it depends.

'I think that Shipman's caution with only altering the records after he had killed someone meant that he wasn't running the risk of altering the records in advance and then for some reason not being able to kill that person and then the changed record by happenstance being open to observation. So what it means is, he could rewrite the record with relative safety.'

Shipman was providing himself with a medical alibi and, even if he knew about the program's security features, the psychologists think he would have believed it impossible for the police to access it. In his mind they simply would not have the skill or intelligence to outwit him. Julian Boon puts it that Shipman thought of the police as 'contemptible plods', nowhere near his level of intellect.

So, when John Ashley arrived at the surgery and announced himself as a computer expert, Dr Shipman was naturally annoyed. 'The first time I met Harold Shipman was when we executed the warrants. Initially he verbally attacked me along the lines of, "This is critical to my surgery, I hope you know what you are doing. I hope you are not going to damage our network or the server or the information." So I responded quite forcefully and told him that I did this for a living and I knew exactly what I was doing.'

Dr Shipman then left the surgery, saying he was going home for his dinner. He returned about an hour and a half later. But this time he was not alone. He had brought one of his sons with him and his demeanour towards DS Ashley was very different.

'His personality had totally changed,' John Ashley told me. 'He explained to the son how I was a computer forensic expert working on his equipment and he explained to me how his son liked computers and tried to engage me in a personal conversation.'

This Jekyll and Hyde personality change comes as no surprise to the psychologists. Julian Boon explained, 'The reaction was one of contrition. As an expert in computers Ashley is, in a sense, Shipman's equal. So, he doesn't treat him in the same sort of condescending way he did Ashley, the police officer.'

John Ashley's visit hadn't gone totally smoothly. The confidentiality of medical records is a very complicated legal issue and Shipman's lawyer had successfully challenged the right of the police to seize them. A few days after the initial raid John Ashley and DI Stan Egerton returned to the surgery and returned the records to a smugly superior Dr Shipman.

'He was quite friendly, but he felt he had won a victory over us because we were returning the evidence. But Stan and I knew we would have the last laugh because we knew we were going to arrest him the following Monday and redo the whole process.'

The computer evidence on its own could not have convicted Shipman, but it was critical to his conviction. It also showed that Shipman had not premeditated his murders. The alterations were made in the hours after he killed, not before. He was simply covering his tracks.

The police now knew how Shipman had probably killed all his victims. The computerised records showed that they had all been visited by Shipman shortly before they died and that after the visit Shipman had returned to the surgery and changed their medical records, going back several years to make it appear they had been showing symptoms of a potentially fatal illness. That illness would then appear on their death certificate. Moreover, these mainly elderly, lady patients were all found in very similar positions – fully dressed either sitting in a chair or on a settee and, as the callers to the Incident Room explained, looking as if they had just fallen asleep.

High levels of morphine, like those discovered in the body of Kathleen Grundy, would easily account for why the dead all looked so peaceful, as if they had fallen asleep. Bernard Postles and his team had the probable method of killing – diamorphine. But could they prove that Shipman had access to that amount of what is a controlled drug?

When the police had first searched Shipman's home they had found a box that contained a number of different drugs. Among them were several ampoules of diamorphine that had been issued to a patient some years before and had obviously been in Shipman's possession ever since. Shipman claimed he did not have access to controlled drugs like morphine. Clearly he did, but the police needed to find proof that he had access to much larger amounts.

Once again, Bernard Postles called on the investigative skills of computer expert John Ashley to find out how much Diamorphine was prescribed to patients and whether any of the victims themselves had been prescribed it.

The computerised medical records listed the amounts and types of drugs Shipman had prescribed. Where he had prescribed Diamorphine for a patient the police could cross-reference this with the prescriptions at the local pharmacies. In that way they were able to work out the quantities that he was actually prescribing as opposed to the quantities he was writing out prescriptions for. The records proved he was over-prescribing for terminally ill patients but then giving them half of what he had written the prescription for and stockpiling the rest.

The amounts were sufficient enough to give Bernard Postles the proof he needed: 'In effect, we had proved he had the weapon in his possession.'

The police had a distinct pattern to the murders. This pattern is known as a serial killer's *modus operandi* (MO). The idea of identifying a killer's MO came from the FBI and was used extensively by their profilers. Colonel Robert Ressler virtually invented the term. 'Usually these things are emotion-driven and they're carried out in a ritualistic, almost compulsive, fashion. It's the basis of why they're doing it and it gives us the modus operandi – the way the killer carries out his murder.'

In the UK our profilers are normally forensic and criminal psychologists like Paul Britton. They examine this MO to gain a profile of the killer. It gives them clues to their personality and can explain why they murder.

'I think we can talk about him having an MO, but it's really crude. We can talk about him tending to elderly people and going to their homes to inject them and usually waiting while they die and sometimes he arranges the people, to make it look as though it's been a casual death.'

I had asked Paul Britton to look at the case for the documentary. He quickly pointed that Shipman gives the profilers a problem. 'When I'm looking at investigating crime, especially if we're looking at murders and serial murders, the thing that is the most important and the most valuable to me is the scene of the crime. It's the remains of the victims; it's where it happened and how it happened and from there I'm normally able to address those key questions: why was it done, how was it done? Now those questions have been undermined by the removal of the crime scene.'

There had been no crime scene. At the time of their deaths, no one thought Shipman's victims had been murdered. No record was taken of how the body was found, no post mortem was carried out, no forensic evidence was gathered. The only medical evidence comes from Dr Shipman himself and therefore is highly suspect, and profilers like Paul Britton are left to get the information they need second-hand.

'There is only what people remember and people's recollections are imperfect. So we must always remember the questions marks that we have to deal with before we look at what he did, how he did it and who he did it to. In the absence of preserved scenes of crime it is very difficult to see all of the psychological characteristics of the perpetrator. It's only because we leave marks of who we are and how we think in our crimes that psychological profiling is really effective. Now Shipman has been able to remove almost all of that.'

When I first met Paul Britton I asked him to give me a profile of the killer responsible for the 'Jack the Ripper' murders in Whitechapel in the 1880s. His conclusion that all the murders had not been carried out by the same killer and that the so-called last murder of Mary Jane Kelly was in fact a domestic copycat killing were extremely insightful and gave a fresh perspective to the case. He pointed out that, even though the Whitechapel murders took place over a hundred years ago, he had more information on those murders than he did on Shipman's recent crimes.

'We are making interesting inferences – if you look at the Whitechapel murders you have a number of poor women who had all been slaughtered in very characteristic ways that allowed you to include this woman, exclude that woman and make all sorts of reasonable predictions about the psychological functioning of the killer. With Shipman you have exactly the reverse: you have almost no victims at all that you can go and look at. You have almost no crime scenes at all that you can go and look at.'

Fellow psychologist Julian Boon believes there are some things that can be ruled out. 'One of the things we look for in trying to understand the motivation of a killer is the precise details of what goes on in a crime. Now one thing that's missing here is evidence of sexual activity: there's no biting, there's no scratching, there's no evidence of torture, there's no evidence of protracting the crime, there's no augmenting the crime, or some embellished fantasy of that nature.

'And he used his professional position as the perfect vehicle to find an outlet for this need. If the vague criteria were right – vulnerable, living alone, not in a position to answer back – where all of that was there, that would be where he would go next. In his normal course of work he would find people who were appropriate to the criteria and then he would pounce.'

Dr Harold Frederick Shipman presents the profilers with another challenge – his crimes suggest psychopathy, but he doesn't entirely fit the profile of a standard psychopathic serial killer. Psychopathy is the psychological term used to describe someone who has no capacity for guilt, for conscience or for empathy.

But that doesn't mean all psychopaths are serial killers. Julian Boon explained that three per cent of the population are psychopaths. 'The vast majority of the population, some 97 per cent, have a capacity for guilt, for conscience, for remorse, for sadness, for empathy, and I don't believe Fred Shipman had anything of the kind in his make-up. People were there to be manipulated by him for his own gains of self-aggrandisement and for gratifying his particular thirst for power over life and death.'

As Paul Britton puts it: 'The thing that I think you have to be so careful about is not to assume that those characteristics in those combinations are only found in people who kill. They're not. If you look at the boardrooms of some of our more successful companies, you see exactly those combinations present.

'Shipman demonstrates some of the features of the established psychopath. He was aloof, cold, calculating and we certainly have seen these characteristics before in people who have killed lots of other people. If, for example, you look at Dennis Nilsen, whom I examined long years ago, you will certainly see those tendencies to be arrogant, self-centred, conceited, and grandiose, the same as in Shipman.'

Until the discovery of Shipman's crimes, Dennis Nilsen's 16 murders made him Britain's most prolific serial killer. In 1992 Paul Britton had interviewed Nilsen in prison and I had spoken at length to Paul about Nilsen and his crimes in a programme in my documentary series *To Kill and Kill Again*.

On February 8, 1983 a Dyno-Rod engineer had found the remains of human flesh and three knucklebones in a sewer drain next to 23 Cranley Gardens, in Muswell Hill, north London. The occupant of the top floor flat was 37-year-old civil servant Dennis Nilsen. When the police came to interview Nilsen he admitted he had strangled four young homeless boys in the flat. The former army cadet cook had then chopped up their bodies and tried to dispose of their remains by flushing them down the toilet.

Twelve more victims, murdered at his previous home in Melrose Avenue in Willesden, had been burnt on bonfires in the back garden, buried under floorboards in the house and dumped inside black bin liners in the local park. He claimed he had killed for company, picking up his victims from gay pubs and bars around London. Nilsen is described as a commonplace man with an inordinate egotism and narcissism. He appears to have had totally inadequate social skills. Work colleagues at the job centre in Kentish Town found him a great bore who wanted to pontificate about anything and everything and brushed off disagreement with the phrase 'We're not on the same wavelength'.

Nilsen was a classic psychopath. As Paul Britton explained, high up on the long list of characteristics used by psychologists to diagnose psychopathy is occupational instability and sexual incontinence. It makes them reasonably easy to spot and singles them out as potential suspects. But Dr Shipman certainly didn't have those characteristics. He had been a successful GP for over 25 years and he had a stable and long-running marriage with children.

The psychopath would also be a person whose occupational competence was often called into question, rather than a person, like Shipman, who was successful in a profession that involved close peer scrutiny and teamwork.

Paul Britton believes that Shipman best fits into a category that would naturally make him a very successful serial killer. 'He is a "complex psychopath". He is able to switch on the professional doctor persona in which he can be warm, caring, charming, all of the things that people look for in their family doctor.

'This is because he's always aware of who he is, he's always aware of what he does and, when he kills, he does it because it pleases or thrills him. He does it because that transition from someone who is alive to someone who is newly dead is something that he simply can't get enough of.'

The psychologists may feel they can only talk in terms of 'a crude MO' but in August 1989 it seemed specific enough to ensure a list of 63 probable victims. The police had used their five-point prioritisation system to decide which deaths should be looked into first. Eleven had scored the maximum five points. They had all gained one point because they had all been buried and this meant now that Postles and his team could embark on the next stage of the investigation.

'I came to the conclusion that the only way that we would get the final piece of evidence would be to exhume the bodies to establish the cause of death.'

On September 8, as Dr Harold Frederick Shipman appeared at Tameside Magistrates Court charged with the murder of Kathleen Grundy, Detective Superintendent Postles applied for an exhumation warrant. 'As he was appearing in court for remand I was in the coroner's office.'

Bernard Postles found himself once more having to explain in detail to the coroner John Pollard why he wanted to carry out another three exhumations. 'We didn't ask to do all eleven at once. We had a long list but we decided to do it systematically because we were learning as we went on. We attempted to choose the ones that had been buried the least period of time because we didn't know what we were going to find.'

John Pollard granted the warrant and the police prepared to go back to Hyde. It was decided that they would only carry out one exhumation a day, so the three would take place on consecutive mornings. The police arranged to meet the forensics team and the men from UK Exhumations on Monday September 21 at St Mary's graveyard. They arranged to meet at 4 am, exactly the same time as the exhumation of Kathleen Grundy.

One reason they were done at that time is because it would be quiet. Later in the morning people would be about and other funerals might be taking place. Another important aspect was that the person's remains were almost always re-interred on the same day. This took place normally early in the afternoon before it began to get dark around three-thirty. Father Maher would attend four exhumations before the year was out, but he was not asked to attend this one – 73-year-old Joan Melia was not one of his parishioners.

Under the glare of the arc lights, the grave was opened up by a small mechanical digger. It was an easy task. The soil was still soft as Joan Melia had only been buried six weeks before. Her body was removed for post mortem, but it was returned to St Mary's and she was re-buried the same afternoon. The soil colour of the freshly dug grave hardly looked different.

The post mortem showed that Joan Melia did have slight emphysema but she did not have lobar pneumonia, the cause of death given by Dr Shipman. Two weeks later, the toxicology results came back. Joan Melia's 'tox graph' could have been the twin of Kathleen Grundy's. The prominent peak of diamorphine could not be missed. Joan Melia's chest infection meant that her lung function was impaired. The pathologist who had carried out the post mortem, Dr John Rutherford, told the inquiry that the administration of morphine while lung function is impaired would have disastrous results. Even a dose that was normally safe might be fatal.

It was then the end of the September and in the two months since Kathleen Grundy's grave had been re-opened the mornings had become a lot colder, but Bernard Postles and his team knew they would become a lot colder still before they finished exhuming the former patients of Dr Harold Frederick Shipman.

He was well respected in Hyde – there's no doubt about that. It was going to be very, very difficult to prove that this man had carried out not just one murder but a number of murders. We had to look behind this façade that had been presented to society of a caring GP who took a great interest in his patients. He might have done that but he also had a sinister side to him and he was systematically killing the patients on his list.

Detective Superintendent Bernard Postles

EXHUMATIONS AND EVIDENCE

In some respects if she'd been cremated we wouldn't have had to go through this but, because they were able to prove that she'd been poisoned, that sealed his conviction as a serial killer.

Danny Mellor, son of victim

Danny Mellor can remember exactly when he knew his mother had been murdered. 'Mum died in the May. In August, I was home from work at lunch time and I always listen to the World at One while I'm having my lunch, and this report came on the radio that a Tameside doctor had been arrested for forging a will. I can't remember the exact wording but Dr Harold Shipman had been arrested and the police were looking into more deaths. As soon as I heard that I knew he'd murdered my mother.

'All of a sudden it started to make sense. I phoned my sister Susan instantly and said what I'd heard on the radio and I said, "He murdered Mum." She hadn't heard the radio broadcast at the time and she was shocked.'

Danny Mellor lives in a tiny Lincolnshire village close to the RAF airbase that is home to the Red Arrows. When we visited him to interview him for the documentary the Arrows were training in skies above his home. Danny Mellor is an RAF Air Electronics Officer, tall, slim, attractive and, because of his military training, extremely articulate. But, below the open and measured approach he has to the retelling of his mother's murder, there is still a lot of raw emotion.

I pride myself on being empathic to interviewee's emotions. I know when to stop and what information to reveal or keep unsaid to protect the feelings of loved ones. But Danny Mellor fooled me and, I am ashamed to say, that

I talked too much and for too long about the case, only prompted to stop by Danny's obvious discomfort. No apology then or now will be enough to allow me to forgive myself, although I know Danny has forgiven me.

When, a few months after our interview, he emailed me to say he had sent the photographs of his mother for use in the programme, he confessed that sorting through all the photos had brought back hundreds of memories. He had found it an extremely painful thing to do.

Winifred Mellor died on the May 11, 1998, at home. She was 73 and was found sitting in her usual chair, her head to one side and looking as if she had fallen asleep. Just over a month later and less than a mile away, Kathleen Grundy's body was found in this same familiar tableau.

But unlike Kathleen Grundy, Winifred Mellor's dead body was 'discovered' by her murderer. Dr Shipman had knocked at a neighbour's house asking for a spare key, saying he was extremely concerned as he had been unable to get his patient to answer the door.

'Winnie' and her late husband Stanley had been patients of Dr Shipman since 1977. 'She spoke very, very highly of him. My father suffered quite poor health before he died and my mum said Dr Shipman was absolutely wonderful. He would do anything to try to get my dad better. I'd never met him. I'd left home to join the Air Force before he became her doctor, but I had this picture of this extremely caring, wonderful doctor.'

Danny Mellor explained that although his mother smoked, she was not a heavy smoker and it certainly didn't affect her health. She thought nothing of a regular ten-minute walk down to the shops in Hyde. 'Mum never suffered any serious illnesses and for a 70-odd-year-old she was very fit, to the degree that she would play quite energetically with her grandchildren, of which she had a fair few.'

Winifred Mellor was well known in Hyde. She and Stan had owned the chip shop in Gee Cross. She had also worked as a nursery nurse at Werneth Grange School for children with special needs. When she retired, she refused to give up working and continued to help children with their reading, but now she worked as a volunteer at St Paul's RC Primary School. 'Mum wasn't the frail old lady that you see doddering down the street now and again. She was a get up and go person. On holidays she wasn't a sit-by-a-pool, read-a-book type. She was off out – something to see, a site to go and view – that sort of a woman, extremely active both in her family life and in her church life.'

'She was quite involved here in our church. She not only attended church on a Sunday but she came most weekdays too,' Father Dennis Maher told me when we met. 'She was a member of our St Vincent/St Paul's Society here. That's a little group of people who look after people in the parish who are living on their own or are house-bound or perhaps bereaved. Winifred was very involved in that.'

Father Maher had been deeply shocked by Winifred Mellor's sudden death. 'The previous Saturday evening she was at mass here. At that time I was organising a trip to the Holy Land and Winifred came in that evening and said, "Have you got my name down? If you haven't got my name down for that trip you're in big trouble.' She was full of life and she said to me that she would never, ever have thought a day would come when she would be going to the Holy Land, something she'd wanted to do all her life. I was very conscious of that when I got the call to go down to the house on the Monday evening.'

Danny Mellor also knows how excited his mother was about her trip. 'I'd speak to her weekly on the phone generally. By chance I'd spoken to her the night before and she was over the moon because she'd just booked a trip to the Holy Land. She was a very devout Catholic and this was something she'd always wanted to do and she was really happy.

'It was a smashing phone call; I was really pleased for her. Then I got a phone call the next day, in the early evening, from my sister to say that Mum had just died. I actually said, "You're joking", thinking instantly after that you don't joke about something like this and she said it was true and that they were all there, my three sisters, in Mum's front room.

'Dr Shipman came round and found her dead. He said she'd died of angina and that she wouldn't take the tablets and she was "a stubborn lady" and that's about as much as I can remember from that because I was deep into shock at this stage, just couldn't believe that the day before she'd been over the moon and really pleased about this trip and then she's dead. There was no logic to any of it.'

While neither Danny nor Father Maher recall Winifred Mellor being at all unwell, on the Monday morning of her death she rang St Paul's School and apologised to the school secretary and said that she could not come in. She said she had a cold and a bad chest and did not want to pass her germs onto the children and was going to see the doctor. However, when the police checked her telephone records there was no call made to the surgery that day and surgery records show she did not attend for an appointment.

It was unlike Winifred Mellor to phone in sick. She loved her work, but her concern for the children obviously made her feel she should stay away. She clearly could not have felt very ill as she did not mention her cold to either of the friends who rang that morning and chatted to her on the phone and made arrangements to go out dancing later that evening. She was also well enough in the afternoon to walk down into Hyde to carry out one of her many parish duties.

Father Maher says, 'The day she actually died she'd been out all day doing things for old people in the parish because, though she herself was seventy-three, she wasn't one of the old people and that paints a good picture of her. She'd been shopping, doing little messages for them, possibly picking up their pensions for them, and didn't get home until three or four o'clock in the afternoon. So she spent the whole day looking after and caring for people and all on a voluntary basis, just because she was part of our parish here.'

Father Maher believes that she died very shortly after she arrived home. 'She had been to one of the supermarkets and, when she got home, she didn't even take the shopping out of the bag. She just put the bag down and went into the kitchen to make herself a cup of tea, because there was a half cup there.'

After Winifred Mellor's death Dr Shipman told members of the family that he had called in during the afternoon at her request. He said that she had called at the surgery at about 2.30 complaining of chest pains and he had arranged to visit her at 3 pm. When he arrived he had offered her a spray to put under her tongue and had suggested she be admitted to hospital. He claimed that she had refused and tried to pass the pain off as indigestion.

While it is unlikely that Winifred Mellor did call at the surgery since no one remembers her visit, Shipman's visit to her flat is confirmed by Mrs Mellor's neighbour, Gloria Ellis. She saw Shipman's car outside the flat at about 3 pm and had assumed he was an insurance salesman. She didn't realise it was the doctor until he knocked on her door later that afternoon to say he needed a key to get into the flat.

Danny Mellor takes up the story. 'Apparently Mrs Ellis had been in the front of the house ironing at three o'clock or thereabouts and had seen him because he had a distinctive people carrier, a big red van-type thing, and he pulled up in front of the house and went in. Then she saw him come out and drive off. She wasn't his patient, so she didn't recognise it was Dr Shipman. But he was quite a distinctive man and she recognised him as the same man who knocked on her front door a few hours later asking her if she had a key to Mrs Mellor's as he was the family doctor and couldn't get in.'

Dr Shipman told the family that Winifred Mellor had telephoned the surgery again about 5.30 pm and he had gone back out to her flat. 'I think it was about six o'clock, when he came back, couldn't get an answer from the door, looked through the window and saw my mum sitting in a chair. So then there was all this pretence of knocking on the window: "Mrs Mellor, can you let me in Mrs Mellor, are you all right in there?"'

Shipman claimed he couldn't get in and had gone round to a neighbour for a key. He seemed aware that the young couple who lived next door to

Mrs Mellor had a spare key to her flat. Danny explained that the couple had become great friends with his mother. 'My mum had become almost a surrogate grandma to their two children and it seemed a good idea for Tony and Gloria Ellis to have a key.

'Anyway, Shipman went round there and asked if she could let him in. They went in and found my mum sitting up in a chair, with a cup of tea alongside her as though she was asleep.'

According to Gloria Ellis's statement to the inquiry, Shipman picked up Mrs Mellor's hand, let it drop, then flicked her eyes and announced that she was dead. The young mother was clearly distressed but said that Dr Shipman was extremely brusque with her. When Gloria Ellis asked him if Winifred Mellor's daughters knew of her death, Shipman called her a 'stupid girl'. It was a silly question, but Mrs Ellis was in shock and Dr Shipman should have been aware of this. His angry tone may have had more to do with the fact that she had recognised him as the man who had called round earlier.

Danny explains, 'I think she said something like, "Oh, you're the gentleman who was here earlier in the afternoon?" He denied it, but she'd actually seen him, although I don't think she could actually put her hand on her heart and say it was three o'clock. He was very abrupt and said, "No, you haven't, it wasn't me", or words to that effect.'

His attitude to Gloria Ellis at last gives profilers like Paul Britton another glimpse at his psyche. 'Dr Shipman was a man who over a lifetime developed this pattern of wishing to kill over and over again. He needed to make sure he wasn't caught. So, if he was in a situation where he was challenged he simply faced it down. And one of the techniques he used was this rather abrasive, abrupt, immediately confrontational response and in the main it worked and the problem went away.'

In this case, Shipman had to calculate fast. It is seems more than likely that he had not planned to mention he had been to the house earlier in the afternoon in case it raised suspicion. He clearly wanted it to appear that he had answered Winifred's call and then found her dead. 'So he gained access and Mrs Ellis was there, nice Mrs Ellis was there as a witness,' Danny Mellor remarked sarcastically.

Shipman had to invent a reason for his earlier visit and why he had left his patient alone. He returned to his favourite lie.

'This is the tale he spun about my mother,' Danny Mellor continued. 'He wanted her to go to hospital and she wouldn't, so he gave her these tablets to take if she ever felt unwell or had an attack and she was supposed to take them and she wouldn't and so no wonder she's dead. No sympathy, no sorrow, no nothing, just she was an antagonistic old woman who wouldn't take her tablets when I told her to. Almost as if she deserved it.'

The police were beginning to see that this was the version of events that Dr Shipman would rely on time and time again to convince the families that the death may have been sudden, but it was not unexpected. 'There were many occasions where Harold Shipman told similar stories to family members that, looked at now, seem incredible,' Bernard Postles told me, 'but here we were able to disprove his account about what had occurred when he had gone to the house.'

Shipman had phoned Winifred Mellor's daughter Kathleen, who lived in Hyde, to tell her of her mother's sudden death. He told them that he would be at the house around six-thirty. Kathleen went round, then the other daughters, Susan and Sheila, arrived, because Kathleen had phoned them, and they rang Father Maher, so he went round and then eventually Shipman arrived.

'It was the first time I had real contact with Dr Shipman,' recalls Father Maher. The priest was surprised to see how scruffy the doctor looked and he also seemed to resent the priest being there.

'Dr Shipman didn't even look at his dead patient. He was arrogant and showed no care whatsoever for the family. He said, "You know why your mother has died, don't you?" Well, they obviously didn't. He said that she had a heart condition and wouldn't accept treatment and wouldn't go to the hospital. This wouldn't be like her at all actually because she was a person who was very sensible. If she was ill she would go to the doctor and she looked after herself so it was totally out of character with her, the things he was saying about her.'

Julian Boon also gains more insight into Shipman the serial killer from this encounter with Winifred Mellor's relatives. 'The way he dealt with the relatives, lying about his movements and saying, "You know what she was like", when all the relatives thought she wasn't like that and that she didn't want to go into hospital when they knew that she would have been only too happy if it had been recommended and so on – this whole palaver of lies yet again emphasises the psychopathic side of Shipman's personality, in the sense that he could act impulsively but only where opportunity presented itself. So it was no accident that he chose vulnerable, principally female, victims. And it is no accident either that he would try to cover his tracks, giving clear evidence that he knew exactly what he was doing.

'It is perfectly clear that he targeted the victims and that he tried to minimise any involvement. Indeed, if anything, he tried to come out as the doctor of the hour who had done all he could to save and support.'

Father Maher remembers that Shipman was more concerned with the paperwork than consoling the family. 'He said there was no need to have a post mortem because he knew why she had died and could sign a certificate. Then he asked if they had an undertaker to take her. I was shocked at this because the family had just found her dead and he gave the impression he wanted her moved as quickly as possible.

'I felt so angry. So I approached him and said, "Doctor, they've just found their mum dead and there's no need for you to get involved in making the funeral arrangements." He never looked at me or said yes or no. He just repeated what he had said and told them to make sure they were down in his surgery at nine-thirty in the morning, and with that he was gone. I came away wondering how could he be so highly thought of and seen as the best doctor in the town.'

But again this description of Shipman only serves to confirm Paul Britton's diagnosis of the GP. One of the strong features of the established psychopath is a complete lack of empathy for other people, who are simply there to serve his purpose.

Winifred Mellor's death certificate, signed by Dr Shipman, put the cause of death as a coronary thrombosis. His claim that she had been suffering from angina for nearly two years was confirmed by a series of entries in her patient record. Detective Sergeant John Ashley found them early on in his investigation. 'In Winifred Mellor's case I remember there were six entries inserted over an 18-month period related to angina. That ultimately led to a cause of death being diagnosed as coronary thrombosis.'

It all came as news to her family, especially her son Danny, who had no idea that his mother had any heart problems: 'I was very surprised when I heard that she was supposedly suffering from angina. Two weeks previously we'd been over there with my two boys, who were teenagers then, and we'd been up Werneth Low, which is a hill at the back of Gee Cross where she lived, and she'd been running around the fields with them. Well, you don't run around the fields at 70-plus suffering from angina.

'But, although I found it very hard to believe, it never ever occurred to me that there was anything untoward in all this and I started to think perhaps she had angina and perhaps she wouldn't take the tablets, perhaps she would consider it a sign of weakness that ultimately cost her her life. But at no time did I ever suspect that there was any sort of foul play.'

Winifred Mellor's death fitted Shipman's MO. 'All these female patients of Dr Shipman were found dressed, sitting up in a chair, quite often a cup of tea would be nearby, a cigarette burned out on an ashtray – all the indications of a sudden death,' Bernard Postles told me. 'But the undertakers and other doctors told us that is not the usual way that people meet their deaths.'

If you ask undertakers and doctors how the elderly are normally found when they die at home they say that they are, more likely than not, to be found in their nightclothes, having died in bed, and they'll tell you that generally the person has been ill for a period of time. Apart from her cold, Winifred Mellor hadn't been ill, but her medical records claimed she suffered from a life-threatening illness.

When John Ashley successfully accessed the software on the surgery computer's server he could clearly see that all the entries relating to Winifred Mellor's angina had been added that afternoon. Shipman changed the records at 4 pm on the date of her death, creating a false medical history, so when he went out to see the body he could then say that he had been treating her for angina and that he could issue a death certificate, thereby avoiding a post mortem.

Following their prioritising system, the police gave Winifred Mellor a point for the medical records, a point because the police were now very suspicious and one point because she was buried. Now all they had to do was check with the family.

Danny said, 'I think they'd been to see one of my sisters first because I lived in Lincoln and a fair way away.'

Their concerns gave Winifred Mellor the full five points. 'One of my sisters phoned me up to say the police had been round and that they were fairly sure and were going to exhume Mum's body. Once she said they were going to exhume Mum's body I knew that they wouldn't do that if they didn't think he'd murdered her.

'To go through a death of a loved one under normal circumstances, to go through the funeral and the burial and the grieving process, is hard work. It's an awful thing for any family to go through and we have to cope with that. Then to find out that the loved one didn't die naturally, that they were murdered, is one more thing to cope with. But it is indescribable to then find they've got to exhume the body and do more tests.'

Danny Mellor's initial reaction was one the police faced in almost every case where they informed the family they intended to exhume the body. 'I said, "I'm going to be there because I'm the eldest of the family. I've got to be there for mum's sake", but the police really strongly advised against it so I was talked out of it and the parish priest, Father Maher, said he'd be there.'

It was early in September when the police went to see Father Maher to tell him that they were going to exhume the remains of Winifred at the end of the month. 'They told me that they'd spoken to the family and had suggested that it would be a good idea that I would be there and the family said they would like that very much.' Father Maher didn't know it then but he would be asked to attend more than one exhumation that year.

'It's very difficult for a family to be approached by the police and told that they are going to exhume their mum who was buried last year. Opening up the grave and taking out her remains, that is very, very, upsetting. So, by way of conciliation, they would say that the priest could attend, because I would normally have presided at the funeral. I was very conscious when I was at the exhumations that I was the only one there who had known this person as a real person.'

Winifred Mellor's body was exhumed from Highfield Cemetery in the village of Bredbury, close to Gee Cross, on September 22. Unlike the previous two exhumations, Winifred Mellor's coffin had to be dug out by hand because it had proved impossible for the mechanical digger to get near the grave.

'For the first time it came home to me what happens even in a short time once you're buried, the amount of decay and disintegration that takes place with the coffin and, of course, the remains. Cemeteries tend to be cold places even at midday but at four o'clock in the morning there's an eerie feeling. It's an experience I wouldn't want to go through again.'

As a priest it was assumed that Father Maher would, like the police, be able to detach himself from the gruesome task that had to be carried out in the early morning light. But he has obviously been deeply affected by the experience. 'To the police and the people actually doing the exhumation and so on it was just another person's remains being exhumed, but I had known her.

'I remember coming out of the cemetery at five o'clock in the morning and it was a bitterly cold morning. Going down through the centre of the town behind me was a van in which her remains were placed. I thought about her, having known her very well, how full of life she was and all the times that she would have walked down the town and been in the market place there, doing her shopping and speaking to people there.

'It was an awful, awful feeling. I remember it was five o'clock in the morning when I got home and there was no way I could go back to bed or anything because I was shaking. When the housekeeper came in that morning I remember her saying to me, "You look terrible, Father. Are you all right?" And I said, "I was out this morning at an exhumation." And even now as I'm talking to you, I can still feel it. I would never, ever again want to go through that again.'

Sadly, he would be called upon many times again in the next few months to go through it again. In fact, just 24 hours after he had watched the coffin of Winifred Mellor lifted out of her grave, he was once again meeting the police in the early hours of the morning to exhume the body of another parishioner. This time the location was Hyde Cemetery and the grave was that of 49-year-old Bianka Pomfret.

German-born Bianka Pomfret suffered from severe manic depression. This meant she was either up or down. When she was up she was forever active in the community, working tirelessly for charity, but when she was down, she was extremely hard to live with. Her illness had cost her dearly. It had ended her marriage and at times kept her apart from her son William, even though he only worked round the corner from her home. Her faith and her church meant everything to her; it was her source of love and support.

'Bianka used to come to mass here every Sunday. A couple of weeks before she died she asked me if I would go and visit her, which I did, but she wasn't in. Next Sunday she waited behind after mass and she said she was sorry not to have been in, but would I come again for a chat.' Father Maher could tell, as he diplomatically puts it, that 'she wasn't feeling marvellous at the time'.

'I remember saying to her that I couldn't go on Monday or Tuesday evening and I had mass on Wednesday evening, so I would definitely go on Thursday evening. She said, "Is that a promise?" And I said, "Bianka, it is a promise and I won't let you down."'

But on Tuesday evening Father Maher got a call from the undertakers to say that Bianka Pomfret had been found dead in her house that afternoon.

'I felt so bad because I felt very guilty and very sad and I immediately began asking myself why I hadn't made an effort to go sooner. I thought she had taken her own life.'

For a devout Catholic, suicide is still a sin and Father Maher felt he might have contributed to Bianka Pomfret taking her own life. So her funeral was particularly poignant for him.

'I can still recall every detail of Bianka's funeral. It was a horrible wet day in December, oh, the rain that day and the howling wind. I felt a real sadness and guilt and when the coffin was lowered into the grave there was water filling in the bottom of the grave. As soon as the prayers at the grave-side were finished everybody left immediately to get back into their cars and the whole thing was a bit indicative of how I felt.'

Bianka Pomfret's son had found his mother's dead body. He had been called by her community mental health support-worker, who couldn't get an answer when she knocked at the door. The tableau was a familiar one – Bianka Pomfret was sitting on the sofa fully clothed. A half-drunk cup of coffee and a burned-out cigarette were on the table. An ambulance was called and the paramedics called her GP.

Dr Shipman claimed that Bianka Pomfret had telephoned him to say she was unwell and he had visited her around 12.30 pm. She had mentioned chest pains but he hadn't mentioned any treatment. He now thought that she had had a heart attack later in the day. He told her bemused son that she had been suffering from angina for about ten months and this, combined with her smoking and the medication for her depression, would have led to the heart attack.

The following day Dr Shipman gave a completely different account to her consultant psychiatrist, claiming that he had found her collapsed, she had been resuscitated and defibrillated, but had died. There had been no need for a post mortem.

But, as Bernard Postles explained, yet again the police were able to catch him out. 'There were lies told on some of the documentation that he'd completed, for instance, the cremation certificate. He had suggested that family members were with him when the individual had died. When the family were interviewed they said they weren't present at that stage, but that they had not seen the document and so they never knew that Shipman had been telling lies. So there were many pieces of evidence that led us to analyse this pattern throughout each of the deaths.'

Detective Sergeant John Ashley had also discovered that Dr Shipman had made several misleading entries for her in his computerised medical records on the day of Bianka Pomfret's death. She also scored the full five points on the prioritising system and she was the third name on Bernard Postles' list.

Father Maher had mixed feelings. At Bianka's grave when she was being exhumed, he wasn't sure how to react. He was glad she had not killed herself, but she was now being investigated as someone murdered by Dr Shipman.

Within a day the police had post mortem reports on both Bianka Pomfret and Winifred Mellor. They revealed no natural cause of death but also proved that neither could have died from heart attacks, as Shipman had suggested. In Bianka Pomfret's case, the pathologist Dr John Rutherford could find no signs of any heart disease. With Winifred Mellor there was no significant abnormality of the heart or blood vessels, such as could account for coronary thrombosis.

Two weeks later, the toxicology results showed huge amounts of diamorphine in both bodies. Significantly, a pre-mortem bruise on Winifred Mellor's arm suggested how the drug had been administered.

'What I wasn't aware of until the trial was that there was evidence of a bruise on her arm,' Danny Mellor told me. 'I didn't know until then that, when my sisters went to the house, they found Mum's sleeve rolled up and a bruise on her arm. They never mentioned that. Of course I'd like to think, if I'd been there, being a more analytical person, I'd have noticed that and asked Shipman about it, but I wasn't there.'

The bruise, linked to the toxicology report, simply confirmed what Dr John Rutherford had already concluded after the first two post mortems on

Kathleen Grundy and Joan Melia. 'Given the circumstantial evidence as we know it, that is that the victims died very rapidly, the only reasonable conclusion to draw is that the drug was injected into a vein. That is the only way it would get into the circulation rapidly.'

Like Angela Woodruff, Danny Mellor comforts himself with the thought that his mother's death was quick and painless. But it is unlikely that Shipman wanted to achieve a quick and painless death for the benefit of his victim, according to Dr Rutherford.

'There are other drugs that could have been used rather than morphine. Some of them would produce fairly rapid death, although not all of them could be guaranteed to produce a relatively peaceful death.' It seems that the use of morphine was for a very deliberate and sinister reason.

'If he'd used a different drug the victim might have made noises or died in a different way, which might have drawn attention to what was happening,' comments Dr Rutherford. Former FBI profiler Rob Ressler confirms that Shipman had a reason for his choice of drug as intelligent as his crimes: he was doing it in the belief that he would escape detection.

'I think he didn't leave the house with her still alive,' Danny Mellor informed me, 'He'd already murdered her. She hadn't even unpacked the shopping because it was in the kitchen still. He pitched up and convinced her for one reason or another that she had to have this injection and then left.'

Father Maher agrees: 'He would have come and rung her doorbell and when she would have seen Dr Shipman there she would have been absolutely delighted. She would have felt very special that he'd have come to see her. And I think one of the things he used to say was, "We're doing a little survey in the surgery and we're visiting some older people among our patients" or it was in order to get a flu injection and to save her having to come down. Winifred would have been absolutely delighted and thrilled that she would be so special that he would come and do that for her.'

'My mum was so trusting of him. It was, "OK, Winnie, I've got your 'flu jab or, I've got a new vitamin injection here that'll perk you up" – that sort of thing, because he could've told her anything and she'd have agreed to it. "Certainly, there you go, which arm do you want it in?" That would've been her reaction because she would never have dreamed of suspecting him of anything. It's very similar to your pet being put to sleep. That's very diffi-cult to live with, to know that somebody came in and put your mother to sleep – because that's what he did.'

Here was another clue for the profilers. Paul Britton concludes that for Shipman, the killing in itself was not valuable because usually it seems to have been conducted as quickly and as efficiently as possible.

However, Julian Boon remarks, 'The simplicity of what went on, the giving of an overdose of an injection, the killing of a patient for no sound reason whatsoever is what was clearly at the root of this. It was something that gave him some form of satisfaction. A need was fulfilled for him by killing an individual. It's that simple. That was the thing that made him tick.'

And as Rob Ressler, explained, 'The bottom line is power control over the lives of others and taking those lives meant something to him.'

If the profilers had more to work with now, so did the police. On October 7, 1998 Dr Shipman was back in the interview room at Ashton under Lyne police station. 'The second time we brought Harold Shipman back to the police station we brought him from prison custody,' Bernard Postles explained.

'It was very similar to when we had interviewed him about the Kathleen Grundy death. We had the toxicology evidence; we had these accounts from witnesses that we wanted to put to him, but in addition to that we also had the computer evidence about the medical records. Bearing in mind we wanted to interview him about three murders, we decided we were going to interview him about the death of Winifred Mellor first, move on to Bianka Pomfret and then Joan Melia. We had also broken it down so that the officers had objectives to achieve after each interview and depending on how that had gone they would move on to the next objective.

'What we wanted to do first was to get Harold Shipman to confirm that he was the one who had actually completed the medical records in relation to Winifred Mellor before putting it to him that in actual fact these had been alterations.'

This time there was a new interviewing team, Detective Sergeant Mark Wareing and Detective Constable Marie Snitinsky. The new pairing had been brought in partly to relieve pressure on the first team, but also to see how Shipman would react to a woman.

Shipman wasn't impressed. 'Answering a detective constable was bad enough, but he considered it even more demeaning to answer a woman. In his body language and in the inflection of his voice answering the male officer sitting next to her,' recalls Postles, who was listening to the interview again from another room.

Police and Criminal Evidence Tapes October 7th 1998
DS Wareing: Can I just hand you the medical records again of Winifred Mellor. Will you confirm for me what you attributed her death to?
Shipman: A coronary thrombosis.
DS Wareing: Were there any other conditions?

Shipman: Listed? No nothing relevant to the cause of death. Doctors don't always diagnose a heart attack; they call it a coronary thrombosis or myocardial infarction to the average GP. They're all the same. The patient's dead.

'Initially, he presented with quite unbelievable arrogance,' psychologist Julian Boon comments. 'Clearly in his eyes these weren't professional policemen doing interviews. They were just contemptible plods who where nowhere near the quality of a medical practitioner.'

But the contemptible plods had prepared a trap for the arrogant GP. DS Ashley's work with the computer had shown the medical records had been altered but, because the evidence was on a server accessed by a number of users, they had to prove it was Shipman who had made the entry and no one else.

'The way the computer network worked was that every user had a personal log-in and their own password. However, the system was so lax that everybody used HFS, Harold Shipman's initials,' John Ashley explained. 'We couldn't just go on the password. We did however know that Harold Shipman was the only person who was consistently at the surgery on each occasion.'

'What we wanted to do was to first get Harold Shipman to confirm that he was the one who had actually completed the medical records in relation to Winifred Mellor,' Bernard Postles added.

Shipman claimed he had made an entry into the computer on May 11 when she called to see him at the surgery:

D.S. Wareing: Where is the record of that visit?
Shipman: The record is on the front of the records there – 11/5/98 coronary thrombosis, cause of death.
D.S. Wareing: So in this case, as well as making a written record on the front of your manila folder, you also made a computer entry.
Shipman: I corrected the date for her death. The date that I made the entry was the 12th.
D.S. Wareing: So you corrected that to the 11th.
Shipman: Yes, to say she died on the 11th but the machine records the entry as on the 12th.
D.S. Wareing: So these would have been done the day after.
Shipman: Yes, I would have gone back to the surgery just to enter it up on the computer.

'He believed that he wasn't going to trip himself up, that what he was going to do was explain away his conduct in relation to each of these deaths. So when it got to the part with the computerised medical records he was almost aggressive with the officer about questions that were put to him. What Mark Wareing was saying to him was, "Who is it who completes the computerised record?" And Shipman said that it was he that did it,' Bernard Postles explained.

The trap was being set. 'Mark Wareing put the question to him again in another way by asking if there were occasions when members of Shipman's staff who actually did the computer entries on his behalf after he had made a written record. Shipman replied, "No, I do it." Wareing then asked the same question again a little later on in a different way and Shipman was quite aggressively forceful, saying, "Can you not understand what I'm saying? I do it."'

'I think when he dealt with the police in the early stages of the final investigation he had no reason to believe that he would be anything other than successful. No reason to believe these people had the intellect to pursue him to conviction,' Paul Britton adds.

But they did. And by lulling Shipman into a sense of false security and by getting him frustrated enough to rule out that the entry had been made by any other person, they had him where they wanted him. 'This was exactly what we wanted. It became very, very difficult for him to deny or to suggest that there was a misunderstanding when it was put to him that whoever made those entries at that time was actually making fraudulent entries which were backdated,' recalls Postles.

The trap was sprung and, listening to the tape, it is clear that DS Mark Wareing cannot help but have a slight smugness to his otherwise emotionless interview tone:

D.S. Wareing: I'm now showing you exhibit JFA42 and it's an insertion behind your computer, a ghost image, and it records what's placed in, when and what's removed. This record of information was created on the 11th of the 5th 98, three minutes 39 seconds after three o'clock by HFS-Dr. H.F. Shipman. Term: chest pain appears okay, angina, date, first date 97, and it's created on the 11th of the 5th 98. Where has that information come from, doctor?

Shipman: I have no recollection of putting that on the machine.

D.S. Wareing: It's your pass code, it's your machine.

Shipman: It doesn't alter the fact I can't remember doing it.

D.S. Wareing: You choose not to remember.

Shipman: It's a rhetorical question.

D.S. Wareing: It's quite correct though, isn't it?

Shipman: I still have no record of entering that onto the computer.

D.S. Wareing: You attended the house at three o'clock and that's when you murdered this lady, and so much was your rush to get back to the surgery and immediately start altering this lady's medical records. We can prove only minutes after three pm on that date you were fabricating that false medical history for this woman. Tell me why you needed to do that.

Shipman: There is no answer.

D.S. Wareing: There is a very clear answer because you'd been to her house, rolled up her sleeve, administered morphine and killed her, and you were covering up what you were doing. That's what happened isn't it, doctor?

Shipman: No.

As a computer expert who regularly exposes computer crime, John Ashley believes pride often comes before a fall: 'Shipman's own belief in his computer skills was far beyond the reality and I don't believe he was aware that these records were actually being kept when he was making the alterations. If he did know, then he was totally dismissive about our ability to find those details.'

As Shipman was confronted with more and more evidence that proved the police did have the ability to find those details, there was a distinct change in his demeanour. It comes as no surprise to Paul Britton: 'By the time he is confronted with the computer evidence, he begins to realise that the world is shifting from his point of view. He has been outmanoeuvred into the provable lie.'

Julian Boon adds that Shipman just could not face the extreme stress of having the tables turned on him by people he would consider to be far inferior to him intellectually, socially and professionally.

On the PACE Interview tapes Shipman's voice has lost its arrogance and for the first time, he now sounds almost confused:

Shipman: I'm sorry, what have you just said? That I recorded what I did the day after she died?

'When he begins to realise that the police officers whom he despises are, on this occasion, actually weaving a web that may cause him difficulty he has to rethink,' Paul Britton explains. On the tape Shipman then completely changes the subject, claiming that all the timings quoted by the police are out by one hour, because the clock on the computer had not reset itself for British summer time.

Shipman: The timing is a little awry, that's what I'm saying, because the clock is not changed or we don't change the clock for summer.

D.S. Wareing: I don't think we should bother about clock timings or anything.
Shipman: Well, you're making a great point of me being there at 7.30 in the morning.
D.S. Wareing: I'm making a great point about somebody falsifying a person's medical records on the date of a death to fabricate a medical history for them.

According to Paul Britton, this was just a stalling tactic for Shipman, who was by now in a state of panic. 'I think he will recognise that from his own mouth and his own foolish behaviour he may have created conditions that will cause him problems. He is probably in shock and is disoriented. He is also aware that he is saying things he shouldn't – "I must stop".'

On the tape at this point Shipman's solicitor's voice is heard for the first time:

Ann Ball, Shipman's solicitor: Can we have a consultation at this stage?
D.S. Wareing: Certainly, time now by my watch is 17.12 hours. I will switch off the tape.

'There was a break requested by his solicitor and they were taken to a side room.' Bernard Postles picks up the story from where the tape was switched off.

Julian Boon comments that the police plan had gone well. 'As predicted, Shipman then went on and, automatically convinced of his own omnipotence and superior intellect and position, went straight for it. For example, where there was an issue over timings on the computer he started to come up with never-ending reasons and he began to overreach himself. So they started to point these things out one by one, hitting him with incontrovertible facts that simply couldn't be. And no amount of "You're just a policeman, you don't understand this" was going to get him out of it.

'At that point, Shipman collapsed psychologically and we'd gone suddenly from this incredibly confident, bullying, bravado character, condescending to everybody else, to someone who was completely a gibbering wreck.'

According to police witnesses at that point Shipman appeared to break down. 'I am told he was in tears and that he was crawling on the floor,' Bernard Postles told me.

Psychologists call this behaviour dissociation. The breakdown is the result of a conflict that is going on in Shipman's head. 'This is a man who believes he is a great saviour, a man who brings and dispenses health and community benefit. He's also probably at a very important fundamental level trying to hold away the meaning of his killing. Dr Shipman is having to contemplate what it is he has done and he is going to have to deal with the fact that he has been the most prolific serial killer on record,' explains Paul Britton.

Julian Boon continues: 'When's he confronted with reality, as opposed to his version of reality, he simply couldn't cope. Very quickly there is only one exit there and that is to quickly dissociate and go right down on your uppers psychologically, which is what he did.'

'It may well be that you can have a crisis of huge proportions, but it will not be extended,' Paul Britton adds, reflecting on the fact that Shipman had regained his composure by the following day. As Bernard Postles bluntly puts it: 'I've got to say that since that moment no productive interview has ever taken place with Harold Shipman.'

But the police weren't concerned that they had pushed Dr Shipman too far. They felt they no longer required a confession. They had all the evidence they needed and on October 7, 1998 Shipman was charged with the murders of Winifred Mellor, Joan Melia and Bianka Pomfret.

For Danny Mellor the arrest came seven months too late.

It was not long before the police would have to admit that, just two months before the GP murdered his mother, a previous investigation had concluded that there was nothing suspicious about, and nothing to link Dr Harold Frederick Shipman to, the sudden and expected deaths of a number of elderly female patients.

It is still a source of great embarrassment to Greater Manchester Police and a subject they do not like to dwell on. 'There had been an earlier investigation of nineteen deaths. I thought that we needed to re-examine those deaths but it was my intention to re-examine them once we'd concluded or gone along the way to concluding the investigation into Kathleen Grundy's death,' Bernard Postles told me.

'But the *Manchester Evening News* discovered that we were conducting this investigation into a doctor and decided to print the story. They were talking about putting in that story the fact that there was a list of deaths that were being examined from some time before, but they were not naming names. And, of course, what that would have done to the people of Hyde whose families had been treated by Shipman was raise the spectre that it could be the death of a member of their family. I took the view that, if that was the case, then they should hear that from the police and not from a newspaper article and I sent officers to see nineteen families.'

One of those nineteen was the family of Winifred Mellor. Danny Mellor says, 'If the police had conducted a proper investigation then we wouldn't have gone through what we've gone through. He would have been arrested before he'd had a chance to murder my mum, Mrs Melia or Mrs Grundy. And we wouldn't have had to have gone through the trauma that we've all suffered.'

There was a huge amount of frustration, backdated frustration if you like, because with the benefit of hindsight in July we could see what we couldn't see in March.

John Pollard, coroner for South Manchester

SUSPICIONS AND STATISTICS

I remember only a couple of weeks into the inquiry when Stan Egerton came into the incident room and said he'd been chatting to a taxi driver he knew and he'd given him a list of names of people he believed Shipman had killed.

Detective Superintendent Bernard Postles

Throughout the 1990s the former policeman John Shaw and his blue Volvo were a familiar sight around the streets of Hyde. Sitting in the back there would normally be an elderly lady chatting away to the large and jolly-looking driver. John Shaw had started K Cabs in 1988 and in true entrepreneurial style, as befitted the Thatcher years, he had identified a perfect business opportunity.

'I found that there was a niche in the market in Hyde of elderly people who wanted just short journeys and who wanted to be able to afford to do it in a taxi. I went around Godley, where I live, putting leaflets through letterboxes to get the business off the ground and over the next eleven years it grew into a substantial little business that would provide me with a living. My clients were for the most part elderly ladies, in a lot of cases elderly widows, and I ran them all over the place.'

John Shaw is a quiet and slow speaker; he thinks before he talks and you could see why his elderly clients felt safe with this man who clearly has a heart as large as his frame. He had a special relationship with most of his clients that extended beyond ferrying them about. 'All my customers I classed as friends. We were in the main on first name terms and they knew that they could depend on me. I also did little jobs for them in the house – they'd ask me to change a light bulb or take the shopping into the house and put it away for them or whatever they needed done. I tried to treat them as I would like my own mother treated.'

But within a few years of getting his business off the ground John Shaw started losing these clients. They weren't being poached by a rival taxi company: instead, it was something far more mysterious. 'I noticed that various ladies were dying suddenly, ladies that I'd seen possibly days before their death or a week before their death when they seemed in good health. I would say that all my customers were not one hundred per cent fit and well, they were elderly, but it shocked me when they died.

'The first of my ladies – I call them my ladies – my customers, to die was Mrs Renée Sparks. I took her into Hyde regularly to do her shopping. She was fit and well but she'd got this arthritic hip or knee and couldn't walk far. On the Wednesday I took her into Hyde and took her back home, went in the flat with her, took her groceries in and spent a few minutes playing with her cat Dinky. On Monday her niece rang me and said that I couldn't pick her aunt up on Wednesday as usual as she'd had a heart attack and died. I didn't suspect anything then; I just accepted that she'd had a heart attack.'

By the time John had lost four more of his clients he was getting suspicious. 'I seemed to be seeing a pattern that caused me a lot of concern. They all died in similar circumstances: they were fully clothed, sitting in a chair. I didn't hear of one of these ladies going into hospital and dying. They all appeared to be dying at home and, in the course of conversation with others, it always seemed to be Dr Shipman who was their doctor.'

John told me that at first he thought he was being paranoid. 'The thought that the doctor might be practising euthanasia was fantastic. My ladies always confided everything to me, even health problems, but I wondered if I was going a bit crazy to even consider that the doctor could be killing these ladies. I simply sat on these ideas. I mentioned it to my wife who said, "If you're wrong about what you're thinking you could get yourself in some very serious trouble."'

But when 82-year-old retired housing worker Joan Harding died suddenly, her regular taxi driver realised he wasn't paranoid. 'Joan Harding was a very bubbly, very outgoing spinster lady. No way was she ready to die.' John Shaw was clearly very fond of the woman he describes as a bit of an eccentric. She was the sort of lady who would come up with some strange ideas. On the way to Manchester Royal Infirmary once she asked him to drive twice round a large roundabout at the end of the M57 so that she would know her way for a future occasion.

On January 3, 1994, John Shaw got a call from Joan Harding asking if he could take her to Dr Shipman's surgery the following morning for an appointment. She told John she needed to be down there by ten o'clock. Unfortunately, John already had a booking to take someone to the airport so he told his regular client he could not take her but could bring her back, if necessary. John made an arrangement with Joan Harding that she would ring his wife Kath if she needed a lift home. When, the following morning, Joan Harding didn't ring for a lift back John assumed she had found someone else to take her home.

He was partially right. Joan Harding had managed to get her friend Marian Bolton to take her to and from the surgery that morning, but Mrs Bolton had not been needed for the return journey. The 82-year-old had died in the consulting room. Dr Shipman said her blood pressure was low and she had had a heart attack. But her medical records, recovered from a Kleenex box at Shipman's home, show no history of heart problems until the day of her final visit.

Friends say that she was a regular visitor to the surgery and her medical notes show that Joan Harding had suffered from recurrent depression, anxiety and a cancer phobia. Why she went to the surgery on the occasion of her death is still unclear. John Shaw thought it might have been because she was in pain from her elbow, which she had broken and had pinned in 1992. The Meals-on-Wheels driver who brought Miss Harding her lunch told the public inquiry that she had complained of feeling sick they day before and her friend Mrs Bolton says she was complaining of back pain. The notes recovered from the Kleenex box seem to suggest she was complaining about her elbow and indigestion, which had left her light-headed.

Whatever the reason for Miss Harding's appointment on January 4, Marian Bolton told the inquiry that, as Miss Harding had to wait, she left her in the surgery and went to buy a paper, brought it back and then went shopping. She told the reception staff that she would be in the car park behind the surgery when Miss Harding came out. She recalls that Joan Harding did not seem seriously ill, whereas the receptionist Carol Chapman told the inquiry that Miss Harding looked 'washed out and pale'.

The practice nurse was seeing a patient in her office when Dr Shipman came in and said, 'I need you now.' Nurse Morgan told the Inquiry that she had replied she would be with him shortly and he had said, 'No, now.' As she followed Shipman into his consulting room he said that a woman had collapsed. Nurse Morgan said she saw an elderly woman laid out on the examination couch, fully dressed apart from a topcoat. The woman was motionless and looked pale and ill.

Dr Shipman knew that the medical procedure in this situation would normally be to try resuscitation, so while Nurse Morgan performed cardiac massage, he conducted mouth to mouth. Shipman carried on the charade for five minutes before deciding to stop. In her medical notes he wrote:

Patient collapsed 11.20
Unable to resuscitate CCM
Self and P/N Morgan present at death.

According to Carol Chapman around 20 minutes had elapsed between Joan Harding going in to see the doctor and his call to ask her to go into the consulting room. Dr Shipman told his receptionist, 'She's dead. Did she come with anyone?' Mrs Chapman found Mrs Bolton and Dr Shipman told her what had happened.

'I knew about one person dying in the surgery,' Len Fellows remembered when I went to interview him. Len had gone to the surgery to empty the Patient Fund pig. 'I said to Carol, one of the receptionists, "Are you all right today, love, having a good day?" And she said, "No, we had a bit of trouble today; a woman died in the surgery." I thought if you're going go you might as well go in the doctor's surgery.'

It seemed that Joan Harding was not the only patient to 'go' in her doctor's surgery. As the police continued with their investigations they discovered that Shipman had managed to have six of his patients die in his surgery.

The first death of a patient of Dr Shipman occurred before he set up on his own in Market Street, while he was still practising at the Donneybrook Surgery. On March 8, 1989 Mrs Mary Hammer attended his morning surgery. According to the Inquiry Report, the 81-year-old looked quite 'normal' when she went into the consulting room. However, a few minutes later, Dr Shipman asked the receptionist to send the next patient in, as Mrs Hammer was undressing in the examination room and would be some time. He saw two or three more patients before telling the receptionist that he thought Mary Hammer had died. Mrs Hammer was lying fully dressed on the couch. He told the family that she had appeared to be having a heart attack; he had given her a small dose of morphine to relieve the pain and went to phone the hospital. On his return she was dead.

It would be another five years before Joan Harding died at the Market Street Surgery, but just eighteen months later 68-year-old widow Bertha (Betty) Moss also died of a massive heart attack in the same consulting room. In the notice of her death in the local paper there was a line that read: 'Special thanks to the family doctor for his care and attention.'

Dora Ashton was 87, but had walked the half-mile from her home to the surgery for her three-monthly check-up. Her son James received a call from the surgery to say that his mother was ill and an ambulance was coming to take her to hospital. When he arrived at the surgery he was told she had had a massive stroke and died in the consulting room. Mrs Ashton had a heart condition and her family accepted the doctor's explanation of what had happened.

The 72-year-old Edith Brady went to the surgery every three months for a vitamin B injection for pernicious anaemia; she died in the examination room on May 13, 1996. Her family thanked Dr Shipman for looking after her so well. Twelve months later, on May 29, 1997, the 63-year-old widow Ivy Lomas turned up for the first appointment of the afternoon session. Surgery started at 4 pm but Mrs Lomas, a regular attendee with numerous minor illnesses and ailments, arrived early. When Dr Shipman arrived at 3.55 pm he invited her into the consulting room. He emerged from the treatment room about 25 minutes later to say he had a problem with the ECG machine. He dealt with three other patients before calling the receptionist to tell her that Ivy Lomas had died from a heart attack.

Outside Dr Shipman's patient list it seems very few people actually die in doctors' surgeries. When I asked Dr Jeremy Dirckze, who works just across the road from Shipman's surgery in the Brook Practice, if a sudden death in a surgery was unusual, he told me, 'It can happen, although in my experience of our practice in fifteen years, we've only had one person die in the surgery and he wasn't actually coming to see the doctor. He was a relative of somebody who was coming to see the doctor and he collapsed in the waiting room. We have had people come in with chest pain who we've treated and had to get an ambulance for but none of them have actually died in the surgery.'

Dr Wally Ashworth, Shipman's own family GP, agrees. In some thirty years it has only happened to him once.

When you rule out accidental death, then all that is left is murder. Harold Frederick Shipman was convicted in January 2000 of the murder of Ivy Lomas. Two years later, in her First Report of the Shipman Inquiry, High Court Judge Dame Janet Smith gave decisions of unlawful killing in relation to the other five cases. In his expert evidence to the inquiry, Dr John Grenville says he has considered all the evidence and says, 'There is a theoretical possibility that Miss Harding suffered a heart attack coincidentally just as she was visiting Shipman about a long-standing elbow problem but this is highly unlikely. In my opinion, it is much more likely that Shipman played a part in Miss Harding's death.'

Dr Grenville is a member of the Royal College of General Practitioners and also the clinical complaints advisor to the Medical Defence Union and he gave evidence at Shipman's criminal trial. John Shaw is just a former policeman turned taxi driver. But he had come to the same conclusion. When he was told a couple of days later that Joan had actually died in Shipman's surgery, he began to think that something was going wrong and became very concerned.

By killing Joan Harding in his surgery Shipman had deviated from his normal killing routine, his MO where he killed his patients in the afternoons in their own homes. But Paul Britton believes he simply felt like a change. 'It's very much to do with satisfaction and thrill and convenience. This man has established an MO that involves killing people in their homes, but the level of sensation sometimes needs a boost and that means you can test yourself. If you look at people who undertake extreme sporting activities they will sometimes make things more and more and more difficult. There is no reason at all to think that he wasn't similarly drawn in his killing of people.

'If you start killing people in your surgery you are able to have what, from his point of view, would be an almost exquisite sensation of doing it literally under people's noses and still being able to carry it through and carry it off. He also seemed occasionally to have an irresistible urge to kill spontaneously and I think that is the height of his risk taking.'

I asked Paul Britton why, after killing a patient at Donneybrook, he had waited five years before killing again in his surgery. He explained that motivation and its drive wax and wane. So, for various reasons, the urge may have eased off, then in the new surgery all of these things became possible again. If Shipman was already killing people at a considerable rate, it had perhaps begun to pall but the change in surroundings and opportunity would stimulate him again. 'For him, killing is an everyday activity.'

John Shaw now had an everyday activity as well: writing up his list. First he backdated his list to include Monica Sparkes, who had died in October 1992. 'I would walk through the door and say that so and so from down the road had been found. Kath would ask who the doctor was and I would reply "Shipman". Then I would write the name on this list of names and approximate dates of death. The list just got longer and longer and, over the next five, six, seven years, I was adding to that list every week or every fortnight. I'd never met the man but his name kept coming up over and over again as the time went by, other ladies kept dying and they were all Shipman's patients and most of them appeared to be dying in the same circumstances and were found in the same positions.'

Looking back, John Shaw thinks Shipman thought he was safe because he believed he was the only person who would have come into contact with all these ladies, so no one would have been able to compare all the deaths and make the connection. He never realised that there was one other man in Hyde who was seeing these people and speaking to them on a regular basis before he killed them.

John Shaw's clients often confided in him about their medical problems, but, as he recalls, not all the conversations were about mere aches and pains. 'I used to take Lena Slater to her sister's every week. Lena confided in me that she'd had breast cancer and was going to Christie's Hospital in Manchester for treatment. Then one particular day I picked her up and she said, "I've got some great news, John. They've given me the all clear from Christie's." I said, "That's great, great news, Lena." Then, a matter of weeks after that, her sister rang me to tell me not to pick Lena up as she'd died suddenly. I asked who her doctor was and she said Shipman. So she went on the list.'

But for the next four years John struggled to come to terms with his conviction that a GP, and one with such a reputation, could really be killing his patients. 'I'd got no one to turn to apart from the wife and she didn't doubt what I was saying, but she said, "If we're wrong, you could find your-self being locked up." I just didn't know where to turn. His eminence as a doctor really stopped me from doubting him and put me in a position where I doubted myself.'

John Shaw wasn't the only one to find it hard to believe a doctor could kill. By 1998 the funeral director Alan Massey was struggling with the same suspicions. Alan Massey has lived in Hyde all his life and is the senior under-taker at Massey and Sons. 'We're a hundred and one years old this year. My grandfather started it – it started off as T & S Massey, Tom, grandfather and his brother. He left the firm and my grandfather carried it on and my dad went working for him – they were cabinet-makers and undertakers then – and I then I went working for my father, leaving school at fifteen, then Debbie came, when she left college. I didn't think she'd last long but she took to it like a duck to water. Then fortunately, when she married, David, her husband, asked if he could come with us, so it is a family business.'

To Alan Massey two facts are irrefutable. The first is that everyone will die at some point; the second was that doctors don't kill their patients. He has had to rethink that last one.

'David was the first of us to get suspicious because he did most of the removals. It was the number of deaths that he was going out on. He used to talk to Debbie at night and he'd come into the office and say to her, "It's another one of Shipman's" and she'd say to him, "How do you know that?" And he'd say that it was always in sort of the same position.

'If people are ill and they die at home, you'll find there could be oxygen bottles, medicines, incontinence pads or anything all round the bedroom. You know that the person's been ill and its common sense that they probably died of natural causes. Now anybody can die in the street, they can die talking, but so many, in chairs, ladies, just sitting there in day clothes, probably a cup of tea, a book, a paper, shopping left unpacked – it's not unusual for one or two a year but, as David said, were getting one a month, two a month. Well, Debbie suddenly realised what he was talking about and she agreed with him, and that's how they first brought it to my attention.

'I just couldn't take it in. But we had more than one chat and it went on for quite a few months and Debbie and David then said, "That's about three or four in such a short time, all Dr Shipman's."'

Debbie was now convinced something was going on and decided to talk to another GP. She spoke to Dr Susan Booth when she came to complete the second part of the cremation form.

Dr Booth worked for the Brook Surgery. She and her fellow doctors countersigned the majority of Shipman's cremation forms. 'Because of the position of the surgeries – we were across the road from Dr Shipman – he would generally bring most of his requests for part two of the cremation form to our surgery,' Dr Jeremy Dirckze explained. 'And we took most of our part twos to him.'

Because forensic evidence of foul play is automatically destroyed during the cremation process, a system of checks and balances has been developed. Before a body can be cremated a form has to be filled in by two doctors. The first is the attending GP, who gives the circumstances and cause of death. A second doctor confirms and countersigns Part 2 of the form. As the undertaker, Alan Massey is responsible for getting the form filled in. 'If the GP has seen the person who has passed away at home we will then take a cremation form down to him which he can fill in at his surgery. Nine out of ten times Shipman said that he could sign the papers so he would come and fill the forms in and then send a second doctor.'

The cremation form is really just an extension of the ordinary death certificate. The doctor who fills out the certificate of death fills in the first part of the form. As well as giving the cause of death he also gives the patient's name, age, occupation, the place they died, how long they had been ill and how long they had a patient of his. The form also asks if there are any suspicious circumstances surrounding the death and who was with the person when they died. The second doctor is brought in to confirm these are all true. Dr Wally Ashworth was very candid about the whole process. 'The second doctor is virtually there to say that he agrees with the first doctor that the cause of death is correct. It's not, in fact, a bad money earner; when I did it there was a fee of about 40 pounds attached to each part of the cremation certificate.'

The money is paid because of the time the second GP is expected to spend on the details of the form. He is supposed to view the body and carefully examine it to make sure the first GP had given a correct cause of death. Dr Jeffery Moysey from the Donneybrook Practice was well known in Hyde for his meticulous examination of bodies. 'I always insist on a full external examination, much to the chagrin of some undertakers. I insist that the patients are undressed, that they're removed from storage and turned over and one undertaker said to me jokingly on one occasion, "There are only two doctors I've met who do that – you and Dr Shipman."' But, it seems it isn't a joke. According to Alan Massey, not all GPs are as thorough as Dr Moysey. 'There's probably a telephone call between them where the first GP says what they've died with and the second doctor more or less endorses what the first doctor said.'

The second GP is also supposed to check with those listed as being present at the time of death to confirm the first doctor's version. All the GPs I spoke to admitted that, unless the witness was another medical professional, they took the decision not to upset a bereaved friend or relative further by asking them distressing questions about the death.

Dr Moysey believes there was a good reason for this, that, until Shipman, the whole basis of certification of cause of death and cremation procedures was based upon mutual trust between patients and doctors and fellow professionals and doctors and undertakers. But Dr Shipman counted on this trust to allow him to literally get away with murder. He constantly lied on his cremation forms. He lied about the cause of death, he lied about who was there at the time and he lied about previous medical conditions that could account for the sudden death.

'His stories and his explanations of death were very detailed and very plausible,' Dr Dirckze told me, and probably because these detailed explanations had always worked with the doctors at the Brook Surgery, Shipman made sure they almost always countersigned his forms. This turned out to be a mistake, because at least one doctor from the Brook had noticed that they seemed to be countersigning an inordinately large number of forms and another was just about have her attention drawn to it.

When Susan Booth went down to Massey and Sons to sign yet another of Shipman's cremation forms, Alan Massey's daughter was waiting for her. According to Alan Massey, 'Debbie said, "You're here a lot" and she said, "Yes, another one of Fred's."' Like most of the doctors at the Brook Practice, Dr Booth was aware that Dr Shipman had a lot deaths, but he was a single-handed practitioner with an elderly patient list. But when Debbie told Susan Booth about her and her husband's concerns, she didn't just tell her about the number of unexpected deaths but also mentioned the way the bodies were found. She told Dr Booth that it seemed that Dr Shipman's elderly patients were always found fully clothed and that there were no signs of any real long-term illness. She compared this to the deaths of other doctors' patients. Usually they would be in bed; they'd obviously been ill for a long time, there would be signs that they were being nursed and a significant difference in the circumstances.

Dr Booth was sufficiently concerned about what she'd been told to talk about it with Dr Dirckze and the other partners. Almost at the same time, another partner, Dr Reynolds voiced her concerns. Dr Linda Reynolds was a newcomer to Hyde and to the Brook Surgery. She had become the fifth partner at the Brook in September 1996, having moved to Hyde from nearby Stockport.

'Dr Reynolds had joined our practice from a practice a few miles away where she'd been for nearly twenty years. She had noticed a different pattern and a different type of death and particularly the numbers of deaths of Dr Shipman's patients compared to what she had been used to in Stockport.

'Dr Reynolds had been getting increasingly concerned about the numbers of deaths that Dr Shipman was asking us to complete the cremation forms for. She started getting suspicious towards the end of '97,' Dr Dirckze explained. 'She told us that it became very apparent to her that there were certainly more deaths from Dr Shipman than she would expect. She wasn't particularly aware at the time of the circumstances of each death, but it was the numbers, and that raised definite suspicions in her mind.'

The information from the undertakers about how the bodies had been found was added to Dr Reynolds's concerns about the numbers. 'As a result of that, we looked at the figures in much more detail. There'd always been a vague feeling of an increased numbers of deaths with Dr Shipman over the previous year or two but that was explained subconsciously maybe by the nature of his practice, the type of doctor he was. He had a large list, he had a lot of elderly people, he had a much more personal approach, and it never reached a level with me that I became overly concerned,' Dr Dirckze admitted.

'I had a look at some rough statistics of our death rates and Dr Shipman's cremation requests and there were some quite alarming discrepancies between his cremations and our total death rate: over the previous year or so, Dr Shipman had requested almost three times as many cremation forms as we had total deaths within the practice.' Dr. Dirckze's figures set it out in black and white. The Brook Practice was three times the size of Shipman's but Shipman had ten times more deaths.

'Dr Reynolds was quite sure there was something more sinister to it. The rest of us didn't dare think that.' Shipman's fellow medics had worked alongside him for years and could not believe he would be able to deliberately kill his patients. 'We agonised at the meeting and tried to rationalise what the reasons for this could be. We looked for anything – initially, his style of practice, his type of patient, his elderly patients, there had been a lot of viral illnesses, flu epidemics over the winter, and much of that period was the winter period. He did practise in a different style – he would often treat patients at home as opposed to sending them into hospital. So, poor medical practice could have been an explanation for some of the deaths. But, even looking at all that, we felt, well, it couldn't account for such a big discrepancy and we felt we had to take some sort of action.

'Not really knowing the ins and outs of the system we felt that the coroner would be the first person to talk to this about and express our concerns. Dr Reynolds was the person who felt most strongly about it and she was the person we agreed would take this on and contact the coroner and see what he had to say.' As well as the coroner, Dr Reynolds spoke to the Medical Defence Union to get some legal advice. Her discussion with them would affect what happened next.

Dr Reynolds called the Coroner's Office in Stockport on Tuesday, March 24. 'I received a telephone call from Dr Reynolds who was concerned that someone should investigate the situation,' the South Manchester coroner John Pollard told me. 'I explained that the only way I could investigate it was by asking the police to act on my behalf to make enquiries as one possible explanation was that the doctor was effectively killing his patients. I hoped I was wrong about the possibility and I think she was also hoping she was completely wrong, and for that reason she asked that the initial investigation should be done in such a way as not to alert Dr Shipman to what was going on and certainly not to identify from whom the complaint had come.'

Dr Reynolds', call to the MDU had made her acutely aware of what the consequences would be if she was wrong. 'At that point there was nothing actually proven and to start making public enquiries would have been quite a dramatic and devastating situation for us,' Dr Jeremy Dirckze explained. 'If there hadn't been any problem, the implications of making an accusation could have been quite far-reaching both professionally and personally for all of us. Of course, you know Dr Shipman was the most respected doctor in Hyde really and calling into question any colleague's practice and behaviour is a major step, especially somebody who's been solid for such a long time. It could have backfired on us.'

Hyde is a small town and Dr Jeffery Moysey from the only other medical practice in the town believes the Brook doctors were right to want the investigations kept confidential and that as few people as necessary should be aware of it.

So, the police were ordered to investigate Dr Shipman, but they were specifically told that under no circumstances were they to do anything that would make him or any of his patients aware that he was under investigation. The investigation initially was to be almost a covert investigation in order to protect the other doctor and the community at large.

After speaking to Dr Reynolds, John Pollard telephoned Chief Superintendent Sykes, Commander of the Tameside Division of GMP. The two men knew each other and were on first name terms. Sykes intended to take advice from Bernard Postles who as senior divisional detective acted as the Commander's crime advisor. But Bernard was away and so the Commander asked Detective Inspector Smith, the only DI available, to undertake the investigation.

John Pollard showed DI Smith the statistics and explained that there were two possible explanations. The first was that Shipman was a caring doctor who looked after his patients in their own homes; the second was that he was killing them. Because of the level of secrecy requested by Dr Reynolds, DI Smith decided to conduct the investigation on his own. As the Inquiry Report comments, this was a mistake as he had never worked unsupervised before.

DI Smith began his investigation with Dr Reynolds. 'They had a talk about the situation, after which he went away and made an investigation into our concerns. I believe it was generally held by the police that the concerns were purely those expressed by Dr Reynolds and not the rest of the practice. That certainly wasn't the case: she was the most vehement in her views and the person who felt most strongly about it, but it was a group decision to take this further and it doesn't appear to me that that message came across because I was surprised that nobody spoke to the rest of the doctors concerned,' Dr Jeremy Dirckze explained.

Dr Reynolds told DI Smith that she thought Shipman was murdering his patients and she thought he was doing it with some sort of drug. She also told him that the bodies of two of Shipman's elderly lady patients, Ada Warburton and Lily Higgins, both of whom had died suddenly, were at the funeral directors'. She suggested they would be available for post mortems. DI Smith denied in evidence to the Public Inquiry that he had been given this information, but Dame Janet Smith, in her Inquiry Report, concludes that he was given it and that, if he had asked the coroner for permission to autopsy either or both, John Pollard would have granted his request.

Ada Warburton had been one of the names on John Shaw's list. A regular client of K Cabs, she had died on March 20 1998. On the day of her death Dr Shipman claimed that she had called him and said she thought she was having a stroke. He claimed he went round, saw no visible signs and said he would come back later. She then died. Miss Warburton kept a dental appointment on the morning she died and her dentist noticed nothing untoward. A friend who saw her that morning also said she appeared perfectly well. Dr Shipman told the police officer called to the scene that Ada Warburton had visited him at the surgery that morning. There is no record of that visit having taken place.

Dame Janet Smith found that both Ada Warburton and Lily Higgins were unlawfully killed by Shipman, but as their bodies were both cremated, without post mortems, we do not know what amounts of diamorphine would have shown up in a toxicology report. Dame Janet also criticised DI Smith for failing to find out more about the statistical evidence or the circumstances of individual deaths and for not interviewing the other doctors at the Brook.

'I was surprised that nobody spoke to the rest of the doctors,' Dr Jeremy Dirckze told me. 'From speaking to Dr Reynolds afterwards I feel that she felt that she wasn't being taken seriously or as seriously as if the rest of the practice had been involved. She commented that they had talked about some of her personal views, that at her previous practice she'd been the junior partner to a very strong-minded male character and had left because of some sort of personality conflict. They were almost hinting that she had a similar problem with Dr Shipman. She felt that they were being over-influenced by this aspect rather than actually listening to what she was saying. I don't think they ever fully appreciated the statistical discrepancy, which is really what was the cornerstone of our concerns, but she was almost being dismissed as a, how shall I put it, a menopausal, emotional woman with an anti-male attack.'

DI Smith went to Tameside Register Office to get copies of all the entries in the register of all the deaths certified by Shipman, going back six months. Shipman had certified 31 deaths but for some reason DI Smith only had copies of 20. It is unclear whether he lost them or wasn't given them in the first place. Smith also requested the medical records for 17 of these patients from West Pennine Health Authority but for reasons of legal confidentiality he was not allowed access to them. Instead, it was agreed that Dr Alan Banks, the Health Authority's medical advisor, would examine 14 of the records on DI Smith's behalf. Dame Janet Smith concluded that Dr Banks's prior knowledge of, and respect for, Dr Shipman made him a very unsuitable person to carry out the examination. He certainly didn't point out to DI Smith the unusual fact that 13 out of the 14 deaths were female, that Shipman had been present in ten out of the 14 cases or that 12 out of the 14 occurred in the patient's home.

While DI Smith conducted his secret investigation, Alan Massey had decided that the whole matter could be simply sorted out by going to see Shipman. While Alan maintains he did not know at this time that the police were investigating Shipman, he knew that Debbie had spoken to Dr Booth. Also, at that time, Dr Shipman was a friend as well as the family GP and Massey probably felt that he deserved the chance to justify himself against suspicion and rumour. Whatever the reason, Alan Massey went to Shipman's Market Street surgery.

'I was really wondering what I was going to say to him, that was the crux of the matter. I stood outside about five, six minutes, just walked past the surgery a couple of times and then I just decided to see him that very evening, after the last patient had left. It was difficult to cope with the usual pleasantries – he asked me if we were busy. I said that we were doing all right and I just said to him that I was a bit worried, or we were a bit worried, about all these deaths of old people, especially ladies.' But the confrontation between the undertaker and the doctor didn't turn out to be at all like Alan had imagined it would be.

'He was nonchalant; he just stood up and said, "There's nothing to worry about, there's all my records, death certificates, and you can have a look at them." And of course it was all in doctors' jargon and he was quite open and jovial about it, no shock. You would have expected anybody to jump at me and ask what I was implying. I felt a great relief and we had quite a pleasant chat for about two or three minutes. I came home and told them there's nothing to worry about, that everything was in order.'

To the criminal psychologists Shipman's casual manner is indicative of a psychopathic personality. Paul Britton explains that Shipman would be able to feign objectivity, and withdraw emotionally to some extent. When his guard was down some of the grandiose elements that figured quite prominently would come to the fore.

Shipman may have been supremely confident but Alan Massey's visit had made him aware he was under some suspicion. After the visit in March, Shipman would wait over a month before killing again. His next victim was Winifred Mellor and he did not kill her until May 11. Dame Janet Smith believes he deliberately chose a victim who would not be cremated, to avoid coming under the scrutiny of either Massey and Sons or the Brook doctors. Certainly, Winifred Mellor had made it abundantly clear that she had a strong preference for burial.

'I don't know whether it had come up or not with Dr Shipman, but she would never have been cremated because of the way she suffered after we were really talked into having my dad cremated,' Danny Mellor told me. 'Because she didn't have a grave to go to, she was deprived of the solace of somewhere to go and be close to Dad and she felt that her children would never suffer in the same way. They would have a grave to visit and to be close to her.'

Paul Britton also believes that by waiting to kill and then choosing someone who was going to be buried, Shipman was minimising the risk. 'If you look at this man he was very careful to protect himself. He was not a man who recklessly or randomly went out and had to kill someone today and didn't care what chance he took. He's a man who had developed a little plan that he enacted over and over again. But he wouldn't enact it until he was reasonably sure he was going to be OK with it, in other words, the chance of being detected was quite low.'

Certainly, the chances of being detected by DI Smith were extremely low. Halfway through the month of April he visited Massey and Sons. 'We had the police come, DI Smith. He just said they'd been looking into some complaints, as far as I can remember. He said they'd looked into Dr Shipman's activities and into some of the rumours that had been going about and they couldn't find anything untoward and that was all. He reassured us that there was nothing to worry about.'

'There were a lot of problems in the way in which the first police inquiry was conducted,' Ann Alexander, the solicitor for most of Shipman's victims, told me when we met up at her elegant south Manchester home. 'The most significant thing for me was that I had always believed that it was a policeman's job to go out and ask questions. And in this particular case Smith didn't ask any questions. He sat and waited for information to be given to him. He just completely failed to get to the bottom of it, failed to make any notes, and because of the way in which he approached the whole thing it was inevitable that he wasn't going to get anything that would have given rise to an earlier arrest.'

It had been just three weeks since the original meeting between DI Smith and Dr Reynolds. He now informed her, according to the Inquiry Report, that his investigation had found no evidence of criminality and no apparent motive, financial or otherwise, for Shipman to harm his patients. He also added that Shipman was well loved by his patients.

'Dr Reynolds mentioned it to the rest of us and then we effectively put it to bed,' Dr Dirckze recalls. 'We were quite relieved; we assumed that our concerns had been fully looked at and that the investigation had been as thorough as was required, and while obviously we felt there was something not right, at least we were happy that there was supposedly a rational explanation for it. I don't believe Dr Reynolds was entirely satisfied. I don't think she felt, given what I've said before about how they'd viewed her, that they had not actually taken her as seriously as she would have liked.'

Linda Reynolds was right. Dame Janet Smith concludes that DI Smith was 'out of his depth'. She criticised CS Sykes for not supervising his work and she also lays some of the blame for the failure of this first investigation on Dr Banks. She acknowledged that Dr Banks's knowledge of and respect for Shipman made it difficult for him to have an open mind, but the 'credibility gap' should not have prevented a professional man from giving a professional opinion.

Bernard Postles was more diplomatic when I asked him what he thought of the first investigation. He admitted that the wrong decision had been made at the end of it: that there was no cause for concern. There plainly was cause for concern because Harold Shipman had been murdering his patients consistently for some years. Postles spoke of his regret that the earlier investigation didn't manage to lead to the arrest of Harold Shipman.

'Obviously they were faced with the problem at the time: doctors don't kill their patients. But it wasn't completely unknown, of course. Beverly Allitt killed some of her patients back in 1994; there have been other instances of doctors and nurses around the world killing their patients,' Ann Alexander reminded me. She believes the decision to respect the Brook doctors' desire to keep the investigation a secret was wrong. 'Murder is the worst crime that can be committed. This is a case where there was a suspicion that Shipman might have been killing his patients. It seems to me that there is absolutely no reason why the police, taking that on board, couldn't have gone behind the request of the Brook doctors for confidentiality and investigated those crimes, because surely they had a responsibility to the public to do so.'

John Shaw also believes that it was the obsession with secrecy that stopped the police from uncovering other leads and evidence. 'Had that first inquiry been done in the open, I would have gone to the police then, but it wasn't, it was hushed up, no one knew anything about it and Shipman took advantage of it and killed again.'

With Shipman's arrest, John Shaw felt able to show his list to an old friend from his police days, a fellow member of his local bowls club, Stan Egerton. 'When Kathleen Grundy died, it brought matters to a head. I couldn't accept that Kathleen's death was natural in so much as I'd seen her, just a matter of weeks prior to her death, and taken her to Stockport station. She was fit and well then. So I broached the matter with a friend who was actually working on her death, Stan Egerton, who was the arresting officer. Stan was shocked when I told him that I'd got a list of ladies that I'd compiled over the past eight years who'd all died while they were Shipman's patients, all in similar circumstances.

'His response was, "Bloody hell, John, what are you talking about?" I said that I had a list and I pulled it out of my pocket. Stan asked how many there were. I counted them and told him that there were twenty and that I had dates going back to 1992. He just said, "Bloody Hell, John," yet again. In some cases they were approximate dates, but it prompted a third Bloody Hell! Nevertheless they were dates close to the times of death going back to 1992. Stan said they were simply looking at what had gone on over the last eighteen months, and I said, "Well, I'm going back eight years. I didn't come to you before because I didn't think you would believe me." Stan's response was, "If you had you come to me a month ago with this I would have had you down as a nutter, with a grudge against Shipman. I would not have believed you. I would have thought you were crackers."'

Harold Shipman would murder Winifred Mellor, Joan Melia and Kathleen Grundy before his crude attempt at forging a will would finally close Dame Janet's 'credibility gap' for ever and it would have to be acknowledged that at least one doctor could and did kill his patients.

Dame Janet's Inquiry found Shipman was responsible for the deaths of more than 260 of his patients. While John Shaw knows his list could not have saved more than a handful of them, the big man with the even bigger heart still feels in some way responsible. 'I'm riddled with guilt. I've been told by the police and by the doctor that I've got nothing to reproach myself for, but I still feel guilty that somehow or other there should have been someone who I could have gone to. I reckoned up that ten per cent of the deaths that he caused were friends and customers of mine – it went absolutely beyond belief.

'Various names kept popping out of the list of two hundred that had had bearings on my life: Harry Freeman, an ex-policeman who I'd worked with as a police cadet in Hyde in my youth; Charlie Barlow, ex-sergeant, big man, strong man, a straight man who'd been destroyed by somebody like Shipman; Mrs Cousins, my ex-headmaster's widow. In our own little cul-de-sac he killed about six ladies – from my front window we could see property where he killed perhaps four of them. He killed three times within twenty yards of my front door.

'How does one soak that up without having some very strange feelings? It's had a very strange effect on me: it's destroyed my religious faith completely. I no longer believe in any sort of religion. After being brought up as a reasonably strong Church of England believer, my religious faith has gone absolutely down the pan.'

When you flick through page after page of the Inquiry Report where Dame Janet has listed the hundreds of names of all of the patients Dr Shipman murdered you can see why John is struggling to come to terms with the enormity of the crimes and the part he played in their detection. There are two names and two deaths that do not appear on that list. But they are deaths that one cannot help but feel are in some way connected to Shipman.

DI Stan Egerton died of a heart attack, carrying a coffin at one of Alan Massey's funerals. He had retired from the police force in 1999 and lived long enough to see Shipman sentenced to life imprisonment for 15 of the murders. In the summer of 1999 Dr Linda Reynolds was diagnosed with terminal cancer – she also lived long enough to see Shipman convicted. She died in March 2000, leaving her beloved husband Nigel to give evidence on her behalf at the Public Inquiry.

Nobody had wanted to believe Linda Reynolds when she said Dr Shipman was a killer. But after the exhumations of Kathleen Grundy, Joan Melia, Bianka Pomfret and Winifred Mellor, they had to. It all came too late for the relatives of Shipman's last three victims. In her Second Report, which looks at the first police investigation, Dame Janet concludes, 'My final words must be for the families of Shipman's last three victims. For them these hearings and readings of this Report will have been profoundly distressing. Once again I can only offer them my deepest sympathy.'

Danny Mellor can only look back now and wonder, 'What if?' 'You become angry, very angry, and you've got to be careful because you could become bitter and angry and twisted and he would have won again. All the anger and all the bitterness in the world isn't going to bring my mum back. You've still got to get on with life and you've got to accept that mistakes were made – now I accept that we all make mistakes, nobody's perfect, but it was the system, apart from individual mistakes, that let my mum down as well.'

But the system was now trying to make sure they were investigating everything properly and Bernard Postles and his team now had new evidence, the names on John Shaw's list.

Certainly it's true to say that no coroner has ever ordered so many exhumations in one year but everybody knew, bearing in mind the earlier investigation in March, that there was the potential here of a very large criminal investigation. But we still didn't know we would be dealing with the biggest serial killer in the history of this country.

John Pollard, coroner for South Manchester

CATHOLICS AND CREMATIONS

People in general have by now become quite grey to him. They're quite shadowy; they're not important. Because of that he's a man who is increasingly alone, he's a man who increasingly occupies a world of one.

Paul Britton, criminal and forensic psychologist

From the air the large area of green, surrounded and hidden from view at ground level by trees, looks like a park, but once on the ground, the gold lettering on the black sign pinned to the equally black wrought-iron gates make it clear that beyond lies the town's main cemetery. The gates seem to be permanently open and, as you walk through, a wide concrete driveway leads up the hill to a red-brick gothic chapel. The ostentatious Victorian building was clearly designed and built at the same time as the town hall, when Hyde knew better days. Row upon row of stone memorials, darkened by the soot of over a hundred years of factory chimneys, also suggest a bygone age of money, wealth and power.

Today, the cemetery is a quiet place. Most of the new graves with their shiny black marble headstones cut as hearts, or ovals, as well as the more traditional oblongs, lie to the left of the cemetery in the area reserved for Catholic burials. On the day we filmed in this section my escort and guide was Father Dennis Maher. He proudly pointed out the area occupied by his late parishioners and their ancestors. 'In our section, the Catholic section, the graves are very well maintained, regularly visited and fresh flowers are continually put on them. There's a great devotion to the dead here.'

Father Maher explained that Hyde has a large Catholic community with more traditional values. 'Certainly one in ten is Catholic, getting on for four thousand in a population of about thirty-five thousand people. There's a big Italian Catholic population in the town and there is a tradition going way back that Irish and Italian Catholics would always be buried. They took the old-fashioned stance on the resurrection of the body at the end of time and the idea of cremation didn't seem to fit in with that. So that would mean that, proportionately speaking, quite a large number of our people here would tend to be buried rather than cremated. And that explains why I was so involved from the very beginning in the exhumations.'

John Shaw's list had added another criterion to the police five-point prioritisation system. Detective Superintendent Bernard Postles now had more names of women, who may well have been murdered by their GP, to take to the coroner. With such a large congregation, it was not surprising that from September to December 1998 Father Maher would find himself returning on a regular basis to the cemetery in the early hours of the morning as yet another parishioner's grave was re-opened by the police and the body removed for post mortem examination. At the end of September Father Maher had been present at the exhumations of Winifred Mellor and Bianka Pomfret and within a few weeks he watched as the body of Marie Quinn was removed from the grave she had occupied for just under a year.

Marie Quinn was 67 when she died on November 24, 1997. A devout Catholic, she was also a fit, active woman. 'The picture that I always have of Marie Quinn is that Marie used to walk very fast – she was like a train. If you met her coming around the corner she was always walking fast and you knew she was on her way some place, she would never just be strolling. I didn't realise until Marie died what a wide circle of friends she had and the number of groups of people with whom she was involved, not just here in the immediate area of Hyde, but all over the place and all over Manchester.' Father Maher compared Marie Quinn to fellow parishioners Winifred Mellor and Kathleen Grundy, 'They were all very into voluntary work. They had reared their families and now for the first time in their lives they were enjoying a little bit of freedom. In Marie's case she had a little bit of money to spare and so was able to a little bit of travelling. Marie used to go to unusual places. She wouldn't be one now that would go and lie on a beach for a week. She'd always go to some place that was interesting. She went off on a pilgrimage to Medjugorje when hardly anybody knew about Medjugorje and I still have a very beautiful candle upstairs that she brought me back from Medjugorje.'

In fact, Marie Quinn's pilgrimage to Medjugorje in Croatia had been filmed for a BBC *Everyman* programme. When, eight years later, I watched the footage for my ITV documentary, I felt for the first time that I was actually seeing one of Dr Shipman's victims as her family and friends would have seen her. With other murdered patients, their relatives and friends had painted me wonderfully rich verbal pictures of their loved ones and I had a whole collection of snapshots, but Marie Quinn walked and talked in front of my eyes. I suddenly started to see why John Shaw would find these deaths so strange.

Marie Quinn was a slim, almost bird-like lady with large round glasses and grey hair that framed her face. She was clearly deeply religious, but no walk-over if the discussion between her holiday companion and herself was anything to go by. She clearly had strong opinions and wasn't scared of speaking her mind. She was also demonstrably fit and active. Decked out in training shoes and slacks, she climbed a mountain, each step faithfully recorded by the BBC *Everyman* cameraman. At the top she sat and watched a sunset, expectant of seeing a miracle. On her return to ground level she mused that maybe she had seen something. Her faith and trust in the power of God was extremely strong, but so it seems was her faith and trust in her GP.

A year after the *Everyman* programme was screened on BBC 1, Marie Quinn, the fit, healthy 67-year-old who had made it to the top of a mountain, was dead.

On the day of her death Marie Quinn had phoned her only son John who lived in Japan, so one of the highlights of her week was speaking to him on the phone. Marie Quinn said nothing to her son that caused him to be concerned about her health. Earlier that day she had attended a funeral and her fellow mourners also thought she appeared to be in normal health. Dr Shipman claimed that at about 5.45 pm, as he stood in reception at the surgery, he picked up a call from Marie Quinn, who was asking for a visit. He said she told him that she had noticed some weakness on her left side. He said he told her to leave the latch on the door open and he would let himself in. Phone records show that no call was made from her home to the surgery that day. Shipman had lied.

He also lied about the time he arrived at Marie Quinn's home. He claimed he arrived at 6.15 pm, but his computerised records show that he was still seeing patients in his surgery at 6.16 pm. In his evidence to the court, Dr Shipman claimed that, when he let himself into her house, he found Marie Quinn on the floor in her kitchen 'close to death'. He considered that she was alive but unconscious and he did not attempt to resuscitate her as he believed that she had had a major stroke and felt that reviving her might lead to irreparable brain damage. He said he then waited two minutes. He claimed that, if she had stirred, he would have called an ambulance, but she did not. The post mortem on Marie Quinn's exhumed body showed no signs of a stroke. The pathologist, Dr John Rutherford, expressed the view that the cause of death was morphine toxicity. Dame Janet Smith in her Inquiry Report states that, as it would have taken Dr Shipman almost 25 minutes to reach Marie Quinn's home and as he phoned her friend to say she had died at about 6.32 pm, Marie Quinn must have died 'very quickly' after Dr Shipman injected her with a lethal dose of diamorphine.

Her death came as a complete shock to everyone, including her priest. 'I remember the undertaker phoning me and telling me that she had been found dead in her house. That's all I was told at the time and I was just very surprised. Again, I used to see Marie very often and she never gave the impression of being sick or said that she was not feeling well or anything and I'd seen her a day or two previous to her being found in the house.'

In the bitter cold of a September morning, as Father Maher watched the coffin with the body of his once active, elderly parishioner hoisted from her grave, his thoughts turned to her GP, just five miles away, in Strangeways Prison. 'I said that, if I had anything to do with this, I would bring him out here, one of these mornings, and just let him stand here and see what he's putting everybody here through.'

The toxicology results from the post mortem on Marie Quinn's exhumed body found 'morphine in the tissues consistent with the administration of a lethal dose'. As the exhumations continued, the results of the toxicology tests on each victim were of the same level and the findings were repeated. Ivy Lomas was exhumed on the same day as Marie Quinn. She was 63 when she died unexpectedly in Shipman's surgery in May 1997. By comparison, Muriel Grimshaw, who died two months later, hadn't been to the doctor for months and was described by family and friends as being in good general health. However, Dr Shipman claimed he had seen the 76-year-old the week before her death. Her body was exhumed along with that of 67-year-old Irene Turner. In July 1996 Irene Turner had been on holiday in Torquay, a week later she was dead, found "laid out" on her bed shortly after a visit from her GP. Lethal levels of morphine were found in the bodies of all three of these former patients.

The amounts being found surprised even the toxicologist. Julie Evans told me: 'We had been involved in exhumations but nothing on the scale of the Shipman case. To have so many bodies to look at in one individual case and to find the same poison in that case was really unique.'

The levels of morphine were all far too high to be accidental or self-administered. They pointed directly at Dr Shipman as the killer and contradicted his medical explanations for the sudden deaths.

Even where his explanation appeared reasonable, the toxicology caught him out. Jean Lilley was only 58 when her body was discovered on her sofa just minutes after Dr Shipman left. The sudden death in April 1997 could have been explained away by the fact that at the time of her death she had been suffering from heart disease and respiratory problems. But lethal levels of morphine proved what the police had suspected and what Shipman's MO suggested – Jean Lilley had been murdered by her GP.

Shipman was now brought back from Strangeways Prison and formally charged with the murders of all five of these former patients. As predicted, he refused to answer any questions about their deaths.

The exhumations with their irrefutable toxicology evidence were proving the key to convictions and, as Bernard Postles explained, the police were using what they learned from the exhumations to decide whether they were likely to be able to recover evidence from those that had been buried a little longer. They systematically worked back until the bodies no longer provided enough evidence.

The police now decided to exhume three more bodies from their list, those of Elizabeth Mellor, Sally Ashworth and Alice Kitchen.

Joe Kitchen says, 'When I'd made contact with the police, they just took some details and took statements off the family. They didn't say then who they were investigating, but then my mum became one of the ones. Then they did say that they might have to exhume her body and they were asking us if we'd mind. Obviously they didn't need our permission but they did ask and I can remember us discussing it as a family. I think the uncertainty had gone on for so long that we had to know one way or the other whether she had been killed.'

The body of Alice Kitchen, the tiny, tough Irish mother of six who, according to Dr Shipman, had refused to go to hospital, preferring instead to wait for her son to come home for his tea, was exhumed on November 11.

'The day my mum was exhumed was very difficult from all the family's point of view. I found it particularly difficult because I had a Remembrance Day service to go to where you're trying to concentrate on remembering those who sacrificed their lives in the War and that day my mum's body was being exhumed to see whether she'd been murdered by her GP. The thing that worried me most was if we went ahead and the body was exhumed and they found nothing, we would have disturbed Mum's body for no reason at all.'

As the undertaker who had buried many of the victims and comforted their relatives before and at the graveside, Alan Massey now found himself dealing with their grief all over again. 'I don't think the families will ever get over that. They weren't there, of course, when we were exhuming the bodies, but to put somebody to rest in their grave and then bring them back up again for a post mortem, it must be devastating for any family. I certainly wouldn't like it if it were anybody of mine.'

But the heartache didn't finish there for the family of Alice Kitchen. Joe Kitchen explained: 'We then had to wait almost three weeks, the longest three weeks of our lives, not knowing whether we'd disturbed our mother for nothing or whether Shipman had actually killed her. One night, I took a phone call from the police, who told me that they'd found traces of morphine in Mum's body that shouldn't have been there and that they were going to charge him with murder. That's how it was left with them and I presumed it was going to court.'

But it seems that the exhumations of his former patients were also causing Dr Shipman some distress. In a letter to a couple of former patients who lived close to him in Mottram, he wrote:

I can't feel anything but sadness when I see the names of the people and the addresses in the papers of those being exhumed – how dreadful for them. I cope well till I see their tears.

The letter, written by Shipman from his prison cell, appears to show sadness for the relatives, but Paul Britton, who reviewed the letters for the ITV documentary, believes that the psychopathic serial killer had no sympathy for anyone else. 'We shouldn't lose track of the fact that this man possesses the capacity for infinite compassion for himself. Remember he lives on a day-by-day basis – people I killed yesterday, they're gone now, they're only grey. But now they're telling him they're going to start looking, to start digging, the victims are all going to come back and you're going to have all those relatives, all those people in the community who are suddenly going to say: "Dr Shipman is a monster. Dr Shipman isn't who we thought he was." Now, he believes he can ride that through, but having to contemplate it is an awful process. Over the years he must have been exposed to some literature that dealt with psychopathology and knew at some level that this behaviour is profoundly abnormal. Now, he is being forced to look at it.'

Julian Boon said that Shipman would not in any way be racked with sufficient remorse as to want to help the bereaved. He would not show any remorse or be even capable of showing remorse.

Shipman regularly corresponded with three of his former patients, a husband and wife in Hyde and a former neighbour from his days as a young GP in Todmorden. The Hyde letters were kindly lent to me by Brian

Whittle and the Todmorden ones are still in the hands of the recipient, Shirley Horsfall, who allowed me to film the letters for my documentary. As a teenager during the early 1970s in market town of Todmorden, West Yorkshire, Shirley Horsfall lived in the same street as Fred and Primrose Shipman. It was Shipman's first GP practice. As well as being a former patient she was also a friend of Primrose Shipman and often babysat for the young couple. 'When it blew up and he was arrested, I just didn't believe it. When I saw the picture in the paper I thought it was just some kind of tabloid-selling material. I rang Primrose and said, "I can't really believe what's happening," and she suggested that I write to Shipman. So I did. He was in Strangeways Prison in Manchester. He wrote back, seeming a little, not distressed but obviously anxious, and explaining what was happening at the time. I wrote back and it just carried on from there.'

The letters are written in the same familiar scrawl I had seen on the hand-written medical notes and the phraseology was remarkably similar. The sentences are disjointed, almost in a personal shorthand. It is a continuous stream of consciousness with bizarre punctuation. While making the ITV documentary series *To Kill and Kill Again*, I received correspondence from both Dennis Nilsen and the Moors Murderer Ian Brady. Both these letters were six pages long, written in a similar scrawl, with the same strangely punctuated stream of thoughts, and Shipman's letters reminded me of them. In each case the writer seemed totally obsessed and believed that his opinion, needs and thoughts were all-important.

When I showed the letters to Paul Britton he found them an extremely useful tool to assess Shipman's state of mind at the time of writing. 'The letters, I think, certainly indicate that there's a man who has a door closed, yet in his letters he *is* talking. If you think of a volcano, one of the mechanisms that prevent the full volcano blowing is that there are vents along the way. And in some ways the letters mirror that venting process. You are beginning to see the expression of opinion and those remaining aspects of himself floating through the letters. Even though he doesn't think it's happening and he wouldn't want to acknowledge it happening, you can see him beginning to build a dependency upon the person receiving the letter.

'Now one of the things that happens in letter writing is that he's able to give the recipient of the letter the picture that he wants to. He's not getting visual feedback: he's not seeing their face, or their eyes. He's not seeing them look horrified so his letter to them in certain ways is him talking to himself. And through that he's talking to us. So, if you understand the vents you can certainly get to know a lot about the volcano. This is very useful as we don't very often have people who are such prolific killers as this man and who have a reasonably scientific background that allows us to study what is quite valuable to us.

'I think that you see a process – a man who at the beginning really didn't think he was going to be convicted. He's a man who took what was in some ways a rational, justifiable position. The evidence against him is what? Well, it's circumstantial apparently – this is his view. He clearly thought, "They can't touch me or connect this to me."'

In the case of Alice Kitchen it seems he was right. Alice had been buried in 1994 and her remains were too decomposed for the toxicology results to be conclusive. Joe Kitchen says, 'Mum had been buried about four and a half years. They said that, although they found traces of morphine, they couldn't work out precisely how much would've been injected into Mum's body and whether it would've been enough to kill her. So they decided not to go ahead with my mum's case and two other cases that were very similar, where they'd been buried a similar time.'

Elizabeth Mellor had been found dead in her own home two months after Alice Kitchen in September 1994; Sally Ashworth had died more than a year earlier in April 1993. Their remains were also badly decomposed and again the toxicology levels were inconclusive. Bernard Postles had come to the conclusion that it was time to stop digging up bodies. 'We reached a point with three bodies that we exhumed where the toxicological evidence wasn't as strong as it had been in the other nine and they tended to be the ones that had been buried the longest, about four and a half to five years. I had already decided that, once we'd reached that point, it would be pointless carrying on with exhumations which were very upsetting for families if there was not going to be any result coming from them.'

The other problem for the police was that the software on Shipman's computer had been updated in October 1996. As John Ashley explained: 'The earlier version of the software didn't record the time and date information relating to creation and alteration of data, so I was unable unfortunately to go further back into Shipman's past to show the same system for records that pre-dated October 1996.' This meant that the police couldn't even prove that Shipman had inserted references to fake illnesses in the medical records of these last three exhumed women to cover up his crime. As Bernard Postles put it, 'We knew he had killed them. They had died unexpectedly after a visit from the doctor and the way they died suggested a lethal injection of diamorphine had been administered. The families were suspicious, but we had no actual hard evidence.'

Joe Kitchen was obviously deeply upset by the decision, but even more upsetting was the way he found out about it. 'We didn't find out that my mum wasn't one of the ones until it was in the press. We heard it there first and not from the police, which was very upsetting. We thought the police would've informed us that they weren't going ahead with it at that stage and the reasons, but the reason they gave was that the Crown Prosecution Service wanted to take the strongest cases.'

The exhumations stopped in December 1998, but that didn't mean the murder investigation was over. The police still had over 50 deaths on their list. These deaths fitted a pattern that Shipman had repeated over and over again.

'It wasn't just a case of finding diamorphine in the bodies that was our primary piece of evidence, but what we also had was a whole host of pieces of circumstantial evidence – bodies found in very similar circumstances, Shipman being the last person to see them alive, Shipman discovering the body. There were also many occasions where Harold Shipman told similar stories to family members, which, looked at now, seem incredible,' Bernard Postles explained.

The toxicology evidence from the exhumations had been strong, but so had the evidence of the alterations Shipman had made to his patients' computerised medical records. The police decided to stop looking at patients who had been buried and instead concentrate on those patients killed by Shipman before October 1996, who had been cremated. This new slant to the investigation certainly didn't rule out Father Maher's parishioners, he explained, 'Twenty-five years ago maybe one in fifty funerals would be a cremation. Nowadays there are probably seventy cremations to thirty burials. This is because a lot of people regard it as a cleaner way of going. It's also a little less expensive than being buried and I know you don't like to think of economics in relation to death but somebody at the end of the day has to pay for the funeral.'

It was an option that Dr Shipman actively encouraged. The police found that, in the cases of a sudden death at home, Shipman had frequently brought influence to bear on family members to have relatives cremated rather than buried. He would give as the reason that it was cheaper for them than a burial service but clearly he was pushing families to cremate.

Ann Smith remembered that when her aunt died suddenly at home Dr Shipman had been very keen to push the idea of a quick cremation. 'He was quite abrupt and just said, "We've no need to have a post mortem; are you going to cremate? The certificate will be ready tomorrow".'

Paul Britton sees this simply as the work of a psychopathic killer who is attempting to ensure that he's destroyed any evidence that might convict him. Shipman's preference for cremation and pushing his victim's families in that direction was entirely to do with self-preservation and nothing to do with managing the family's grief.

As Bernard Postles commented, 'Obviously there was finality to this as well, to anybody wanting to come along and exhume the body.'

Even if the ashes of a suspected victim had been preserved they were useless to the toxicologists, who needed tissue samples to detect diamorphine. But Bernard Postles and his team refused to give up and let Shipman get away with murder just because the bodies had been disposed of. Without the forensic evidence the team started to look at the 'similar fact' evidence of how the body had been found, whether the patients had been visited by Shipman before their deaths and whether their patient records had been altered. 'Although we didn't have a body, what we were able to do was to show the circumstances of death were almost identical to the circumstances of deaths where we'd actually exhumed the body,' Bernard Postles explained.

In his letters written from his prison cell, Dr Shipman makes it clear that he was aware that his modus operandi was being used to identify his victims:

Critically, I can see the police case. It is who saw her last, who has access to drugs, who repeats the action – he's guilty. We all have routines. It's the way we live, our tendency, our ability to do tedious jobs, just the way we do it so it is properly done. The police have to prove this routine was made up to hide the murders. Not much hope of that, I hope.
   That's all
   Fred

The police looked at six cases where the patient had been cremated, but where the similar fact evidence pointed to it having Shipman's MO. When 77-year-old Lizzie Adams died suddenly at her home on February 28, 1997 her relatives and friends believed Dr Shipman's diagnosis of bronchopneumonia as a cause of death and, as her death had occurred while he was making a house call, he was able to sign her cremation form. But when the news of Kathleen Grundy's death hit the headlines Lizzie Adams's eldest daughter started to make her own enquiries. She discovered that her mother's doctor had lied about ordering an ambulance and about carrying out an examination of her body after death. She contacted the police.

Lizzie Adams had been a professional ballroom dancer and was still teaching dancing all over the area well into her late seventies. Bill Catlow had been Lizzie Adams's friend and dancing partner for 17 years. When I interviewed him at his home it was clear that the couple were extremely fond of each other. 'She always used to say that life begins at sixty. That's when I met her, of course. She loved her dancing and when she got into teaching she felt she had the world in her hands. We were great together, really. I'd always known her from being a teenager and her husband as well; he died when he was in his fifties. I'd not been in the ballroom for about four years because my wife died in '95 and I didn't want to do dancing again. My niece asked me to teach her to dance, so we went to Oldham Civic Centre and of course Betty [Bill had always called his friend by her nickname Betty] was there. So I had a couple of dances with her and she said, "Will you be coming again?" Then I went the following week and had a few dances with her and when they started tea dances Betty jumped at the chance to go.'

In 1982 Betty Adams passed her teacher's exam and she and Bill Catlow started up some dance classes. 'We were doing night schools – on a Monday we did modern ballroom, on a Tuesday we did easy sequence and old time, for beginners, you know. On a Wednesday we did all the top sequence, the new dances that were coming out about every month. And I had the town hall and did sequence on Monday afternoon, Thursday afternoon and Saturday. And we did that for sixteen years.'

The couple even danced to raise money for Dr Shipman's surgery fund. 'When he started up on his own he had little dances at the Queen's Hotel, so we went to support him. We'd get up first so that then the crowds would get up. He used to buy all sorts with the proceeds. That's how he bought all his equipment for the surgery.'

Just two days before her death the active and fit 77-year-old had returned from a dancing holiday in Malta. 'She was fine in Malta. We were dancing every day, having a drink or two, travelling around the island, and she was fine. We left Malta on the 27th and she was dead on the 28th. There was a coach, because this party we'd gone with were what they call the Over-50s Club, and they dropped me off at Betty's. I had a big case and so she used to roll up some of her dancing clothes, the pleated things, and put them in my case. So I had to take all them out and a pair of shoes she had in, had a cup of tea and I was back home before two o'clock.'

On her return from Malta Lizzie Adams was troubled by a cold and a cough and her daughter picked up a prescription for an antibiotic for her from Shipman's surgery. The following morning she told her daughter that the antibiotic had 'nearly blown her head off'. Bill Catlow told me that the tablets were giving her headaches and so she rang the doctor to tell him.

A note made by the receptionist on the visits request form states that the patient felt dizzy, sick and wobbly and wanted a visit. Shipman told the jury at his trial that, when he arrived early in the afternoon, Lizzie Adams was obviously poorly. She came to the door slowly to let him in; he then said that she led him into the living room at the back of the house. She told him she was breathless, she felt unwell and had a cough. He claimed that on examination he found her heart was racing, she was clammy to the touch and looked pale and her lips were blue. He said he had told her to go to hospital but she refused. He told the jury that at this point Bill Catlow arrived.

Catlow says, 'She had said not to go round until two o'clock and, if Betty said two o'clock, it was two o'clock, not ten past or ten to. She said, "I've got all my washing to do," and I said, "Well, I've got all mine to do as well," so it was about five minutes to two I left here.'

Bill was shocked to find his friend's front door open. 'Then I noticed when I went through the front door the vestibule door was open. And Shipman's there looking into this cabinet – she was a collector of Royal Doulton and cut glass. The place was full of it. He said, "Who are you?" and I said, "You know I am." He did know me; he didn't know me well but he knew me by sight because I'd been to his dances and whatever. Then he said, "I'm sending Mrs Adams to hospital. She's ill, very ill." I said, "You've got to be joking, she was all right yesterday." So I pushed past him into the living room and she's sitting in the chair asleep. I thought she was asleep. So I just shouted at her, I said, "What's going off?"'

Even seven years after his friend's death it was still obviously extremely upsetting for the 90-year-old to tell me what happened next.

'She didn't answer so I went across to where she's sitting in the fireside chair in what she called her working gear, a top and slacks. Her washing was on the lines outside, the ironing board was out and her iron ready for ironing. I just bent over her and said, "Doctor, I think she's fainted."' Like almost all of Shipman's victims Lizzie Adams looked as if she had just fallen asleep.

In his evidence Dr Shipman claimed that he undertook a modified examination – he looked at Lizzie Adams's pupils, her retinas and listened to her heart. Dr Jeremy Dirckze told me, 'In order to confirm death there are certain set examinations that you would have to do – examine a pulse, check pupils, look for signs of breathing. It would be impossible to make sure without some sort of examination for the vital signs.'

Bill Catlow said her GP did none of these things. 'He came walking back in, looked, bent over to her and said, "She's gone." Then I said, "I can feel her pulse." He said, "No, that's yours."' Her oldest and dearest friend couldn't believe she was dead, but it seems her GP knew she was and was so confident of the fact that he didn't even check to see if Bill Catlow had felt a pulse. Shipman knew Lizzie Adams was dead, he had killed her.

Bill Catlow is an elegant man, who I am sure, can still twirl around the dance floor with grace. He is also a proud man and it was that pride that stopped him moving in or marrying the woman who had been more than just a dancing partner to him. He explained to me how Betty had her own home, a far nicer home than his, in his mind; she also had savings, much more than he had. He had felt he could not ask her to give it all up for him. But he also wonders whether, if they had been together, Shipman would have targeted Lizzie Adams.

And, with hindsight, Bill Catlow also now realises the whole scene that greeted him that day was very wrong. 'You can't imagine a woman who's ill getting the ironing board out and doing her ironing. The clothes were all on the line ready for doing. So that was a lie in the first place, what he said. He turned away then and said he'd cancel the ambulance but we now know he had never called an ambulance. And that was it. So I said, "Well, I'll go for her daughter. I know where the youngest daughter works; it's not five minutes from here." He said, "Don't do that. You stay here and I'll ring them." So he must've been looking at her phone book because he rang right away and he was mumbling something over the phone about cancelling the ambulance and as we know now he didn't order an ambulance. There was nothing wrong with Betty, I think. He killed her for calling him out.'

Lizzie Adams's medical records, found in Shipman's garage after his arrest, showed that she had suffered from a number of chronic conditions, none of which related to her death. In her Inquiry Report Dame Janet Smith concludes that 'a natural death at home during a doctor's visit is an extremely rare event'. She also explains that deaths from bronchopneumonia are not as sudden as Lizzie Adams's death was, but the way she was found was 'entirely typical of those observed at the deaths of other Shipman victims'. She points out that yet again Dr Shipman claimed that his patient had refused to go to hospital and that he lied about calling an ambulance.

Bill Catlow had stumbled in on a murder and he is not the only friend or relative who now realises that they arrived just a few seconds too late.

On the day of her death, March 6, 1995, Maria West had invited her friend Marion Hadfield round for tea. The two ladies watched television and waited for Dr Shipman to arrive. The 81-year-old widow had asked to see her GP because he had prescribed some pethidine tablets, but they had not agreed with her and she wanted them changed. Although she used an inhaler for asthma and took anti-inflammatory drugs for arthritis, she was fit for her age and led a busy social life. She certainly didn't appear to have been ill that day and had told her friend she was just about to book a holiday at Butlins.

Marion Hatfield was in the bathroom when Shipman arrived. She heard his voice and remained in the kitchen so as not to intrude. Shipman then appeared in the kitchen and seemed surprised to see her. He said that Mrs West had collapsed on him and that he was going upstairs to find her son, who was staying there at the time. When her friend asked if there was anything she could do, Dr Shipman used a familiar phrase, 'She's gone.'

Marion Hatfield found her friend sitting exactly as she had left her. Shipman did not attempt resuscitation, merely raising Mrs West's eyelids and pronouncing that there was no sign of life. In typical Shipman brusque style he told her son that he had expected her to die and had not tried to revive her as she would have been a vegetable if she had been brought round. On the cremation form he lied, saying that Mrs Hatfield had been present at time of death.

John Nuttall still wishes he had not gone out to feed the ponies on the day his mother died. On the morning of January 26, 1998, 64-year-old Norah Nuttall had gone to see Dr Shipman after she had developed a cough. At lunchtime, she told her son, who lived with her, that the doctor had given her some medicine. She did not say she was expecting the doctor to call and her son was not concerned about his mother's health. He left the house for 40 minutes and on his return he saw Dr Shipman's car outside. The doctor was leaving the house and said that Mrs Nuttall had rung him and that he had rung for an ambulance to take her to hospital. John Nuttall ran into the house and found his mother slumped in the chair, apparently asleep. Shipman said she had taken a turn for the worse, then touched her neck and said, just as he had said to Bill Catlow, 'She's gone.' No record of any call to the ambulance service was found.

On her cremation form Shipman stated the cause of death to be left ventricular failure of 15 minutes' duration, due to congestive heart failure of three years' duration. He claimed to have carried out a full external exam-ination after death and that John Nuttall was present at the death. Dr Jeremy Dirckze signed the second half of the form and, although he had no recollection of the case, he admits he would have relied entirely on what Dr. Shipman told him.

Pamela Hillier had spoken to her daughter just before the doctor arrived and killed her. Jacqueline Gee had spent the morning with her 68-year-old mother sorting through her accounts. About a week before her death Mrs Hillier had fallen and hurt her knee. It had become quite painful so she had asked Dr Shipman to call in to see her. When Mrs Gee couldn't get hold of her mother in the afternoon she sent a neighbour round. Pamela

Hillier was flat on her back on the bedroom floor. When her daughter suggested a post mortem was needed as it was such a sudden death, Shipman said it would be an unpleasant thing to put her mother's body through and that he was sure of the cause of death – she had had a stroke as a result of high blood pressure.

When John Ashley accessed her medical records he discovered a number of backdated records designed to give the appearance of a developing problem with high blood pressure. Shipman had created one final entry for the day of her death, suggesting that her blood pressure was very high and that he had advised her to increase her medication. They were all written at the same time shortly before Pamela Hillier's body was discovered.

A week later Dr Shipman called on Christine Simpson, the warden of Ogden Court, a block of sheltered housing flats in the centre of Hyde. He told the warden that he had just found 57-year-old Maureen Ward dead of a brain tumour. The warden was surprised that Shipman had gained entry to the flat, but Shipman said that Miss Ward was expecting him to drop off an appointment letter and had left the lock 'on the snip'. He told his receptionist, Carol Chapman, that he had seen an ambulance outside Ogden Court and the paramedics had told him Maureen Ward was dead.

Maureen Ward was lying on her bed fully dressed in day clothes. Her eyes were closed and she looked, as Mrs Simpson put it, 'completely straight and tidy'. In the kitchen were signs that Miss Ward had been interrupted while spooning some cat food into a dish. At the time of her death, she appeared to be in good health; just hours before she was found dead, she had helped an elderly resident by carrying a bag of heavy bedding across to the laundry. She was about to leave Hyde and most of her belongings were packed ready for her move to Southport. Some time before her death she had suffered from cancer, but had been treated successfully. Shipman certified her death as due to carcinomatosis, which is the expression used to describe cancer that has become generalised. Patients who die of carcinomatosis do not die suddenly.

DS Ashley uncovered several false entries in Maureen Ward's computer medical records designed to show that during the previous two months she had exhibited signs of a brain tumour. At his trial Shipman would claim that it was only after she died that he recalled her mentioning a whole host of symptoms that could have led to a brain tumour and thought he should amend his records so they were not misleading. The jury clearly didn't believe him.

Kathleen Wagstaff died on December 9, 1997, the day before Bianka Pomfret's body was found. The 81-year-old widow had been in good general health and had gone shopping in Hyde on the day she died. At about 1.45 pm that day Shipman left the surgery without saying where he was going. A neighbour saw Mrs Wagstaff letting him into her flat some time between 2 and 3 pm. The neighbour recalled that she seemed surprised but pleased to see the doctor. Another neighbour saw him in the car park outside the flats about half an hour later. In the mid-afternoon Shipman went to see a neighbour and told him that Mrs Wagstaff had died. He said he would inform the relatives.

Her son Peter says, 'My mother was slumped in a chair and everybody was wondering what had happened because there was nothing wrong with her. We went to see Shipman the following morning and he said to us, "Of course, you knew she had heart disease." But we didn't know. He explained that in certain cases some elderly people just get over it and others die instantly.'

Shipman certified the cause of death as coronary thrombosis.

'He actually put down on the cremation certificate that there was a neighbour present at my mother's death.' There had been no neighbour present but that wasn't the only lie Shipman told Peter Wagstaff. 'He told us that he called an ambulance and cancelled it later, but there was no call listed. He said she had phoned the surgery but there was no record of that call either. He took great pains to say that when he called at my mother's door she said to him, "What are you doing here?" He explained that away to us by saying that when he was paged from the surgery he was just around the corner. He was making out that it was more of a surprise how quickly he had got there. What we didn't know was that the neighbour had actually seen him at the door and heard my mother say, "What are you doing here?" That all came out much later but at the time we just accepted everything he said and it was more a relief that my mother had had Dr Shipman with her when she had died, that she had not died on her own.'

As if that wasn't adding enough insult to injury Peter Wagstaff explained, 'We didn't have flowers at he funeral. We thought it quite appropriate that, as Dr Shipman had been such a caring doctor to both my parents, donations should be to his Patient Fund.'

Len Fellows, who ran the fund, remembers that they donated about two hundred and seventy pounds to the fund on behalf of Mrs Wagstaff.

It seems Shipman's surgery often benefited financially from his murders. Fellows added, 'There were no end of cases like the Wagstaffs. After this all started I began to go through all the correspondence of people who I had written to, thanking them for their donations when a relative had died. I find it very sad that Shipman had murdered the relatives of a lot of the people who gave money to the fund and they were utterly betrayed.'

*

In February 1999 Dr Harold Frederick Shipman was charged with the murders of Kathleen Wagstaff, Lizzie Adams, Maria West, Nora Nuttall, Pamela Hillier and Maureen Ward. The six cremated patients were added to the nine cases where police had been able to exhume the body. Shipman now faced 15 charges of murder.

Hyde's most popular GP spent the next eight months on remand awaiting his trial. During this period he wrote frequently to his friends in Mottram and to Shirley Horsfall. The early letters were mostly about the impending trial. He was also concerned about the way the press were harassing Primrose and his family.

In a letter to Shirley Horsfall, Shipman arrogantly claims that, because the expert evidence on the typed will suggests it was written with just one finger and was badly spelt and punctuated, no jury could possibly believe that he, an educated doctor with good computer keyboard skills, could have typed it. He also bizarrely refers to himself at this point in the third person as 'a doctor'. Later he refers to a deal with the Crown Prosecution Service, but seems to believe it is designed to catch him out by admitting he had morphine in his possession.

9.8. 1999.

Dear Shirley,

Somehow you've slipped through my net of who to write to, since last time a lot has happened. The present situation is there, there was nine bodies and six cremated ones, charged with murder. A trench of fifteen and eighteen put in as evidence, evidence? To show that what I did in 1977, I do now. The police are looking at another fifty three, trial October 4th to February 28th, that's the court booking. Since they set off with four weeks and now five months, don't hold your breath, another Christmas in here to look forward to. The good news that they're expert on typewriters says the will and the letters were typed by one finger on the machine, they were new to, and the phrases and the punctuation showed they were not literate.

A letter typed by a doctor has some similarities of course but in all probability he didn't type the will or the letters, so who did? Not bothered as long as we prove it wasn't me. The GP expert for us came today, I got on with him at once …

The CPS have offered a deal, admit I carried drugs, morphine and they'd volume eight alone. This is the twenty six, sixth cases which are similar, I hope so, I haven't changed how I practice. It will also mean I was in contact with morphine and by inference stole it. If their case is so strong, why the horse trading. I get a three legged horse, motive, opportunity and method. If we challenge them the worse is, is I get guided by my QC is how I work, what my ideals were and admitting in court that yes, I was in contact but didn't take

any. My QC says it will damage our case, how? We're having a few days apart
to think about it, hopefully sort it out by October 5th, the first day of trial,
    That's all,
    Fred

Paul Britton explained, 'I think that when he talks of himself in the third person as "a doctor" you have to remember he's a person who is used to communicating professionally about other people. He will have been writing letters to consultants and others over the years, so he will have a certain formal way of writing. It's also the case that part of his armour is to externalise whatever it is, so that he's not even letting aspects of himself in. He's able to talk about "a doctor" and to feign objectivity, to an extent to withdraw the emotional part that would go with the "I".'

In another letter sent to Shirley Horsfall he talks about the impending trial and the possible verdict. He even jokes about the odds being offered against the verdict at his trial. He also seems resigned to the fact that he won't practise again.

HMP Strangeways, 3.8. 1999.
Dear Shirley,
Got your letter yesterday, thank you yes, I feel better both in anti-depressants
and the case moving have helped. Only sixty three days to go for the start of
the trial at Preston. It looks very likely that they'll change to Manchester.
Prosecution say they need three months to present their case another Christmas
in here. Then we need six to eight weeks and no verdict until when? How long
does it take you to say guilty, guilty with one guilty, with all of them or not
guilty? The way it's going to be presented will mean experts coming to listen
to experts, for them to tell QC's of error and risky questions to ask.

    William Hill fifteen to one – innocent, two to one on guilty. I know they
only have the prosecution's side but it doesn't look good. At least I'll have some-
thing to fill the hours after the trial either way, I'm pretty sure I'll retire
completely, not even locum work.

Julian Boon also looked at the letters for my documentary. 'The letters show firstly a complete lack of any remorse or capacity for conscience what-soever. Secondly, you see the complete lack of any acceptance of any involvement in it or, and this is equally indicative of his arrogance given my personal conviction that he knew exactly what he'd done, even deigning to discuss it or allude to it, beyond how it affected him. So there's ample discussion about appeals and how that might come to his favour, discussion in terms almost like a horse race in terms of betting odds, always how it affects him – him, him, him, him, him. And you could begin to understand the sort of egocentricism that leads him to believe the world out there is simply to be manipulated for his purposes.'

In another strangely schizophrenic letter it appears that he is admitting his guilt, by saying that the Medical Association should have picked up on him earlier, but within a mere comma he has changed it back to the fact that the MA have not supported him.

The MA will be hammered afterwards for not picking me up earlier, for not standing by me and having a suspension placed on me.

As Paul Britton remarks, 'I'm sure that at some points along the way those advising him would have discussed the case against him. Whatever their advice was, he clearly thought that the very worst they could do was to catch him with some administrative issues, some drug-related problem. He will be thinking, "I've been interviewed, I've been over all these different things. They are nowhere near linking me to the crimes."

'But, as time went on, I think he will have come to understand that there was a different process going on in the world outside and that there had been a step-change in the nature of the way that he and the case were being viewed. Because I think that, by the time the trial was well under way, he couldn't have been acquitted and I think towards the end and in those letters you begin to see the recognition of that. Now you have a man who's proud, a man who's arrogant, a man who's conceited, so at some level it will come as a huge shock to him that those grey, shadowy nonentities out there have actually caged him. His position is very likely to be, "They didn't catch me fairly. If they had used the rules, they would've known they couldn't prove anything." So technically, from his point of view, he should've gone free. His view would've been that they caged him on prejudice.'

And, as the trial got nearer, Dr Shipman seems to be less jovial.

Only eight days left, feeling anxious, a little worried, rather like waiting a test result. Life here goes on regardless of how I feel, most if not all specialist reports are read, shredded and re-written. The biggest problem other than the morphine in the body is that I've always said I didn't carry any. The police took my drug bag, my other two bags, searched house and home, found an M and S bag with returned drugs.

Shipman Letters

95

CHAPTER SIX

TRIAL AND RETRIBUTION

I think from the early stages of the investigation there was a realisation by myself and others who were working with me that this would not just finish with the trial.

Detective Superintendent Bernard Postles

In the year that followed Dr Shipman's initial arrest the police were constantly compiling evidence against him. Their list of 60 deaths had now risen into the hundreds, but they did not know exactly how many of these cases they could actually take to court. For the relatives it would be a roller-coaster rider for their emotions.

'Once we knew he was guilty we were in regular contact with the police,' Peter Wagstaff told me. 'We knew there were a lot more cases than even probably the press were aware of because we were getting information filtering through from police officers. We were told at one stage that they were going to do a major charge of 30 victims and then the information came through that the CPS were looking at the more damning indictments where the evidence was stronger.'

The Crown Prosecution Service had ruled out charging Shipman with murder of the three final bodies to be exhumed as it was felt the forensic evidence was too weak, but would they go with Bernard Postles's plan to charge the GP with all the deaths where the bodies had been cremated and there was no forensic evidence?

For Peter Wagstaff it was a tense time. 'We were just waiting to find out whether my mother was included in that. But I think there was always an indication that the evidence was strong, so I felt, and the inference from the police was, that the charge was going to come.' When their family doctor was formally charged with the murder of Kathleen Wagstaff, Peter and Angela Wagstaff came face to face with the reality of what had happened. 'I can't tell you the feeling when they actually said they were charging him. All of a sudden there was a very strong realisation – this is going to court. Whereas at one stage we had been fully supportive of our doctor, now we were going to be giving evidence against this man we trusted.'

The trial of Dr Harold Frederick Shipman started on October 5, 1999. In the end, the 53-old GP faced one charge of forgery, relating to Kathleen Grundy's will, and 15 charges of murder. The CPS had felt this would be more than enough for a jury to cope with. Bernard Postles explained, 'The decision to restrict it to fifteen counts of murder in the indictment revolved around the ability of the jury to actually understand the evidence. That's not an attempt to suggest that they didn't have the intelligence but it's very, very difficult to weigh up the evidence in relation to one case without that influencing your decision in relation to another. There was a wealth of evidence that was presented over a lengthy period of time and the decision to restrict it to 15 was a decision made between the prosecuting counsel, the Crown Prosecution Service and the police on a basis of practicality about what could be achieved in the time.'

Nine exhumation cases had been brought to court: Kathleen Grundy, Winifred Mellor, Joan Melia, Bianka Pomfret, Marie Quinn, Ivy Lomas, Jean Lilley, Irene Turner and Muriel Grimshaw. In addition, along with Kathleen Wagstaff, the CPS had decided to prosecute on five more crema-tion cases: Norah Nuttall, Maureen Ward, Pamela Hillier, Maria West and Lizzie Adams.

On the first day of the trial a white prison van heralded the arrival of Dr Shipman at Preston Sessions House, almost two hours before the hearing began. This would become a daily routine. The van would bring him from prison to the court and take him back at night, with this regular arrival and departure greeted by a firework display of flashbulbs and a crescendo of camera clicks. The world's media had descended on Preston for what ITN described in their ten o'clock news bulletin as 'one of Britain's biggest-ever murder trials'.

After the van disappeared from view the press turned their attention to the Shipman family and especially to his wife, Primrose. A large plain-looking woman, who seemed to wear the same dark, shapeless raincoat to court every day, Primrose Shipman evokes a range of responses in those who have met her. To some she was a wife dominated by a far more intelligent, bullying husband, but to others she was the one who controlled the marriage and what she lacked in education she more than made up for in natural intelligence and confidence. However, there are two things that everyone I spoke to agreed on. Firstly, she was, and still is, fiercely loyal to her husband, secondly is a very good mother to her children. Her marital loyalty was displayed by her constant attendance at the court, while her maternal instincts clearly went beyond her immediate family. As Brian Whittle recalls, 'It was it was quite surreal. Primrose was handing out sweets to the press, chatting to them and asking them about their families.'

At first Primrose Shipman attended Preston Crown Court's Courtroom One with her children. Sam, 16 years old, and 17-year-old David were with her for most of the time; her daughter Sarah and older son Christopher attended less often. As the trial continued she also relied on friends like Shirley Horsfall for a public display of support. 'I did go to the trial with Primrose one day. Obviously, friends did go with her and it was a long trial so I attended it during the October half-term holiday.

'I was very nervous going into the court and spending time with another of Primrose's friends in a small room. I found it very difficult going to get a cup of coffee in the main hall when people were really queuing to get into the courtroom because, as soon as I went into the room with Primrose, everyone started saying, "There she is." They all turned round and started pointing and I found it extremely uncomfortable. Primrose was having to face this day in, day out and I think she had got used to it. In the court with Primrose it wasn't too bad because we were sitting right at the front, with people behind, so that made things easier.'

Preston Crown Court was no stranger to high-profile trials – the two young boys accused of killing toddler Jamie Bulger were convicted there. This case promised to be no less traumatic for the witnesses and families of the bereaved. Leading the prosecution team was Richard Henriques QC, who told the jury they would be hearing testimony from a 'small army' of sons, daughters, friends and neighbours. Shipman's defence counsel, Nicola Davies QC, tried to get the trial stopped on the grounds that the press reports of the police investigation had been sensational. She also requested that the trial should be divided into three: the first trial dealing purely with Kathleen Grundy; the second with the exhumation deaths; and the third with the cremation deaths. Finally, she asked that evidence relating to how Shipman had stockpiled morphine should be withheld as it referred to cases he had not been charged with. The judge, Mr Justice Forbes, denied all three requests.

At the beginning of the trial the defendant spoke only once, when asked by the court clerk to confirm his identity as Dr Harold Frederick Shipman.

'He was insignificant. He could have been somebody up on a motoring charge,' Brian Whittle told me. 'When we first interviewed him, he had been wearing a sports coat with leather patches on the elbows. When he appeared in the dock obviously he smartened himself up but he was no longer ebullient. He'd lost a lot of weight and was alternately attentive and nervous. He asked for pen and paper to be given to him so he could make notes as he went along, but really he looked a pretty forlorn and dejected figure.'

For Danny Mellor this was the first time he had ever seen his mother's murderer in person. 'He was sitting off to the barrister's left. I'd seen him on television, obviously. I looked at him but he wasn't looking at me. He certainly didn't make any eye contact with me, fortunately. Later, when I went to the public gallery, I sat directly behind him and then most of the time I think he was writing, his head was down and he was making notes.'

'Throughout the trial Harold Shipman was taking notes. Certainly in the early stages, he was taking a full and active part in his defence and conversing with his barristers. Most of the time, though, he appeared detached, almost superfluous to the proceedings going on round him,' Bernard Postles recalled.

But it seems Dr Shipman was aware of at least one other person in the courtroom. 'Fred did look up at Primrose but he never looked up and never acknowledged that anyone else was there,' Shirley Horsfall remembered.

Primrose Shipman had visited her husband constantly while he was on remand in prison, but for those who had known him before and not seen him for months there was a dramatic difference in his appearance.

'I was amazed how much weight he'd lost. Looking at him from the back, a suit that used to fit him seemed to be hanging off him,' Len Fellows told me.

Angela Wagstaff, who had rung a newspaper to defend the GP who was now in the dock accused of killing her mother-in-law, said, 'He looked like a little old man, not the doctor we knew. He had gone grey and he looked as though he had lost weight.' DI John Ashley, who was called to give his expert evidence on the alterations to the computerised medical notes, hardly recognised the high-handed GP he had met a year before. 'In his surgery, his own environment, he was very domineering. Now, in the dock he'd taken on a pallor. He was grey, he was small. But he was still defiant.'

Shipman's appearance may have changed but it seems his attitude had not. Father Maher was also called as a witness. 'I went to court and I couldn't get over his whole demeanour in the court. He was staring at me, trying to intimidate me and piercing me with his eyes. I wasn't the only one that he did this to. He showed no sort of feeling at all. Just as he did when I was in the house the day when Mrs Mellor died, he just showed no emotion, no feeling, totally cold.'

Bill Catlow was called by the prosecution to give evidence in the case of his old friend and dancing partner Lizzie Adams. 'When I got up to the stand Shipman said at first that he didn't know me. His lawyer started asking me questions but he did a very foolish thing: he got on to dancing and I said, "You name it we do it – Old Time, Ballroom, Sequence, Latin." I said she was a member of the International Dancing Teachers Association and she was also a member of the United Kingdom Dance Teachers Association and I said we danced every day.'

The defence case was that Lizzie Adams had been very ill with a chest infection when Shipman had called to see her on the day of her death so the fact that she was a regular dancer seemed to interest the judge. 'The judge looked at me and said: "But Mrs Adams was a very sick woman?" I said, "Well, sick or not, we danced seven days a week and that includes Sunday." I told him that, when we were in Malta, we danced every night and then, two days after we got home, she was dead. So Shipman's barrister is pulling at his wig and he didn't know what to say, he's stuttering, and the judge looked at me and he looked at him and the judge said, "You may stand down, thank you very much."'

But not everyone found the experience of giving evidence as smooth as the 90-year-old dancing teacher. All of the relatives I interviewed for the ITV documentary had their own memories of their day in court and most found it traumatic. 'It was quite surprising: you give a statement and a very detailed statement on something as traumatic as that and a day or two later you've forgotten what you said or you've forgotten the details. Of course the statement's been written down, so some months later some very clever barrister comes and pores over that statement and drags this information out of you,' Danny Mellor explained.

'I was very nervous, obviously, because it's not every day you go to a Crown Court and I was giving my evidence and I just looked away at Shipman. The barrister was asking me a question and it went completely over my head. I wasn't listening; I was just focused on this man who had murdered my mum. I had to snap myself out of it and ask him to repeat his question.'

Len Fellows hadn't seen his old GP since they had discussed the police investigation of Kathleen Grundy's will. 'I never even looked at Shipman. I just looked at the jury, the judge and the barrister for the prosecution and the barrister for the defence – all he said was no questions. I never actually looked Shipman in the face at all. I didn't want to be thrown by looking at him. I left the box and went and sat up in the public gallery.'

Danny Mellor also found himself watching proceedings from the public gallery. 'I gave my evidence first of the family and after that you're allowed to sit in the public gallery. I spoke to my sisters in great depth, after my mum's death and before the trial, and we went over all sorts of things, but when my sisters gave their evidence, there were details coming out that I didn't know about, like when I heard about the arm and the bruise, which was very surprising. I can understand why there was so much that was new to me that they already knew about, because it's such a traumatic thing to go through you that just don't want to remember it.'

In the weeks that followed, relative after relative, witness after witness, would have to remember. 'Angela was a wreck when she had to give evidence, but we both felt we were doing the right thing because we were a hundred per cent convinced that what we were saying was true,' Peter Wagstaff told me. 'The first time we got there we were met by Witness Support and there were a lot of relatives there. You are very nervous and upset and they ask you to look through the door and you see inside the court and you can see the back of Shipman's head, which was strange. We went when the prosecution presented my mother's case and we went during the defence for my mother's case.'

Even Angela Woodruff, a lawyer by profession, found the proceedings intimidating. 'I obviously had to give evidence and that was the first time I'd seen Dr Shipman since I knew that he'd killed her. So just going into court and seeing him was scary. But, once I got my confidence, it was OK giving evidence. It was very interesting to hear all the evidence, if you could distance yourself a bit. And it was lovely to hear lots of my mum's friends and colleagues talking about her and bringing her to life again.'

Throughout the weeks of witness evidence Shipman constantly made detailed notes on what was being said and passed on comments and suggested questions to his defence team, seated in front of the dock. But it seems he was also using his letters to comment on the trial. He wrote a number of letters from his prison cell to a man who ran a framing shop in Hyde. Shipman had been a regular customer and he and his wife became friendly with Fred and his wife Primrose and they corresponded. In these letters Shipman gave a good account of what was going on at the trial. The letters are now in the possession of Brian Whittle, who kindly allowed me access to them and spoke about them in his interview for the ITV documentary.

In these letters you see Shipman's bizarre sense of humour. Talking about the judge, he comments that in court you didn't need a Mogadon to get to sleep, you only had to listen to Mr Justice Forbes, the judge.

From the letters it appeared that Shipman was in good, even jovial, spirits, and he seemed to convey this upbeat mood to his wife. 'At lunchtime Primrose went down to spend time with him. She went to see him at every possible opportunity. Obviously, she was concerned, but she thought he was holding up well,' Shirley Horsfall explained.

Paul Britton believes that at this point Shipman was confident. 'He had no reason to believe that he would be anything other than successful. No reason to believe that these people had the intellect to pursue him to conviction. I think that bravado is the wrong word to use for this man. The characteristics that we would think of as bravado are much deeper in him – arrogance, conceit, the belief that there is a huge distinction between his ability to carry things off and that of those around him. I think it's so large that mere bravado doesn't catch it.'

Despite his psychopathic belief that he was above the law his defence team clearly thought it necessary to brief him at length about the trial. Brian Whittle explained, 'He referred in one particular sequence of letters to a briefing by his legal team and this was a bit like something out of a John Grisham novel where the subject is rehearsed in the kinds of questions he's going to be asked.'

The past week has been barrister and solicitor week. Monday we did one case! The way was I read very carefully the notes, then we all read every page together, then Ian asks questions. First, just for informalities, then he played being the QC for the prosecutions and then for the defence. He liked it, waving his arms about, pointing his finger, shouting and saying things like "You took yourself off after deciding that you would kill ..."

Paul Britton believes the defence team needed to ensure that he was well briefed from a psychological point of view. 'He will perceive that there is a huge difference in the elevation between himself in the dock and the judge up there on the bench and he will resent the fact that it's the judge who runs the court. It is important that he knows that, if he irritates the judge, it will not go well for him. He must also know that there are twelve people sitting over there, any one or more of whom may be looking at him at any time. He will know that people make judgements about other people on what they see. A witness makes a particular remark and people will look at him to see what he does, how he looks.'

The letters show he had taken the advice on board but still felt extremely frustrated by the proceedings:

The other big stress is just to sit and hear witnesses speak and not to answer, nod or shake my head and calmly take notes.

According to Paul Britton this is the more familiar side to Shipman's persona coming through. 'This is a man who is unable in the main to tolerate other people's intransigence, foolishness, other people's resistance. He has no regard for people in their own right, only insofar as they give him the rewards or status he wants. Now he is in court, which in our system is one of the most formal, rule-bound situations of all, and I think the person in the dock, even though he seems the centre of attention, is in fact almost the least attended person. He is a viewer or an object.'

For Julian Boon it is all about Shipman's desire to control. 'Control is a main engine of his sort of psychology. As soon as he loses control that sort of personality simply cannot cope.'

Shipman clearly could not understand why the witnesses were being called. In another letter he reveals that he believes he is the only person the jury should be listening to:

The court is a stage. The bit players are now, the stars are both there already – the big star has yet to come (me).

'I think that, when he describes himself as the star in the court and the witnesses as bit players, that is a reflection of his tendency to be grandiose and his urge to be centre stage.' Paul Britton again sees this as typical of Shipman's psychotic view of the world. 'But the ones who are centre stage during the trial process really are counsel and the judge and the people who pass through the witness box periodically. They really are the powerful centres in the court and this tends to be an affront to his sense of importance.'

Finally, it was the turn of the 'star'. After six weeks, 26 days and 120 witnesses, the prosecution case was closed. There was no opening address from the defence, Nicola Davies merely announcing, 'I call Dr Harold Frederick Shipman.'

To start with, dressed in a pale brown suit, with his hands on top of the witness box, he played the role of a small-town GP, answering his counsel's questions quietly but firmly. He even described Marie Quinn as having 'dizzy dos'. But, as he continued, his arrogance started to show through – he used medical terminology in a superior manner with condescending asides and lectured the jury from the witness box.

Bernard Postles recalls, 'When it came to giving evidence I believe that he displayed many of the characteristics that he displayed when he was interviewed by police officers. He was going to verbally spar with prosecuting counsel and he was going to win – which I think was an incredible mistake on his part because it was apparent again that he was lying throughout. So I think that Harold Shipman displayed all the characteristics of Harold Shipman when he took part in the trial.'

Julian Boon believes this was to be expected. 'Shipman was presenting to himself and the outside world as a man who was above everybody else in terms of intellect, of professional status, of being an authority figure, and this meant an enormous amount to him.'

In one sickening moment that Peter and Angela Wagstaff will never forget he told the jury that he had made a mistake on Kathleen Wagstaff's cremation certificate because 'this was one of the few times I was possibly more upset than the relatives'.

Shipman, under pressure because he had lied about the neighbour being there at the time of the death, was trying to explain it away by saying that he was very upset.

Then, at the start of December, two months into the trial, there was a dramatic development. 'There was an incident involving a local radio station where the presenter said, "What do you think about this Shipman business? Isn't it incredible? Why don't they just lock him away and get on with it. He's obviously guilty as sin." So, everybody who listened to the radio could then hear this presenter shouting, "Guilty, guilty." Given our country's laws of prejudice that was incredibly prejudicial to the trial,' Brian Whittle explained. 'The radio station was in court the next day for the most unbelievable dressing-down by the judge, who then called in the jury and said, "Did anybody hear this broadcast?" And they all truthfully said no. Which was very lucky because there have been famous murder trials where the case was thrown out because of prejudice. So the trial could have been aborted at that very point.'

In this case the trial continued into its fourth month and the judge finally finished his summing up on January 24. 'Then the time came for the jury to go out and consider,' Danny Mellor recalls. 'It got to lunchtime and the judge asked the jury whether they had reached a verdict. They had not so there was a break for lunch and everybody went off.'

Peter and Angela Wagstaff told me this procedure was repeated more than once. 'We'd usually call in about quarter past four. The judge would come in and thank the jury for their deliberations and dismiss them and then tell everyone to come back the following morning.'

Back in Hyde the wait was just as unendurable. 'When the jury was sent out I think most people expected a verdict by the end of the week and it didn't come,' Father Maher told me. 'I remember that weekend in particular – most people by this stage had made up their minds and, having been in court myself as a witness and seen him there and also the evidence, I had no doubt whatsoever in my mind that he was guilty. My own feeling and that of people I spoke to was that the following week was one of the longest weeks in my life. As each day went on, the elements of doubt began to arise in one's mind, and not just in my mind but in everybody you spoke to, people were wondering if it was possible that he could be found innocent or that he wasn't guilty because the jury was out for so long.'

Brian Whittle says, 'I don't think anybody in the press doubted that he was guilty.' But, as explained, he and his colleagues from the media also knew that being guilty didn't necessarily mean he would be convicted. 'I think where you have 15 murder charges and the evidence is obviously largely circumstantial and largely forensic there's always a doubt that one of the cases or two of the cases might fail. When you have 15 murder charges, you may have a dozen that are absolutely cast-iron, but there's always a chance that one or two of them might not be proven and therefore the jury would have to come back and it would get rather complicated.'

From his letters it seems the defendant was convinced that he knew what the verdict would be:

> *No verdict till when? How long does it take to say guilty, with one guilty, with all of them.*

'I think by the time the trial was well under way he couldn't have been acquitted. It was simply not possible and I think towards the end you begin to see the recognition of that,' Paul Britton surmises.

Julian Boon suggests, 'He's given the incontrovertibles, things which simply cannot be explained in any other way than his guilt. Even Shipman by that stage had to see it.'

Back at the court, Angela Wagstaff was also confident of the outcome, but she also knew the first case the jury would look at was that of her mother and the forged will. 'That was awful time, absolutely awful. I'm not a criminal lawyer, but I was the one who kept trying to convince everyone who was thinking the jury would come back after a day or something. I kept saying, "But there are 15 murder counts and one forgery account, and they've got to look at each one carefully, or else they wouldn't be doing their job." So it didn't really surprise me, although it seemed a long time when you are waiting.'

Bernard Postles also wasn't worried by the wait. He too had expected it. 'They were considering 15 counts of murder and accounts of forgery. There was an incredible amount of evidence that had been presented; the case had run for just over three months; evidence had been taken for around about ten weeks with witness after witness on behalf of the prosecution. I've got to say that I believe that the jury took their responsibilities seriously and what they decided to do was to weigh the whole of the evidence in each case before they decided whether Harold Shipman was guilty or not. I'm sure it would've been very easy to have come to the conclusion, after considering the first count, that Shipman was guilty of that particular count so he must've done the others.'

It took exactly six days for the jury to reach a decision on all the cases and on Monday, January 31, 2000, they finally came back with a verdict. Danny Mellor and his sisters were gathered with the other relatives. 'We were all called in and everybody expected that again there would be no verdict and that we would be dismissed for lunch again. We all sat in the pubic gallery and one o'clock came and nothing happened, quarter past one came and still nothing happened, and of course then there were all sorts of buzzes going round. "What's happening, what's the delay?"'

'The judge's clerk came into the courtroom and went to talk to some-body, one of the court officials, and walked out again and Kathleen, my sister, was convinced that they had reached a decision and she was shaking,' Danny added.

Peter Wagstaff remembered. 'The lady from witness support said the jury had made a decision. At that point everybody was in a state of emotion and anxiety. There was a sense of urgency; the judge's clerk was running around talking to barristers; the press were getting all hyper-active.'

'It was bedlam, because it was it was half past four, just after half past four, everybody was ready to go home and then they came back in.' Brian Whittle remembers that the press were right up against their deadlines.

Danny Mellor continued with his memories of that afternoon. 'So the jury came in and the judge came in and said, "Mr Foreman, have you reached a verdict?" Answer – "Yes!" They read out each one in turn, but they don't say the "murder of Mrs ...". It is on count number one, murder, "Do you find the defendant guilty or not guilty?" "Guilty!" And I was thinking, "Oh, which count is my mum?" Because Mrs Grundy was count number one, then there was the forgery of the will.'

Luckily, the relatives had Angela Wagstaff. 'When the verdict came it was just such a relief, it was wonderful. My way of coping with the trial had been to write everything down, so I wrote all the evidence down. I think I've got about seven A4 books of it. And when I knew the verdict was coming, I wrote down in my notebook all the counts and the names against them, because I knew that they would do it by count number. So everyone was looking at me, and I said, "Yes, yes, that's yours, that's yours, that's yours."'

Danny Mellor is still grateful for her foresight. 'Mrs Grundy's daughter Angela was sitting just in front of us and Kathleen, my sister, leaned over and said, "What count is me mum?" And Angela said three, or perhaps four. And it came two, three and then four: guilty, guilty. And we didn't know how to feel. The first four or five were from the bodies that had been exhumed but the other verdicts were on cremations and we didn't know whether, when it came to the cremations, they might say not guilty because it couldn't be proved, but of course they didn't and it was guilty on all counts.'

Peter Wagstaff's mother Kathleen had been cremated. 'My mother was the thirteenth charge and we had to sit and wait for that. At that point you are waiting for a verdict and it is very difficult and surreal. You want a guilty verdict but you don't want to realise that your mother has been murdered. So we were waiting for the first 12 verdicts and, as each one was given, everybody was getting more and more upset. Then the guilty verdict came out and I think we burst into tears.'

'Guilty, guilty, guilty, 15 times, and then there was the sentencing and it was, press-wise, the most unbelievable scramble and of course there was all the background material that had been waiting to be published and the TV background ready to go out – it was a fairly sensational night.' Brian and the rest of the press made their deadlines and later that night the 'bongs' on *News at Ten* would reveal: 'Guilty.' Trevor MacDonald would start the main news with the sentence, 'Tonight the doctor who is Britain's worse serial killer was found guilty of the murder of 15 of his female patients and told he will spend the rest of his life behind bars.'

Mr Justice Forbes sentenced Dr Harold Frederick Shipman to life imprisonment with the words, 'None of your victims realised that yours was not a healing touch. None of them knew that in truth you had brought death, death which was disguised as the caring attention of a good doctor.'

The families listened to the words, but they were still coming to terms with what had happened. 'At the end of it all, when we walked out, it was total raw emotion. Everyone was hugging one another; everybody was crying; the stenographer was crying; the judge's clerk and the police were all visibly moved. It was the end to a horrible period. It was the verdict everybody wanted because everybody believed it was the only just verdict,' Peter Wagstaff remembered.

Danny Mellor struggled to explain the cocktail of emotions he experienced. 'I don't know how I felt really. There was a great sense of relief that he'd been found guilty – I don't know how I would have lived if he'd been found not guilty because I was convinced he'd done it – so it was a sense of relief, but also terrible dejection as well. I really didn't know how to feel because it's a feeling that you don't go through more than once in your life and you shouldn't ever have to go through it.'

Outside the court Angela Wagstaff made a short statement. 'I'd written a little speech before, on the basis that he was going to be found guilty, and I just wanted to thank lots of people, but I know that the media don't like thanks, so that didn't appear very much. But I also just wanted to paint a picture of my mum and it was a little bit of therapy for me, I suppose.' The speech didn't go quite as planned as, three-quarters of the way through and fighting back the tears, the emotion caught up with the woman who had set the whole case in motion.

For a few, who had stuck by and defended their GP throughout the trial, the realisation finally dawned – the perfect doctor had also been a serial killer. 'I never doubted that he would be found guilty, I had no doubts whatsoever, not like quite a number of people,' Len Fellows said. He told me about one former patient who had steadfastly refused to believe that Shipman was guilty. 'There was a guy, Bill, who used to have the newspaper shop near him, a good friend of mine, a smashing guy, and Shipman used to go there every day to pick up his *Yorkshire Post*. Bill kept swearing to me that Shipman had never done all this, right the way through until the day or two days before the verdict, and then he said to me, "Len, I think I'm going to have egg on my face. I've been defending Shipman all these months and I think I'm really going to look silly." I said, "Don't worry, Bill, you're not alone. I know quite a number of people who couldn't accept that he was guilty." I knew, having been in the CID, that he was certain to be found guilty but people still trusted him, you see.'

But the case would not end at the trial. In all, 45 of the investigated cases had not gone before the jury and at least 50 more former patients looked likely to have been victims. Outside the court, when Angela and Peter Wagstaff addressed the crowd, Peter had not forgotten those other victims. 'The result was the right result; it was the only result there could have been. But our hearts and sympathies go out to all the other families that are involved in this and have not yet received justice.'

When I interviewed Peter at his home I asked him why, after the trial, he hadn't just gone home and closed the doors. He replied, 'We couldn't do that because there were too many other people involved in this who knew that they were in the same situation, but obviously they couldn't have had all the charges at once.'

Danny Mellor felt the same. 'We'd had a straightforward, legal decision: this man murdered my mother, which was what we wanted. These other people didn't have that. They had very well-founded suspicions, especially as he'd then been found guilty of our murders, but they didn't have that final legal decision that he was responsible for their loved one's death. And that must be terrible to have to live with. I felt terribly sorry for the people who did not have the relief and the release that I and my family had.'

Still, there seemed to be hope for relatives like Joe Kitchen, whose mother Alice had not been one of the 15. 'They led us to believe that further prosecutions could happen, so we were still hoping that that would be the case.'

But, as Bernard Postles explained, it wasn't to be. 'What we couldn't have was a series of trials. After the publicity that surrounded the trial, he would never have got a fair trial in relation to any additional counts of murder – which was obviously the basis of the argument from the Director of Public Prosecutions that he should face no further charges.' On February 18, 2000 the DPP announced that no further criminal proceedings would be initiated against Dr Shipman because of the inability to guarantee a fair trial.

Because of his deep involvement in the case, Brian Whittle knew most of these families personally. He says, 'I think this was pretty tough on the relatives because there were 23 or 24 cases waiting in the sidelines that the police were ready to prosecute with.' Instead of a trial and with no further criminal proceedings, the South Manchester coroner John Pollard was actually able to hold inquests on 27 new cases. He was also able to deliver verdicts on the three exhumed patients that were not included in the criminal charges. Along with Sarah Ashworth and Elizabeth Mellor, John Pollard recorded a verdict of unlawful killing in the death of Alice Kitchen.

Joe Kitchen explained, 'In our case an inquest was opened and at least we got a verdict from the Coroner's Court of unlawful killing so I think we've come to terms with it. I know that doesn't bring people back but it satisfied us to some extent because obviously now we can understand why that happened. He'd been charged with 15 murders and he was likely never to get out again, but at the time we were very annoyed.'

As well as the 27 inquest cases, the police had to deal with hundreds of anxious relatives, alerted by the publicity surrounding the trial, convinced they had a new murder to add to the list. With no chance of further charges being brought, some families tried to get the answers from the former GP.

But as Julian Boon explained, this would never be an option for Shipman. 'I think he was always going to remain quiet because this is his internal world, an intensely private world. There are criminals, for example, I think, Dennis Nielsen, who are only too happy to talk about their crimes in nauseating detail, but Shipman would not want ever to share this with anybody at all.' So while the relatives' letters were greeted by silence, Shipman wrote these cold, comfortless words to his friend in Hyde.

A few letters from relatives asking if I murdered their aunt, uncle, mother, father etc, no answer there, if I deny or admit it, the press will start all over again. To admit anything is silly because I've always denied the charges and it looks like I'll have to keep going. Hopefully not needing to do so after the appeal.

Julian Boon continues, 'Notice no concern for the relatives, no concern for whether or not he actually did it, that isn't even discussed. It's just a question of whether a technicality can get him off being convicted. He never acknowledges any guilt whatsoever. He didn't before, he didn't during interview, he didn't during the trial and he didn't subsequently in the letters. For this reason I don't think, for example, that his relatives would've known or his nearest friends about this private world. And that's not simply self-protection because quite easily he could've told about it and made life easier on himself if he'd put his hand up and said, "Look, this is my particular sort of quirk that I like this power over life and death and exercising it."'

Paul Britton agrees, 'His position is very likely to be that hysteria was at work and consequently he's now caged. But already he's talking of appeals. He is now hoping that he's going to get to a place where there are wiser, more rational, more easily managed judgments.'

There would be no appeal, but it seems there would be an inquiry. On February 1, 2000, the day after Shipman was convicted, the Secretary of State for Health announced in the House of Commons that he was setting up an inquiry under the chairmanship of Lord Laming of Tewin.

Danny Mellor was not happy. 'Initially, immediately after the trial, we were told we were going to get an inquiry and it was referred to in parliament as a public inquiry. Some time later, it said on the radio that Alan Milburn had just announced that the inquiry into the Shipman murders would be conducted in private and I was appalled. We were promised a public inquiry. Well, that started a big fight.'

Danny Mellor was joined by Peter and Angela Wagstaff. 'Alan Milburn said the Laming Inquiry would report back by September. We couldn't believe that could possibly be the case. There was too much involved. I think generally we agreed that what we needed was a public inquiry and that you couldn't have an independent inquiry behind closed doors. It had to be transparent so that we could see what was going on.'

The Laming Inquiry had already begun its preliminary work when Alan Milburn was forced to admit that it would be held in private and that members of the families of the deceased former patients would not be permitted to hear or read the evidence given to the inquiry, or be allowed legal representation. The families contacted solicitor Ann Alexander.

'I was first approached by the son-in-law of one of Shipman's original 15 victims. Following the conclusion of the trial the families had got together and decided that they needed some help because they were looking for a detailed inquiry into what had gone on. Peter Wagstaff contacted me and invited me to a meeting then later it became apparent that the government had no intention of holding a public inquiry, which was what the families wanted.'

In April 2000 Alan Milburn wrote officially to Ann Alexander, as the solicitor representing the group, now known officially as 'The Tameside Families Support Group', stating that he declined to change his decision to hold the inquiry in private. 'It became apparent that we couldn't persuade the Government to change their mind in correspondence and so we had to issue proceedings for a judicial review.' On July 20, the Divisional Court set aside the Secretary of State's decision and resubmitted it to him. He then had little choice but to announce on September 21 that a public inquiry would be held into the issues surrounding Shipman's crimes and it would be chaired by High Court Judge Dame Janet Smith.

Ann Alexander is the sort of glamorous legal eagle you feel would be perfectly at home on the set of *LA Law*. She clearly loves her work and devotes huge amounts of time to it, but it is more than a career. It was clear when I met her that she cares deeply for her clients. 'We succeeded and following on from that we negotiated with the Department of Health for the setting up of the inquiry and, most importantly, for the appointment of a leading judicial figure to chair it. The families were absolutely delighted with the appointment of Dame Janet Smith. She was everything that they wanted.'

Danny Mellor and the other relatives in the Tameside Families Support Group had won a well-deserved victory. 'We certainly had to fight very hard to get that judicial review and when Dame Janet opened the Inquiry it became quite apparent that this was going to be a very, very thorough inquiry.'

The terms of reference for the Inquiry were simple. It would investigate three key questions: how Shipman's patients died; why he wasn't stopped earlier; and what needs to be changed to stop this from happening again.

But, although the terms of reference were set by the Department of Health, Dame Janet Smith went into everything in a lot more detail than the relatives had originally anticipated. 'I'm assuming that, being the sort of woman she was, she determined what she was going to cover and not the Department of Health, because it was not in the interests of the Department of Health and the Home Office to have such a wide-ranging public inquiry,' Danny Mellor told me.

The most important thing Dame Janet did as far as the families were concerned was to look into every single death of a patient of Shipman's throughout his career. Ann Alexander told me, 'None of us ever expected that would happen. I think the most that we expected was that she would look at the deaths that had been reported to the Greater Manchester police. But she went far beyond that and looked into a total of 887 deaths throughout the whole of his career, went into it in enormous detail, called witnesses, took statements and identified whether or not in her opinion he'd been responsible for the death of the patient.'

Dame Janet would spend three years investigating the 25 years Shipman had spent as a GP. In all, her team investigated 887 deaths and one attack on a living person that all occurred during that period. The team now had access to 2311 witness statements taken by the police and 362 sets of GP notes as well as a substantial number of further records. The coroner John Pollard had 52,500 files covering a period of 21 years alone.

As the solicitor representing the relatives, Ann Alexander was involved in the Inquiry from the beginning. 'First, there was all the paperwork that had to be amassed to identify what records were still in existence in relation to each death. That involved looking for medical records, both the General Practitioner records, any relevant hospital records that there might've been, the death certificates, the cremation certificates and so on. Then, in relation to each case, the Inquiry had to identify who the relatives were, who were those people who could give information as to what had happened round about the time of the patient's death and then every single one of those people was interviewed, a statement taken and all of the background information was then put together. So, in effect, she did a mini-murder trial in each case.'

As Ann Alexander explained, this amount of work required a vast team of legal staff. 'In the inquiry team there were counsel, leading counsel and junior counsel who were involved in the Inquiry on a day to day basis. They were supported by a team of solicitors and then there were para-legals in the inquiry offices, who were responsible for doing a lot of the background checking, and support staff, secretarial staff and so on. Then they also out-sourced some of the work to another firm of solicitors who went out and took statements. In our firm we had something like two hundred relatives that we had to interview as well. So even in my firm with all those relatives to interview we had a staff of about twenty at its height, who were involved in doing nothing else but work on this case.'

The main job of Ann's team was to take statements. 'We went to see every single client who contacted us and it didn't really matter how old, or how long ago the death was. There were some who had reported what they believed to have been a suspicious death. Some of those families found out that another family member who had also been a patient of Shipman's had died and that the inquiry thought that that death might be suspicious as well and for them that was very shocking. There were a number of incidences where more than one family member's death was examined by the inquiry, if it wasn't a father or a mother, it might've been an aunt or an uncle. And, of course, everyone knew somebody else even if it wasn't a family member.

'I had a team of para-legals and we arranged for them to do bereavement counselling before they went out to see anyone because of course most of them were very young, they hadn't encountered death and it was going to be a very stressful situation to sit and talk with families who were very deeply distressed about what had happened.'

As the local parish priest Father Dennis Maher found he was also involved in counselling relatives. 'It came as a terrible shock to them when they got a letter from the inquiry to say that their loved one who possibly died sixteen or twenty years ago was part of the Inquiry investigation. To suddenly discover that your mother or grandmother didn't die from natural causes, but might have been a victim of his, came as a cruel blow to many families here. It opened up a whole new area of grief and sorrow and sadness. I remember one very nice lady saying to me one day that receiving this letter from the Inquiry gave rise to feelings worse than when her mum died. She said, "We presumed she died from natural causes and, although we were very sad at the time and we didn't want to lose her, we accepted it and we've done our best since. We've never forgotten her but we've got on with life. But suddenly now, 19 years on, we have this letter here saying that she was almost certainly a victim of Dr Shipman. You have no idea, Father, what this has done to us as a family."'

Ann Alexander's team now faced the hard task of extracting as much information as possible from the families. 'It was really a question of our being able to talk to them and take them back in time and assist them in remembering what had happened. We did make sure that everyone had proper training in that before they went out and I also used to send them out in pairs, so that one could concentrate on the questioning while somebody else was taking the detailed notes. But it had to be very thorough and, of course, once we'd taken the notes, we then had to send the statement out to them. In some cases we actually had to go through it with them in person because it was very distressing for them to remember what had happened and then to have to see it all written down on paper just brought it all flooding back.

'I think it was quite difficult for some of them to remember everything that had happened, but we did have the benefit of having some of the documentation, the medical records and so on, which made it often easier for them to remember because we were able to prompt them a little bit. We also had to make sure that the people doing the interviewing had proper skills to help people remember things that perhaps they thought they'd forgotten but were actually still in their memory, and that way we got an enormous amount out of them. Once they started to remember it became much easier over a period of time for them to remember more and more detail.'

The Inquiry had discovered that out of the 888 cases there was compelling evidence that Shipman was not responsible for 394 deaths. That left 493 deaths and one attack. An overwhelming 335 of these deaths had occurred suddenly in the patients' own homes. One hundred and twenty-four had occurred in residential homes and a further 15 took place at a Hyde nursing home.

Dame Janet made full use of Shipman's MO in assessing these cases, as Ann Alexander explained: 'There were a lot of patterns right from the beginning – people being found in chairs, fully dressed, looking very peaceful, often with the lights on, the television on, in the middle of doing something, Shipman turning up unexpectedly, all this kind of thing. So we actually made a list of all the features that we found and we were just able to tick them off and of course the information the police had from their original investigations was very helpful to us.'

For Bernard Postles, the Inquiry was able to pick up where his investigations had had to stop. 'I think in the early stages of the investigation I found it difficult to believe that Harold Shipman was a killer. But as the evidence mounted I've got to say that there is no doubt whatsoever in my mind that Harold Shipman killed all those people and that's been borne out by the results of the Public Inquiry.'

Ann's legal team, along with others working for the Inquiry, ruled out 210 deaths that were clearly from natural causes. That left 283. Dame Janet concluded that 215 of these were definitely murder, with 45 more there was a 'real suspicion' but the evidence was not sufficiently clear and in 38 cases the evidence was either of such poor quality or simply not available so she was unable to reach a decision.

As someone who never had his day in court because of lack of evidence, Joe Kitchen reserves his greatest sympathy for the 38 cases where Dame Janet couldn't reach a conclusion. 'I honestly feel sorry for those who didn't get a verdict where there was a possibility that he could've done it, but there wasn't quite enough evidence there.'

But, as Danny Mellor explained, for most relatives there was at last an answer to the question they had been asking since Shipman's arrest. 'I'm sure there are some people who are still convinced that Shipman murdered their mother, father, whatever, and the public inquiry has not been able to say yes. But two hundred-plus families have now had that certainty. He's been proved to have killed their relative.'

I asked Ann Alexander when she had realised the enormity of the case she had taken on. 'I think the first point at which I realised that it was going to be a very difficult case and that it was going to involve an enormous number of people was during the course of the first meeting that I had. There were only about a dozen people there at that first meeting but a couple of the people had to leave the room because they were actually too distressed to remain. Then after that the phone just started ringing and it was really scary how many people there were who thought that their relatives had been killed by Shipman. Once Dame Janet had completed her investigations and we then did an analysis of all of the people that we acted for, the vast majority of them had had their relatives killed by him.'

Dame Janet Smith now knew approximately how many patients Dr Shipman had killed, but she didn't know why. The profilers know that no one factor makes someone a serial killer. Instead, it is a chain of sometimes linked and sometimes unrelated events that shape the mind of a psychopath. To find the first link in that chain you need to go right back to their childhood.

> *The work of the investigation and decision writing proved far greater than I had anticipated and has taken longer than I had hoped. I believe that this First Report provides as complete and accurate an account of Shipman's criminality as it will ever be possible to give.*
>
> *Dame Janet Smith*

INFLUENCES AND ADDICTIONS

Serial killers will start killing generally towards the end of a cycle that will start in pre-adolescence.

Rob Ressler, FBI profiler

The criminal psychologists who study serial killers often go back to their childhood to try to find clues to how it all began.

Julian Boon explained, 'It doesn't suddenly start on your forty-eighth birthday and you realise you've got a taste for killing people. It's much more likely to be early on in life. There are some instances where subjects as young as six or seven years of age have had fantasies to do with death and the enactment of death, killing themselves, killing other people and so on.'

Paul Britton puts it another way. 'It is when you begin to look at the unique life-path of this person that you begin to see how he gets from being this grubby but largely blank canvas to this fully painted, terrible, serial killer.'

The blank canvas of Harold Frederick Shipman's life began on January 14, 1946. He was born into a world that had just survived a world war and was full of hope for the future. He was the second child, but the first boy, of his parents Vera and Harold, who gave their son his father's name, which was why he was always called Fred by his family to avoid confusion.

When Brian Whittle first went to Nottingham and started knocking on doors people didn't know who he was talking about when he asked them about Harold Shipman. 'Because the name appeared on the charge sheet that way – Harold Frederick Shipman – the media at large called him Harold, but he's always been known as Fred to his family and friends.'

Brian Whittle had followed the story of the Hyde murders from the beginning and after the trial he decided to write a book on the case. It included detailed research into Fred Shipman's early life.

'He was brought up on a council estate, a decent council estate in Nottingham. His dad was a lorry driver and although the Shipmans were no better or worse off financially than their neighbours, they were regarded as a bit standoffish.'

The family lived in the Sherwood district of Nottingham but, although the area takes its name from the famous forest where Robin Hood and his Merry Men supposedly robbed the rich to give to the poor, in reality this city suburb, raised slightly above the centre of Nottingham, provides a never-ending vista of pre-war council housing.

Longmead Drive is a long, sweeping crescent with small cul-de-sacs pointing off it in both directions. When I arrived to film a short sequence on old black and white film, a reconstruction of the 1960s, I was struck by how little seemed to have changed there over the years. Only the satellite dishes and the PVC windows and doors updated the Edwards Estate and, once shot through the lens of an old Super 8 camera, they went unnoticed against the classic dated background.

The old gate at number 163 is probably the same one that young Fred Shipman would pass through on his way to and from school, the same gate that would have been opened by the family GP when he came to administer morphine to Vera Shipman, as she was dying.

But that is getting too far ahead; we need to sketch in some lines before we start to paint this life picture. 'What we're trying to do is to reconstruct the life, the early experience, the educational experience that we would expect to see in the growing child and the young man,' Paul Britton explains

And for that, it is back to Brian Whittle. 'Fred Shipman was a middle child and his mother doted on him. Vera was a small, slim woman with the same dark eyes and hair that Fred had as a boy. She was very clear about the standard of behaviour she expected from her children. If you look at early photographs of him aged seven years old, he's wearing a crisp white shirt, neat little short trousers and a bow tie, a little bit affected, but his mother wanted him to be perfect. She saw him as the clever one, the one she had plans for.

'A neighbour told me that she thought Vera wanted her children to be different; she didn't want them to be like other kids on the estate. They never mixed with the other kids in the street. He didn't play out. He'd be in the house with his older sister and younger brother, doing his homework.

He had a couple of close friends and this applied all the way through junior school and grammar school, but that was all.'

'He was always on the fringe, but he placed himself on the fringe,' his old school friend, Bob Studholme, recalled. 'He wasn't prepared to laugh at the daft things that we, as adolescent boys, were all up for, you know, our first smutty jokes. I remember once in the changing rooms, after a practice, a chap was telling a dirty joke. We were all guffawing at the punch line and I happened to turn away from the group, because I was aware that Fred was sitting just behind me. He'd heard all this and he looked at me and smiled as if to say, "Don't worry, you'll get better as you get older."

'I don't believe there was anyone who was a super-close friend with Fred. He would always be there, towards the outside of the group, standing calmly and looking quite content.'

At eleven, Fred Shipman passed the entrance exam to High Pavement Grammar School in Nottingham. His parents were extremely proud – according to some sources, sending her son to the traditional, boys-only grammar had been a priority for Vera Shipman and knowing he had pleased his mother must have been an added bonus for young Fred.

The school had been founded in the eighteenth century and was the first non-sectarian school in England. It had been named after its original location between the city's castle and the old medieval city centre, but after the war it had moved to new buildings in the Bestwood district. Although this meant it was less than a mile away from Longmead Drive, Fred Shipman still had to be up and dressed before 7 am to get to school on time.

By the educational standards of the mid-1950s it was modern in outlook and approach. It had earned a reputation for providing a good education for bright kids from less well-off backgrounds and over sixty per cent of its pupils came from working class homes just like the Shipman family. *Virtus Solas Nobilitas* (virtue is the only nobility) was the motto of a school that had been built on a tradition of combining academic with sporting prowess. This was fortunate because, as Bob Studholme told me, 'Fred was good at sport but not naturally academically bright. He was in a science class, after year three, so his strengths were obviously in science, but he wasn't in the highest class. I also had the feeling from seeing him in the sixth form later that he didn't find it that easy. He had to work.'

Brian Whittle's research also revealed that English was Fred Shipman's weakest subject and certainly his letters from prison show a man ill at ease with both grammar and punctuation. 'Fred was placed in the C stream at school. I think he was a person who worked very hard for his knowledge. He had five "O" levels, and never rose above it.'

Bob Studholme by comparison was good at English and went on to become a teacher himself. He believes Fred Shipman and he became friends because he was older than their fellow classmates.

'Fred was a year younger than me but I had been seriously ill at school and I had to repeat my second year. When I came back after being hospitalised, there was this young man, who was very gifted at games and had wonderful sideboards, at that very young age, of which we were all envious, and he was certainly a person within the year group who commanded quite a lot of respect. He was a very calm person and far more mature than us. He was physically more mature; perhaps he shaved the edges of those sideboards and things, which made the rather immature adolescents very envious.

'My relationship with him was basically on the sports front. He was a talented sportsman. He was a very good rugby player so we travelled in teams together. He was a great guy to play with, he really was. He played county rugby. As we all grew later on, we tended to surpass him physically, but even if he was physically not big, he was well built and hard, didn't mind taking the rattle. If it meant it benefited his side he was a gritty rugby player.

'He was a man of few words, a man of action, very determined, hard and quick; he had a real streak of ruthlessness. In a game of rugby, there is always an opportunity where you come up against your opposite number and it's you or him. Fred always made sure that it was him. He was a lamb in the house and a lion in the field, I think is the expression.'

That determination and streak of ruthlessness would be seen later in his MO, but more important to the profilers is Fred Shipman's relationship with his mother. 'What you can see clearly is the particular strength of the relationship Shipman had with his mum. The influence of a strong mother character in their early lives is something that a great many serial killers have in common. Dennis Nilsen has a strong mother, so did Fred West,' Paul Britton explained.

It is clear that Vera Shipman's relationship with her son made him feel superior and it was then that he started to develop the feelings of self-importance, while the arrogance and haughtiness that would figure so prominently in his adult persona clearly have their origins with the little boy who from a very early age had set himself apart from the rest.

But the greatest effect on young Shipman would have less to do with the relationship with his mother and more with the tragic events that would overtake this close bond.

Fred was 17 years old and in his first year of sixth form when his doting mother was diagnosed with terminal lung cancer. In the 1960s such a diagnosis meant a slow, painful and inevitable death. The whole family would have been well aware of the shadow that hung over them. But it seems that the family that neighbours described as 'standoffish' kept their troubles to themselves.

'We didn't know an awful lot. We were semi-aware that his mum was ill. And there were a few incidences of people who had members of their family who were ill; at the time tuberculosis was still in evidence. We assumed that it would be that,' Bob Studholme explained.

'I don't think I ever saw his dad. I think he was a busy man, working, particularly as the mother's state of health deteriorated. I think the father had an awful lot on his plate. They weren't the sort of people you'd recognise at a school concert, or at the school play, or anything like that.'

Harold Shipman was a busy man, and so it was Fred who would be the first of the family to return home in the afternoon and, according to Brian Whittle, he had a regular routine of making his mother a cup of tea and waiting for the doctor to arrive. Vera was in extreme pain and her only relief was daily doses of morphine.

'Vera's death came before the hospice movement.' Brian Whittle explains. 'The attractive house-proud woman was now emaciated, gaunt and debilitated, putting all her energies into coping with the pain. Seeing Fred at the end of his school day rallied her, but as the weeks went by she could hardly raise the energy to sit up and spent all her time in bed.'

Brian Whittle's research has revealed that normally Vera Shipman's son would be present when the morphine was administered. 'The routine would be that the local doctor would call on her most days in the afternoon, but medical protocol demanded that somebody else would have to be present when she was given the morphine injection. You didn't have diamorphine pumps in those days, it had to be an actual injection, so young Fred would witness the injection being given, easing the terrible pain she was in. It must have made a profound impression on him. That was his first experience of seeing that particular drug at work.'

The criminal psychologists see no coincidence in the fact that in later life Dr Shipman chose the afternoon as the time to administer his lethal injections, or the fact that he used the same drug – diamorphine. Julian Boon believes the emotional impact of watching the effects of such a strong, painkilling opiate would have made a huge impact on a 17-year-old traumatised by the imminent death of his much-loved and doting parent. 'There was a fascination with drugs and the impact of drugs and that may well be linked to watching his mother being treated in the days leading up to her death.

A smiling Fred Shipman (bottom right). His friend Bob Studholme (middle row second from end on right).

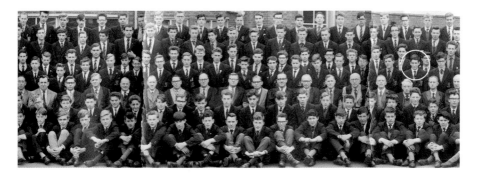

Above: High Pavement Grammar School. A teenage Fred Shipman in the fourth row.

Below: Shipman married at 20. His bride, Mary Rose Oxtoby, was 17.

ℒast 𝔚ill & 𝔗estament

RESIDUE TO ADULT (FORM 1)

PRINT NAME AND ADDRESS	THIS Last Will & Testament is made by me KATHLEEN GRUNDY of LOUGHRIGG COTTAGE 79 JOEL LANE GEE CROSS HYDE CHESHIRE SK14 5JZ I REVOKE all previous wills and codicils.
EXECUTORS' NAMES AND ADDRESSES	I APPOINT as executors and trustees of my will HAMILTONS WARD & CO and of CENTURY HOUSE 107-109 of MARKET ST HYDE CHESHIRE
SUBSTITUTIONAL EXECUTOR'S NAME AND ADDRESS	and should one or more of them fail to or be unable to act I APPOINT to fill any vacancy of
SPECIFIC GIFTS AND LEGACIES	I GIVE ALL MY ESTATE, MONEY AND HOUSE TO MY DOCTOR. MY FAMILY ARE NOT IN NEED AND I WANT TO REWARD HIM FOR ALL THE CARE HE HAS GIVEN TO ME AND THE PEOPLE OF HYDE. HE IS SENSIBLE ENOUGH TO HANDLE ANY PROBLEMS THIS MAY GIVE HIM. MY DOCTOR IS DrH.F.SHIPMAN 21 MARKET ST HYDE CHESHIRE SL14 2AF
RESIDUARY GIFT	I GIVE the residue of my estate to but if he/she or any of them take more than one person and if them fails to survive me by 28 days or if this gift or any part of it fails for any other reason, then I GIVE the residue of my estate or the part of it affected to MY DAUGHTER
FUNERAL WISHES	I WISH my body to be ☒ buried ☑ cremated other instructions
DATE	SIGNED by the above-named testator in our presence on the 9th day of JUNE 19 98 and then by us in the testator's presence
TESTATOR'S SIGNATURE	SIGNED *K. Grundy.*
WITNESSES' SIGNATURES NAMES AND ADDRESSES	SIGNED ▓▓▓▓ SIGNED ▓▓▓▓ of ▓▓▓▓ of ▓▓▓▓ occupation *Shop Keeper.* occupation *Moving + Handling Co-ordinal*

Greater Manchester Police photocopy of Kathleen Grundy's will.

Kathleen Grundy and grandson. The mayoress of
Hyde who would be Shipman's final victim.

Winifred Mellow with
her son Danny and her
grandchildren.
Shipman was convicted
of her murder after
high levels of morphine
were found in her
exhumed body.

Val Cuthbert. The
former Hyde publican
who pulled strings to
get back on Shipman's
patient list. He killed
her a year later.

Kathleen Wagstaff. Shipman was convicted of her murder even though she was cremated.

Kathleen Wagstaff and Ann Royle. The two mothers Shipman mixed up.

Lizze and Bill. Dear friends and dancing partners. But Bill Catlow arrived too late to save Lizzie Adams.

Alice Kitchen and her sisters. Alice Kitchen was not one of the 15 cases taken to court – her body had been buried too long.

Arthur and Hetty Stopford. The deaths of both these grandparents were investigated by the Inquiry. Shipman had planned to use Arthur to get more diamorphine but his family became suspicious.

Lucy Virgin. She called her niece minutes before her death.

Betty Royston. Did her dementia mean she could see a side to Shipman his other patients couldn't?

Joan Harding. Died in his surgery.

John Shaw. The taxi driver who spent six years compiling a list of elderly female clients who had died suddenly.

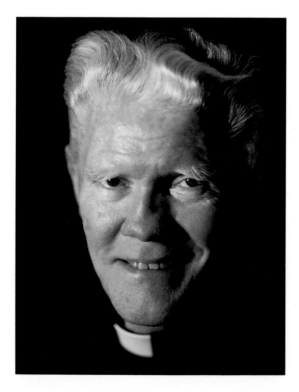

Father Dennis Maher. A great many of his elderly female parishioners were patients of Dr Shipman. Tragically, he was to attend the exhumation of four of them.

'The maternal attachment is an extremely important thing. His mother was receiving injections of morphine and he was witnessing that and he may well have got some sort of buzz out of it. This would have been very much in his inner world and it may well be that this, inter-linked with his fascination with death and the control over life and death, may have been something which gradually became the stronger and stronger engine in terms of personality and then one day he begins to acts it out.'

Paul Britton comments, 'When you look at his choice of morphine, he has a history with it. From his point of view it's effective, it works easily and quickly; it's not messy. It's something he's comfortable with.'

Finally, on Friday, June 21, 1963, Vera Shipman passed away in a morphine-induced coma. Both Fred and his younger brother Clive were with her. The family GP, Dr Andrew Campbell, is no longer alive, but it is likely that, like most caring GPs, when it was clear the pain had overcome all of his patient's strength and sheer exhaustion meant she could fight no more, he would have administered one final, larger dose of morphine. He would have also injected it slightly more quickly into the skeletal arm of his dying patient.

The injection is never meant to be lethal in itself – it is merely meant to help ease the patient on their way. For obvious reasons, it is a subject few GPs will talk about, much less admit to publicly, although it is still, as I understand it, common practice and it was one of the possible explanations that his fellow medics originally came up with for Dr Shipman's overuse of morphine. I watched as just such an injection being given to my terminally ill father. In his case, as I am sure happens many times, his GP had been slightly premature and he survived a few more days.

'The death of his mother and especially the nature of her dying must be significant,' Paul Britton told me. 'I think that, if we could know how he felt during the time before her dying, through her final treatment and immediately after her death, we would see that he moved from a sense of anguish to a release from that. So there would at least be the beginning, the signals of that sense of peacefulness that he went on to develop later.

'Shipman will be visualising how his mother looked in death and this, I think, is one of the key drives for the man. Other people who kill under similar circumstances need some motivational drive, for the peaceful joy that comes from that death and dying process. I can think of one man who killed animals at a very early stage and he was able to remember the great pleasure, not of the killing but of the warm, waxy, the floppy remains of the animal and how much pleasure and contentment, how much peace he got from that.

'I think Shipman had the same deep and profound joy in the presence of death and in particular seeing the transition of someone from life into death.'

Paul Britton believes it was the result and not the actual act of murder that drove Shipman to kill and kill again. 'I can't see anything that indicates that killing in and of itself was valuable, because usually it's conducted as quickly and as efficiently as he can. What he's looking for is that great peace, that joyfulness, that sense of everything being as he would want it to be when the victim is dead.'

Paul also believes that the way the bodies of his victims were found links back to how he saw his mother after she had died: 'I believe sometimes he arranged the deceased person, moved their limbs to exactly where he would like them to be. I think that's the tableau, that little scene.'

While Paul Britton believes that Vera Shipman's death helps to explain why Shipman killed in the way he did, the profiler is quick to point out that it is one event in a long chain that eventually led to his overwhelming desire to kill and kill again. 'It would be wrong to think of this as a seminal trigger.'

Young Fred Shipman's reaction immediately after his mother's long-expected death is also extremely significant for the psychologists. 'He was 17 at the time. He didn't tell anybody she'd died but just went to school as normal on the Monday,' Brian Whittle told me.

Bob Studholme remembers the story their mutual friend Michael Heath told him the following day. 'They were walking to school, because Michael's bicycle was broken. And Michael said to him, "Was there anything exciting at the weekend, Fred?" "No," he said, "my mum died."

'Michael was absolutely staggered by this and said he spent the next few seconds wondering what to say. So then he said he was sorry at the news and asked Fred what he done. And Fred told him that he had gone out for a run.

'Apparently he'd left home, some time after his mother had been declared dead, and set off on this enormous run, out through the northern part of the city of Nottingham, over the country boundary, out across some agricultural land, back through an old mill village, and back home, which would be a minimum of ten miles. The friend asked him if it had rained and Fred said, "Yes, all the way."'

'He was an excellent middle-distance runner and he just went out and ran miles and miles, round the streets of Nottingham, in the middle of the night, presumably to try to fill his mind with something else to concentrate, to take the pain away,' Brian Whittle added.

Julian Boon feels this emotional distancing is a major clue to Shipman's psychological profile: 'This is evidence of psychopathy. Most people aged 17 or whatever would be devastated by the loss of a relative in those circumstances. Yet he isolated himself. He went out on a very long run. He appeared to lack any signs of grief or emotion and was remarkably quiet about his mother's death when he got back to school on Monday.'

To Paul Britton it is clear that the shaping of Shipman's personality had begun in his childhood. The death of his mother had taught him that he could isolate himself from his emotions. He would later use this ability to deal with any stressful situation and it would prove extremely useful to him once he began killing.

'This is a man who, from his very earliest years, learnt to deal with intense, internal feelings so that when he dealt with other people he could be matter-of-fact and calm and controlled.

'This is something that he would come to rely on. I think that when you look at his behaviour with the bereaved families, after the deaths he brought about, you have to understand that for him the value of the death has largely gone, certainly for the moment. Very often, after high-impact events, people do have a "down time" when their personality comes to the fore and I think with the families it would be important to give no inkling at all that this deceased person might have any particular value to him.

'Also, I think you have to look at his behaviour at the end of the first significant police interview when he had his crisis, after which he shut down yet again.

'I don't believe that his reaction to the death and the treatment of his mother at her dying was indifference. We don't know how he truly felt in the period immediately after his mother's death. It is simply the case that part of his armour is to externalise whatever it is so that he's not even letting aspects of himself in.'

His old school friends would experience this emotional distancing again when, almost forty years later, they tried to contact him. 'At the Old Boys' Rugby Club, there were of course several people who remembered him and were very concerned. There was a degree of sympathy for him,' Bob Studholme explained.

'They were bullying me into writing to him. So I did. I didn't write a long letter and I began it with the first line of our school song. After that I wrote, "Fred, there are lot of people in Nottingham still thinking about you in a 'very positive vein'." I suggested that if he would like to get in touch, he should not hesitate to do so.

'But I had no response from that at all. Another friend had indicated that he had written and Fred had written back to say that he had no memory at all of his fellow pupil. He seemed as if he wanted to keep us out of the situation. The whole thing surprised us – to suddenly shut off what had been, I would think, a very positive and pleasant part of his life – lots of support, good pals, a good and positive school. It was a disappointment to us, in fact, we felt rejected.'

The death of Vera Shipman would have one more obvious effect on her son – Fred Shipman had a sudden desire to become a doctor. Brian Whittle told me that, according to his family, seeing the GP minister to his mother appears to have had a profound effect on his future career plans. 'After his mother's death it became his avowed ambition to be a doctor. There's no mention of that prior to that. So it may be simplistic but maybe the wonders doctors could do for their patients was something that made an impression on him. He was taking his "A" levels at the time or studying for them – he took chemistry, physics and biology – and in fact he had to re-sit them to get into medical college.'

Finding out thirty or so years later that his old friend had become a GP was a shock to Bob Studholme. 'Fred never said he wanted to be a doctor. I assume that he did much better at his "A" levels than in 1964. He must have upped the grades to see if he could get a place in medical school.'

Bob Studholme went off to university after taking his 'A' levels and had lost touch with Fred Shipman. 'There was an element of confusion here, because I left High Pavement in 1964 and I believed that Fred had too. It was only when someone pointed out to me on a prize-giving programme that Fred had returned to the third-year sixth that I realised he'd gone back and had another go at his "A" levels. I thought, knowing Fred, because he was in science, he'd look at something with chemistry perhaps.

'For years, I looked when I was playing rugby at uni, and asked players on other teams: "Where's Fred Shipman?" But we never found him. I always thought he'd pop up somewhere. When the news first broke on the television and it said Dr Shipman, I assumed it was an academic Dr Shipman, and not a medical one. It was that much of a surprise.'

For relatives of his victims, it is easy in hindsight to look cynically at Shipman's choice of career, as Danny Mellor pointed out: 'It raises the question in my mind about his motives for entering the medical profession, whether it was on the basis that it would give him a ready supply of victims.'

But Paul Britton believes that, at this early age, the young Fred Shipman would not have been aware enough of his dark desires to plan ahead that much. 'I think it's highly unlikely that Shipman determined to become a doctor so that he could begin a life of killing people. If he had had that as an urge, then he wouldn't have been able to resist it for the five, six years that you need to go through training. It's something that would have had to express itself in other ways.

'One effect of his mother's death would be to make him quite lonely, so that the vocational urge may very well have been present. It's important not to make the mistake of thinking that from the very beginning this was a sinister man who was heartlessly manipulating the entire world just to put old ladies in front of him so that he could kill them. I think that training and practising and qualifying as a doctor are much too demanding for that to be the only motivation. There are much more simply acquired technologies that would allow him to become a murderer. I'm reasonably sure that he did see himself as an important heroic medic at some points. He went into medicine almost certainly with a vocational prompt. I don't think he went in to become a serial killer.'

But the path he had chosen meant that, within five years, Shipman's vocational prompt and his psychopathic desire to kill would coincide.

In September 1965, just two years after his mother's death, Shipman left Nottingham and headed north. He had gained a place at Leeds University's Medical School. 'I think it's important to remember that the training of a prospective doctor includes a lot of working with the dead,' Paul Britton explained.

'There are post mortems. They are working with remains, visiting sick people in the hospitals, quite possibly being present as people die. So by the time he finished his early medical training, he would be quite familiar with death. What we don't know is what exactly gave him the thrill sensation.'

But we have a clue. According to some of his fellow medical students Fred Shipman was fascinated with corpses. It appears that, unlike many of his colleagues, he was not squeamish about handling a body and he is said to have stayed in a hospital morgue after other students had gone home, claiming he had stayed behind to spend more time studying the body. If this were true, it would provide the thrill sensation Paul Britton was looking for.

Shipman's time at Leeds certainly provides the psychologists with yet more clues to how and why he killed but it also provided him with a single event that would shape the rest of his life.

Brian Whittle explained, 'He shared a house on the outskirts of Leeds, on the Wetherby Road, just off the ring road leading into central Leeds, with another student. They got a regular bus to the medical school, the number 38.

'On the back of the bus was a girl called Primrose Oxtoby, who was 16. She didn't have any qualifications but she'd shown a bit of a flair for art and had got a job as a window dresser. She came from a very strict background;

her parents were Methodists, God-fearing people. She couldn't wear make-up or go to the local hop. This was the Swinging Sixties when it was all happening or supposedly, and she didn't get a taste of it at all. But as she'd got a job and a bit of freedom, she had a few friends and so there were giggly girls at the back of a bus.'

A giggly girl is a far cry from the media image of the large, sour-faced lady in the dull, shapeless raincoat, with her equally shapeless haircut, the woman who attended the trial of her husband every day, but who refused to talk to the press, to give the emotional interview we all secretly hoped to bag. But who knows how any of us would react to the revelation that our husband, and the father of our children, is the country's biggest serial killer? No one can doubt the damage that could do to the strongest personality.

According to the hints dropped by Dr Wally Ashworth during his interview with me, at this stage in her life Primrose Shipman hardly had a strong personality. 'She was a patient of mine and therefore I'm restricted in the things that I can say, but a lady who I think was carrying a lot upon her shoulders. For me to make any statements as to whether she was depressed would be entirely wrong, having been her doctor. But I suppose one could conjecture that she was.'

Brian Whittle told me, 'I think originally she could have been quite a fun-loving person and girlish, not unattractive. In early pictures of her, when they were married, she could look quite attractive, dressed up to go to a medical reunion. She went to several, there are pictures of that and they were very happy together. They had a good social life, although it did revolve round the family.'

Her old friend Shirley Horsfall, who first got to know Primrose Shipman as a young mother, believes that the media thought that the woman they saw had always been like that. 'Watching the television drama they did in the not too distant past and the way that Primrose was portrayed, I was amazed. Where did they get this character from? It was nothing like the Primrose I knew. They portrayed Primrose as dowdy and unintelligent and she's not a bit like that. The character would have been better played by Pam Ferris or Pauline Quirk than the person they did use.'

Wally Ashworth also sees Primrose differently from how she was portrayed in the documentary: 'I suppose one could say that she was a motherly sort. She was a nice enough woman who had other interests apart from his surgery, although she frequently went with him to his interests and became socially involved with, for instance, the rugby club. But to me she always looked rather nervous. It was a little difficult to be certain who was dominant in the household. One would naturally have thought it would have been Fred, but then, if I was guessing, I would have thought that perhaps his wife was somewhat of a dominant feature in the household.'

But seems everyone has a different opinion of the dynamics of the Shipmans' marriage. 'Fred himself was a terrific disciplinarian and she was a good mother,' Brian Whittle told me, 'but over the years I think they lost the plot a bit. I don't know whether they lost interest in each other but obviously she put on a huge amount of weight and I don't think her relationships with her own children were as good as they might have been. They did all at some point attend the trial and she's tried to keep the family together, with some degree of success.'

What we do know for certain is that Primrose Oxtoby was poorly educated in comparison to Fred Shipman. Unlike her future husband, she had failed her eleven plus and had gone to Wetherby Secondary Modern, where the emphasis was on practical rather than academic skills. Classmates there described her to Brian Whittle as 'a rather butch-looking girl, sturdily built, but not fat. She had a pudding basin hairstyle and a scrubbed face. She was remembered as wearing twin sets and pleated skirts, quiet, plain and forgettable.'

But clearly not everyone found her forgettable – she was after all voted vice-captain of her school house and in this role she would organise teams for sports days. Her fellow Guide pack members also recall her as a sensible organiser.

In 1964 Primrose Oxtoby started to catch the 38 bus into Leeds every day because she had won a place on an art and design course in Leeds. It probably wasn't exactly what she had planned as her mother Edna had insisted she combine the one-year course with a catering qualification. At the end of the course, armed with a certificate, she got a job as a window dresser. Her new job and her income apparently gave her more confidence and the Primrose recalled by Shirley Horsfall is much more akin to the giggly girl Fred Shipman must have seen on his daily bus journey to medical school: 'Primrose is a bundle of laughs really, very good company, good fun. Very down to earth, very jolly, very bubbly and vivacious. We used to spend quite a long time just chatting and she managed to make humour out of anything. It was good fun being there and I enjoyed her company.'

Shipman also bore little resemblance to the bearded, bespectacled GP who became familiar to the world. 'As a young man Fred Shipman was quite a handsome guy,' Brian Whittle explained. 'He had a mop of curly black hair and he dressed smartly. There are some pictures taken of him on a rugby tour where he's wearing a yellow waistcoat and really posing for the camera and he looks the business. He stands out in that particular group. He was stocky, but quite well made. He was a good rugby player and pictures of him at that age – 17, 18, 19 – show him to be quite handsome, quite a catch, especially to a 16-year-old girl, a giggling teenager getting on the bus, going to work with her friends.

'He caught her eye and they got together. They got talking, went for a coffee in Leeds and they quickly became boyfriend and girlfriend. Within a very short space of time they became more than that. Primrose obviously fell for him and he got her pregnant. She was 17, he was 20 and they were in deep trouble.'

However, Primrose appeared very happy with her unexpected condition. 'She wasn't fazed about this at all, but she told her girlfriends, "Guess what? I'm pregnant."'

No one knows what Fred's reaction to the news was but, according to Brian Whittle, Primrose was not the girl he would have married had he been able to explore other options. 'Many years later Fred told a nurse he was working with that getting Primrose pregnant was a mistake. He said, "I was a bright boy, I should have known better, shouldn't I?"'

Primrose had never had a boyfriend before, and it seems she was Fred's first girlfriend. 'I would say, knowing Fred as well, that there was perhaps little experience on either side when they first met. He certainly never had a girlfriend a school, as far as I am aware. When we had our sixth-form dances he would bring his sister along,' Bob Studholme told me. When eventually he saw his old friend's wife on television he was shocked. 'I thought that, although she looked a very motherly type of lady and he had all the signs of being cared for, I thought he might have married someone small, dark, petite. But it's that chemistry isn't it, and there must have been at that time some chemistry between them.'

Len Fellows was also bemused by his doctor's choice of wife. 'She was not on the same intellectual level as Shipman. She obviously wasn't a well-educated lady. She was always pleasant and polite to me, but she was rather a dowdy sort of person. She was rather heavily built, plainly dressed, frumpish is the word you might use. You'd wonder at what chemistry brought these two people on different intellectual levels together. I would've said that Shipman and his wife were chalk and cheese.'

Chalk and cheese now had a bigger problem than differing personalities. Brian Whittle says, 'Obviously, they had to break the news and her parents were absolutely mortified, as indeed were his.' Harold Shipman senior had much higher hopes for his doctor son and Primrose's family were not only strict Methodists but had the strong morals to go with their old-fashioned, working-class values. 'Her father George worked for the local council, although he had been a farm labourer. They were a hard-working family who'd made their way, had a nice house in Wetherby, due to an inheritance, and they wanted their daughter to be brought up the right way. She'd learned to play the piano and went to Sunday School – they tried to do all the right things.

'Now her father, George, had a soft spot for Primrose, especially as her elder sister had died of multiple sclerosis. George doted a bit on Primrose but her mother certainly didn't. The shame sat very heavily on Edna Oxtoby. It seemed the very first time her daughter was let off the leash, and goes out to work with a bunch of girls, she falls for this handsome guy who gets her pregnant virtually first time. She was not impressed.

'She took an instant dislike to Fred because she thought he was smarmy and superior. You see, he'd become a medical student and that was a very much a kudos thing and he fazed about the fact that he'd got their daughter pregnant. They were going to stick together and make the best of things and in fact that's what they did for the rest of their lives. But the resentment Edna Oxtoby felt lasted all through her life.

'Years later, after Shipman committed suicide and his wife went back to the area and tried to make amends for things and make up with her mother, a very strange thing happened. Just a few weeks before her death Edna Oxtoby, who had gone into a nursing home but still owned a very substantial house in Wetherby, re-made her will, leaving her money to a neighbour with a number of other very small bequests. She did this knowing that Primrose was in dire financial straits, knowing she had four grandchildren, two of whom she'd never seen, and in that will Primrose didn't get left a penny. So that's indicative of the deep resentment felt by Primrose Shipman's mother.' Brian explained.

Harold Shipman married Primrose Oxtoby at Barkston Ash Register office, ten miles from Wetherby, on November 5, 1966. Some accounts of the wedding have the bride in a long blue dress and the groom in an ill-fitting black suit that was either borrowed or the one he had worn at his mother's funeral. He could certainly not have afforded a new one. The copy of the marriage certificate we acquired for the ITV documentary simply records the groom as Harold Frederick Shipman, aged 20, a bachelor whose profession is described as medical student. He had given as his residence at the time of the marriage his digs in Wetherby Road. The bride, Primrose Mary Oxtoby, gives her age as 17 and her occupation as a window dresser. Her address is her parents' home in Wetherby. Harold Frederick Shipman, lorry driver, and George Oxtoby, Highways labourer, are listed both as the fathers and as the two witnesses.

Brian Whittle says, 'Obviously there had to be a shotgun wedding and this was a cause of great shame to her parents, who wanted it hushed up. So they got married out of the area, rather than in Wetherby where Primrose came from, and none of their friends attended this wedding. As far as I am aware, there are no photographs in existence of it.

'But Shipman and his new bride were very happy together. They were an incredibly close couple. I think it's just possible she was in total thrall to him and that they lived almost inseparable lives. Primrose spent almost forty years with this one man – they did everything together. Primrose even stood in at the surgery on Saturdays. There was obviously a bond that lasted until the very moment he died.'

Shirley Horsfall recalls her friend's steadfast loyalty to her husband even after his arrest. 'I think Primrose was always hopeful that something would turn up that would allow Fred to go free. The impression from Primrose was that it was just a nightmare that we would wake up from and that Fred would be released. I think Primrose truly believed that evidence would turn up that would prove Fred to be innocent.'

Back in 1966 the young couple were just starting off on their married life with no hint of what was to follow. 'They got student accommodation near the medical school, a cosy little flat,' Brian Whittle explained. But this was hardly a picture of perfect domesticity. Fred Shipman was just two months into his second year of medical training – his lecture schedule, 8.30 am until 4 pm with more lectures on Saturday mornings, meant the young married couple spent little time together.

Wednesday afternoon was traditionally reserved for sports, but the excellent rugby player could only wonder how things would have been as Wednesday afternoon was also half-day closing and he would spend the hours with his new wife. Even after she became too big to squeeze into the windows to dress the dummies Shipman would continue to spend his free time with his young wife, who had moved back in with her parents for the final weeks of her pregnancy.

There he was greeted with silent disapproval, something Shipman would have found extremely annoying. His attitude appears to have been that, if he wasn't welcome at the house, he would stay away so the couple would meet in nearby cafés. But it was not too long before they would be joined by their baby daughter, Sarah, who was born on Valentine's Day the following year, and the couple then moved back into their cramped flat together.

But if life for the young couple was hard, life for the trainee doctor, who had always needed to spend extra time at his studies, was much harder. 'He didn't have the social life a normal medical student would have. For him, it was study, study, study and then home to nappies and domesticity,' Brian Whittle reminded me.

Paul Britton believes that Shipman's psychopathic personality would have resented the constraints that had been put on him by the unplanned pregnancy. 'His position is very likely to be that he is caged. So he appears to accept that. But you have a person who is in many ways pent up by now. He has huge self-esteem. He's already arrogant and self-regarding but he's developing in a box, the box of his particular social setting. I don't think you can describe it in terms of being a classic killer anger. I think what you can do is understand that the man is a narcissist, overwhelmed by self-regard, who genuinely cannot understand why other people don't feel the same about him. So that anything that takes attention away from that is seen as deviant, as hostile, as deliberately not giving him his due.

'Now the things that have been mentioned, like the resentment, the frustration, those conditions affect thousands and thousands of people. If it was the case that every narcissist, everyone who had the resentments and the other things, became serial killers, there'd be none of us left. It's not like that. The man has a particular pattern to his personality; he has a particular way of interacting with the world. What's necessary is to understand how that is related to the circumstances that trigger and then drive his tendency to kill.'

In the space of just four years Shipman had lost his mother to cancer, met his first girlfriend, lost his virginity, faced the stress of an unplanned pregnancy and forced marriage and was trying to study in a sphere that more than stretched his limited academic ability.

'Anything that entails personal internal trauma and upheaval will push these people to these acts of violence.' Colonel Robert Ressler, who has personally interviewed most of America's serial killers, believes that this stress combined with frustration and anger in a psychopath is a potentially murderous combination: 'Because they're mad, they're angry, it leads them, pushes them to their first offence.'

Shipman was still some way off his first offence but, according to Paul Britton, the frustration he must have felt at this stage in his life provided yet another link in the chain. 'I think that we see a person who was certainly damaged in his childhood and a person who was not able to make the appropriate social relationships with his peers, a person who became psychologically relatively isolated because of the social pressures around him and that was accompanied by this growing sense of self-esteem. I think that he always thought that he was good enough and also thought that the structure of the system meant that there would always be people who would refuse to give him the recognition that he needed and the chances that he deserved.

'I think that if you were to sit down with this man over a cup of tea and he was to talk directly, at some point he would describe himself as a cheated man. What is interesting is that in the main he controlled it all. If he hadn't been able to do that, I don't think he would have seen himself through his young years and his medical training as solidly as he did.'

*

But the 'control' he was exhibiting clearly needed some help. Faced with the stress of trying to study for his medical exams and the responsibility of a wife and new baby, the young medical student had begun taking drugs. Psychologists such as Paul Britton say that this is far from unusual. 'I think we know that medics are particularly susceptible to their products. The training helps people to understand how different medications work.

'The training in the early years is very stressful and brings a great burden of responsibility so people do get depressed. He has personal experience of that family of drugs so he knows what it's likely to do. People sometimes comment on the black humour that is shared by young doctors and medical students – of course, it's a way of managing stress and I think that the use self-medicating comes out of that.'

Most medical students use alcohol as a release and it's true that to start with the young Fred Shipman did escape from the flat and his wife and child to spend the odd evening getting drunk with his fellow academics. But whether his financial commitments meant he could not afford to make alcohol his release or emotional pressure from his young wife perhaps made it difficult for him to get drunk very often, it seemed whatever the reason, the young doctor found the easily accessible and, we must assume, free supply of drugs a more convenient option.

Brian Whittle's research again provides clues as to how Shipman might have discovered this vent for his problems. 'I don't think it's known exactly when he started taking drugs, it but it could have been during a trial at medical school in Leeds. They worked in groups of four students, so two would actually sample the drug and the other two would monitor it. This was quite common at that time.'

Shipman's drug of choice was pethidine. A strong analgesic, used mainly in childbirth, it has a pleasant side-effect of euphoria.

Dr John Michael Grieve, who gave Shipman his first GP job, in Todmorden, says pethidine was normally the chosen narcotic used by another overworked medical profession. 'I thought that pethidine addiction was something that only afflicted midwives, because it is the drug that midwives are allowed to prescribe, and it relaxes spasm and relieves pain, so a midwife with a painful period is often very tempted to take a bit of pethidine. One was told all sorts of stories about midwives who were incapable of working because they were addicted to pethidine, because it was the drug that was available to them and the only one.

'This was a very useful drug in the right circumstances. I found it very helpful when I had my appendix out and they used it as a pre-med on me.

I just went into the operation on a lovely blue haze. It's comparatively short acting, and I suppose this is why he took it.'

'That's one aspect but also pethidine is a drug that can keep you going through very long hours of work,' Brian Whittle added.

Here was another link in the chain. The young boy who considered himself superior and who had learnt to shut down his emotions had discovered a fascination with the effects of morphine. Now, frustrated by his personal life and overcome by the stress of his studies, he had accidentally found that the calming effects of pethidine helped him through long hours of study.

But he had also discovered that pethidine had the sinister effect of mirroring the effects of morphine. 'I think that you can certainly argue that what he gets out of his personal use of pethidine and what he gets out of the tableaux he later creates are parallel,' Paul Britton explained.

He does not believe that Shipman took pethidine for the same psychological reasons that drive most addicts to continuously use drugs. 'This man didn't put himself on the line over and over again in order to feed his craving. I think it's something that it is much more studied than that. I've certainly come across many, many people who have a deep need to keep repeating a particular process.'

In 1970 Shipman sat a month of final examinations and, while others in his year achieved honours degrees, he scraped by with a pass. Yet again, he probably felt he had been cheated. But his feeling of superiority would have been bolstered by his ability to successfully conceal his drug habit.

He had now been taking pethidine for several years. He had disguised his addiction throughout the rest of his medical studies and it seems he also managed to conceal his drug-taking from fellow medics during his three years of clinical work mainly carried out at the nearby Leeds General infirmary. We have no idea how he fed his habit during this time but he did, so there must have been plenty of undetectable ways for a young trainee medic to get hold of the painkiller.

So, when it came to starting his first proper job, as a pre-registration house doctor at Pontefract General Infirmary, Shipman must have been confident that his addiction was under no threat of exposure and that at last he would be free to write prescriptions for his own habit. He would have felt confident and in control as he, Primrose and three-year-old Sarah left their small flat in Leeds for a much larger doctor's staff house in the grounds of the hospital. He was above the system; he had fooled doctors supposedly older and wiser than him, doctors who had not given him the academic credit he deserved.

But, even without academic honours, his training had put him in a position of respect, trust and above all power. 'If you look back at the beginnings of the training in Shipman's day, medicine was a family occupation and it was certainly understood that you needed to be the right sort of person to be considered for training. So then you went through five years, six years before you were let loose on your own in the community,' Paul Britton told me.

'You also need a strong vocational requirement as GPs and medics aren't particularly well paid. I know there'll be all sorts of dissent to that but in the main if you take a person who has spent as many years as that learning skills they could expect to earn a great deal more money doing something else. So that, if you have a hero doctor who has been well trained, well filtered and is now going off to work in a relatively impoverished place, they've got to be a good chap, haven't they? Then remember that Shipman by now has become a skilful liar.'

Until now Shipman's lies had merely covered up a relatively harmless drug addiction. But his cravings had never been just for the personal effects the drug had on him: they were linked to a much bigger craving and a fascination with drugs and death.

Now, for the first time since his mother's death, he would be given the opportunity to watch the effects of drugs like pethidine and morphine on a regular basis. In fact, he would even be responsible for their administration.

'He is involved directly in determining the future of patients,' Paul Britton explained. 'Now, for many people in medicine, especially at the beginning, this is a huge experience and brings quite a lot of anxiety – if I get it wrong, is this person going to die on me – and they're very concerned to get it right. But what they do have is an enormous feeling of satisfaction, of making a difference.

'For Shipman this then begins to move into that pathological direction where, yes, you can make a difference, but actually you can begin to play the person. It is a bit like a musical instrument, at the end of it, they're just a biological system. If you press this button, they don't breathe so easily; if you press that button, they're smiling and joyful. And what's the thing that makes the difference? One of the things is the drug. You can try it with whoever is the patient and you can influence the way that they are and it's only a short step from there to beginning to link all these together in the first attempts to hurt somebody. From there, it's a very rapidly escalating process into this dark pathway of his killing.'

It seems the chain now had more than enough links in place.

You have a person who is in many ways pent up by now. At the same time he is developing his need for recognition and this then comes together when he is involved in the direct, hands-on, determining of the future of patients.

Paul Britton, criminal and forensic psychologist

BEGINNINGS AND ENDINGS

The signs are there. Something seriously criminal was going on during Shipman's time at Pontefract.

Detective Superintendent Chris Gregg.

On August 5, 1971 the General Medical Council provisionally registered a batch of successful graduates as new doctors. Number 1470473 on that list was Harold Frederick Shipman. But before Dr H.F. Shipman could enjoy full registration he would have to spend a year working in a hospital. His six months of medical experience and six months of surgical experience, working under a firm of consultants, was how he would learn to be a real doctor.

Junior doctors have traditionally worked exceptionally long hours and it seems that Shipman's first year at Pontefract General Infirmary was no different, as Brian Whittle found out. 'Many years later, when he was in Strangeways Prison, Shipman joked to a doctor friend that if you could cope with the junior houseman regime, then prison life was certainly no worse.'

The young father had originally chosen Pontefract General Infirmary because it offered accommodation for the whole family, but it seems he was comfortable there because, after his first compulsory year, he remained at the hospital for another two and a half years, qualifying as a senior houseman and acquiring diplomas in child health in 1972 and obstetrics and gynaecology in 1974. His interest in childcare and obstetrics could have had something to do with the fact that, nine months into his first year at the hospital, Primrose gave birth to their second child, a baby boy called Christopher Frederick.

Pontefract is a large Yorkshire market town between Wakefield in the north and Leeds to the south. Until the recent investigation into Shipman's activities at the hospital, the town was known mainly for Pontefract cakes, the flat, round liquorice sweets that are made in the town, and for the Pontefract Races, the largest flat-track, circular racecourse in Europe. Like most Pennine towns its older buildings have been darkened by years of industrial soot, but the General Infirmary, sitting astride Friarwood Lane below the market, is a collection of much more modern buildings. The rented accommodation for doctors and their families was in the form of a complex of 1930s council-style houses, not dissimilar to the one Fred Shipman was brought up in. The main part of the hospital has, however, a late-60s style to the architecture and must have been relatively new when Shipman arrived there in 1970.

It is clear that, during this period, Shipman was still abusing pethidine and he now had a ready supply of the drug. Pethidine was frequently used in most departments at Pontefract General Infirmary for the relief of post-operative pain and certainly widely used in the Obstetrics and Gynaecology Department, where he worked while gaining his diplomas.

In July 1975, when Shipman was first interviewed by Home Office inspectors and the police about his drug abuse, he told his interviewers that he had taken pethidine once at a party when he was a student, but had never taken it since. That was, of course, a complete lie. Dame Janet Smith, in her Inquiry Report, surmises that the fact the Shipman began to obtain pethidine within six weeks of leaving Pontefract and starting a new job in Todmorden suggests he had been acquiring the drug for some time.

The procedure in the Obstetrics and Gynaecology Department at the time was that a record of each dose of pethidine supplied for use was entered by the pharmaceutical staff into the controlled drugs record kept on the ward. The drug then had to be signed out for use by two registered midwives. Also, when doctors administered injections, there was normally a nurse present.

But while most of the staff who worked at Pontefract at the time believe it would have been almost impossible for Shipman to obtain pethidine for his own use, there are a few who are not so sure. Dr John Turner, a consultant physician under whom Shipman worked immediately after he qualified, told the public inquiry that he believes that, in general, it was relatively easy for a member of the resident medical staff to acquire drugs, if he or she was minded to do so, simply by colluding with the nursing staff.

What seems likely is that, if he had either the help of a nurse or had found a way of distracting his co-worker, he would adopt the ruse that he would use later as a GP. Shipman would prescribe a pethidine injection for a patient, then administer half of the injection to the patient and keep half the contents of the syringe for himself.

The condition of Shipman's veins, when his drug abuse was eventually exposed in 1975, suggested he had been taking pethidine for at least five years, which supports the theory that he was abusing the drug heavily while at Pontefract. What is also interesting is that he told his interviewers in 1975 that he had acquired his preference for pethidine while working in a hospital. At the time it was thought he was referring to his prescribing practice, but was this may have been the arrogant Dr Shipman attempting to spar yet again with his interviewers. Could his use of the word preference actually be referring to his drug abuse?

Very little else is known about his time at Pontefract General Infirmary. The books written about his crimes devote, at most, a couple of pages to these three years and even Dame Janet Smith appeared to believe that it was too early in his career to be significant to her investigation. In her First Inquiry Report, under the heading 'Shipman's Professional Career: Training', she writes:

From Leeds Shipman moved to Pontefract where he was employed for 12 months as a pre-registration house doctor before being fully registered with the General Medical Council GMC in August 1971.

She goes on to list his diplomas. In her summing-up of the case, Pontefract appears under the heading 'Shipman's Unlawful Activities: The Early Years'. Dame Janet explains:

The Inquiry received information about one death which occurred at the Pontefract General Infirmary in 1973, regarding which a relative was expressing concern. On investigation, the death proved to be completely unconnected with Shipman. There were no grounds whatsoever for suspicion of his involvement and the case was subsequently closed. No other suspicious deaths occurring in Pontefract have been brought to the Inquiry's attention.

The Inquiry has had difficulty in obtaining information about Shipman's time in Pontefract, as it is over 30 years since he started work there. Most of the consultants under whom he did his training have now died and few staff who worked with him can be traced. Few relevant documents have survived. However, the Inquiry has been in touch with a retired consultant obstetrician and gynaecologist who recalls Shipman's time in his department, and with other medical professionals who worked with Shipman. None was aware of any sudden or unexplained death for which Shipman may have been responsible.

I conclude that there is no evidence that Shipman killed any patient while at the Pontefract General Infirmary.

Ann Alexander explained that because of this Dame Janet had decided to begin her investigations in earnest with Shipman's move to Todmorden as a GP in March 1974. 'Dame Janet decided to go as far back as Todmorden because that was when Shipman first worked as a general practitioner and it was quite easy for her therefore to identify his patients and who had died.

'But since Shipman killed himself there has now come to light further information as a result of which she believes that incidents may have occurred in Pontefract. So the inquiry is currently looking into that with a view to considering whether in fact his crimes might have been even more serious.'

In 2003 a new witness contacted West Yorkshire Police with an unbelievable story. It caused a major rethink of Shipman's three years as house officer at Pontefract General Infirmary.

'Following Shipman's suicide, a lady contacted us and explained that she'd been a health worker at the Pontefract hospital in the early 1970s. She recognised Shipman as the doctor who she believed was dealing with a lot of female patients and, in her view, the patients died suddenly and unexpectedly when being dealt with by Shipman.' Detective Superintendent Chris Gregg was the senior office in charge of West Yorkshire's investigation into possible murders carried out by Shipman during his years as a GP in Todmorden. He now found himself looking at yet another possible location and another possible set of suspicious deaths.

'It's certainly conceivable that Shipman's killings could have started at Pontefract. There had to be a trigger somewhere, for this man to start his serial killing. We know it finished at Hyde. But it certainly started somewhere. It could have been very, very early in his medical career and it could have been as early as 1970 in Pontefract.

'We went to see the lady and we spent some time with her, talking her through her concerns, and we've passed those concerns over to the Public Inquiry. Now, we are working closely with the Inquiry to see exactly what's been going on at Pontefract and, at this stage, we wouldn't exclude any possibility.'

In my interview with Chris Gregg in the spring of 2004 I asked why it had taken so long for the woman to come forward, after Harold Shipman's face had been all over the front pages of the newspapers and on television as early as 1999. 'The witness who contacted us said that she hadn't seen Shipman previously and it was only following his suicide that she actually realised that this was the doctor who'd been working alongside her at Pontefract hospital in that period, 1970 to 1973. And she hadn't got any knowledge of the Shipman case prior to that. So it sounds quite remarkable but we are taking the lady's concerns very seriously.' His answer was cryptic but it was clear that the unidentified witness was somebody who commanded enough respect to be believed.

The woman was able to give the Inquiry details that they had not been able to access before and it made the job of an initial cursory investigation much easier. 'Shipman's time at Pontefract is being looked at very closely. The wards, the areas where he practised at the hospital, are now being explored.

'We know he certified a considerable number of deaths while he was working over the three years as a houseman at Pontefract Hospital. Are those deaths suspicious? Or are they natural? At this point, we wouldn't exclude anything.

'We are only just beginning to understand what was happening at Pontefract hospital during that time. We are just taking the lid off. The work now is in recovering and retrieving the documentation, the medical records, and unlocking any evidence that may demonstrate whether his killing started during his time at Pontefract.'

Certainly, the criminal psychologists believe it is more than likely that Shipman first started to experiment with murder while at Pontefract. Colonel Robert Ressler believes that there is a key age when most serial killers move from merely thinking about killing to the actual act of murder.

'What I have determined is that generally between 12 and 15 years of development occur from the time that a person starts having these early motivating fantasies to the time they step over the line and go into human offence. So it is generally the mid-to-late twenties or early thirties when they start killing.'

Shipman was 24 when he arrived at Pontefract and 28 when he left.

Paul Britton adds, 'We know that he was still taking Pethidine during his three and a half years at Pontefract, so the need to suppress resentment and anger were still there, in fact they had probably got much worse. The work load certainly hadn't got any easier and he now had two children under five to cope with as well.' Paul Britton also believes that he would have found the role of a junior doctor an affront to his feelings of superiority. 'He would find that medicine was much more rigorously hierarchical than he could cope with.'

Shipman was now dealing with patients on a day to day basis for the first time in his career. 'There's no reason at all to suppose that he didn't begin to hurt people during that stage. He may well have killed them. I would be surprised if there wasn't at least some element of him rehearsing the early stages – he could interfere with people's respiration, for example. I'm quite sure that knowing that he could introduce this medication or that medication would have been significant,' Paul Britton concludes.

Julian Boon agrees: 'We know from other offenders that you may have what apparently seem to be a fantasy-driven desires gradually being expressed, then being perfected infrequently and then with ever greater frequency. It is my view that Shipman has had this for the bulk of his life and I would be very worried about what went on when he was a junior houseman.

'There would be opportunities there – people coming in from road accidents or whatever. And, if you are Shipman and you have those proclivities, there is the temptation to push them over the edge and then come out and be the hero of the hour and say, "I did all I could to save them, Mrs So and So, but unfortunately there was nothing I could do. We did everything possible."

'For Shipman, now he's got the taste, then there's no way back. You've done it and then all you can do is slowly perfect it and feed that need more and more frequently because you get very good and adept at dealing with it.'

'The thrills that are associated with the killing and the sense of peacefulness at the end would have been more intense in his younger days than they would later,' Paul Britton explains. 'Remember that at an early stage, the variation in the attempts to hurt someone, the uncertain outcome and perhaps the sexual element that has been hinted at although not properly explored is something that would be associated with much higher peaks of pleasure than later on.'

It is important to make clear here that when the psychologists refer to a sexual element or motive, they are talking about the high associated with the murder, which they say is akin to a sexual high. 'To be a serial killer doesn't automatically put you into a particular personality box,' says Britton. 'There are many serial killers who certainly kill out of sexual delight. But people's sexuality is expressed in many different ways. For most people, it involves some direct sexual experience, some contact with a partner, but for some people, who are somewhat unusual and usually quite disturbed, that can extend to direct sexual contact with a person who is very ill or who has just died and we call that necrophilia of one sort or another.'

But Paul Britton believes that Shipman's high was achieved by the exact opposite of direct sexual contact. 'Now, it's perfectly feasible and we see it from time to time that people have the same satisfaction, the same sexual pleasure from no contact at all with the remains, beyond being close to it, and it may very well be that the killing, the injection, is as close a contact that is ever required or made. So that the sexual fulfilment is entirely a cerebral and mental experience with no physical contact at all necessarily.'

'But having acted it out, you can't go back, you've done it. It's a bit like losing your virginity, it only happens the once and the likelihood is that you will act it out again. You carry on with increased frequency to feed the habit as it were,' Julian Boon explains.

But it is unlikely that, if he started to kill at Pontefract, he could have begun this escalation or made a 'habit' of it. Paul Britton worked for a number of years in the NHS: 'Remember that, under the hospital system, work is not often conducted alone. There's normally a team of nurses present and certainly when you have the younger, less experienced medics, you will usually have other healthcare staff around while something is happening.

'There will be people checking doses, there are medicine cupboards, there are trolleys, everything has to be booked in then and there. It makes the actual killing, using his later methods, much more difficult. The medical records are very much more controlled so that he would be on duty on one shift and someone else on another shift, so that what's written in the charts is routinely looked at by someone else, every shift.' Yet he had managed to misappropriate pethadine within the same system.

The key to finding proof that Shipman did start to kill while at Pontefract could lie in these medical records. But there was a problem: between 1970 and 2000 the health service had gone through a number of restructures, the hospital authority had changed and there was now a health trust in charge, and over the years records were lost or simply not kept in the first place.

'We found that medical records were destroyed after fifteen years, so there was no chance of being able to piece together the medical background of any of the patients,' Detective Superintendent Gregg told me, 'but what still did exist were cremation records – death certificates and burial certificates – and we had to piece together the information that was contained in those documents.'

West Yorkshire Police had the cremation certificates but, like the Manchester team, they needed more evidence.

The investigation of Shipman's time at Pontefract was what the police call a cold case – a crime that has taken place many years before. Several television dramas now feature cold case squads who appear to make the fact there has been a passage of time between the crime and the investigation a minor problem. Chris Gregg says this can be the case, especially with high-profile murders.

'When dealing with cold case murders, invariably there is little evidence to go on, other than scientific evidence, and this, after advances in scientific techniques, can possibly bring some results. Also, there may be witnesses to a murder that has happened years earlier, and it will be imprinted in their minds and will stay with them for ever more. So you can often revisit the victims; you can often revisit the witnesses and you can often look at the scientific evidence to see if there is any progress that can be made there.'

But at Pontefract in the 1970s no one knew there had been any murders – the deaths had seemed routine and hardly memorable. Gregg explained, 'In this particular case, there was no scientific evidence, because it wasn't known at the time that any of the particular people who'd died were the subjects of a murder. It was just a natural death as far as the relatives and the friends of each of these people were concerned. There was no scientific evidence such as you might get in a murder – clothing, murder weapon, the scene, samples taken from a murder scene – all the things that you would ordinarily get in a routine cold case murder just weren't available in this case.'

During the three and a half years he spent at Pontefract General Infirmary Shipman also did a bit of medical moonlighting, occasionally doing GP locum work for a general practice in Tanshelf. The Public Inquiry's investigations into Shipman's time in Pontefract included interviews with a member of staff and another doctor who also did locum work for the same practice. They said that no concern was ever expressed about Shipman's work there and the Inquiry found no evidence that would support the view that he did kill while working as a locum.

Dame Janet Smith also considered the possibility that, between the end of his employment at Pontefract and his arrival in Todmorden, Shipman might have worked as a locum for a general practitioner practising in the Boothtown area of Halifax, who had been injured in a road accident. But the Calderdale and Kirklees Health Authority has no record of a Dr Harold Frederick Shipman working in their area and none of the general practitioners who were practising in Boothtown at the relevant time remember him being their locum. Primrose Shipman also told the Inquiry that her husband never worked in Halifax.

Dame Janet concluded:

> There is no evidence that Shipman killed any patient while working as a locum doctor in Pontefract. I think he probably did not work as a locum in Halifax.

Dame Janet's report on this period of Shipman's life is being published separately.

PRACTICE AND PETHIDINE

The first homicide is very frightening, they surely believe that the next knock at the door will be the police and it'll all be over. When this does not happen they start feeling an immunity. They've stepped over the bounds of taking a human life and gotten away with it and by the time they've had three or four homicides they're feeling like they're walking with the gods.

Colonel Robert Ressler, senior FBI forensic profiler

The Pennine Hills form the backbone of northern England, at the base the pretty rolling hills of the Peak District gradually increase in height and flatten out to form Saddleworth Moor, infamous as the location chosen for the burial of the child victims of Moors Murderers Ian Brady and Myra Hindley. North of the Moor the Pennines start to form peaks and troughs that run east and west and divide Lancashire from Yorkshire.

The troughs are steep-sided valleys, their bases filled by rivers. These fast-flowing watercourses provided water for the cotton and woollen industries and with the mills came the small market towns that spread out along and up the valley sides. Todmorden is one such town. At the westernmost end of the Calder Valley, where it joins two other Pennine passes, the town serves as a gateway between the counties of the red and white roses. The cotton mills, the postcode and the accent all suggest the town is Lancastrian but, since the end of the nineteenth century, Todmorden has been in the county of West Yorkshire.

An impressive arched viaduct that carries the Manchester to Leeds railway line dominates the town. It is made out of the same pale grey Pennine stone as most of the rest of the buildings and its magnificence suggests that, like

Hyde, Todmorden has known much better, more prosperous days. Close to the central arch, in the centre of the town, is the Abraham Ormerod Medical Centre. A flat-doubled fronted building with a carriage drive, it is named after a local benefactor who paid to have it built. In the 1970s it was the home of the town's doctors and in 1974 it was here that Shipman came in answer to their advertisement for a new GP.

'Our practice was in rather a difficult situation. We'd lost a lot of manpower and we were looking for a new assistant. It was a temporary job, and he was filling in for the latest partner who'd had to retire due to ill health.' Dr John Michael Grieve stills lives in Todmorden. His wife was the Lady Mayoress and he remembers well the first time he came into contact with the 28-year-old Harold Frederick Shipman.

'This brand-new doctor who'd done his hospital jobs and qualified himself very well for general practice, including getting his membership of the College of General Practitioners, answered an advertisement – I think he was the only one at this point – and he came to see us and seemed admirably suited, an almost insignificant individual, you might say, but he knew the right answers to the relevant questions and seemed quite keen.'

Dr Grieve can't recall whether they ever did get any other applications, but it didn't matter – the job was Shipman's. Paul Britton believes it was inevitable that Shipman would become a GP. 'Shipman's move into general practice was a career choice that took him away from the very rigidly struc-tured hospital hierarchy. That is a hierarchy that would irritate and cause psychological difficulty for a man of Shipman's temperament. He doesn't like authority unless it's his.

'The consultant system in the hospital means that authority is very firmly vested at the top of the hierarchy. The move into general practice means that he's much more his own man and more able to direct and develop his personal contacts.'

People tend to stay put in the Pennine valley towns, Dr Grieve can remember delivering the grandmothers of some of the babies born today in the town. It is a close community where strangers are immediately noticed, as Shirley Horsfall told me when I visited her house halfway up one of the valley sides. 'Todmorden is a very small town and everyone gets to know about anything that happens very quickly. So the vacancy for the new GP was very well known and who filled it was very quickly known.'

The new GP certainly seemed to settle in very quickly. Dr Grieve comments, 'When Fred Shipman came to this practice he did a very good job. When something needed doing he would always be the first one to volunteer. One was very much impressed by his enthusiasm – if there was a knock at the door, a lot of professionals would tend to sneak out the other way, but Fred would be running to open it and offer his services.'

The twenty-something, newly trained doctor was also offering suggestions for modernising the practice. 'Things were improving all the time and Fred was right in on it. Things were so different then. It was before computers but they were on the horizon and Fred was very keen that we should be ready for them when they came, so he used to take sheaves of notes home in the evening and summarise them, cutting out the dross so that the written notes became more streamlined and we were ready to go on to computer once it became available.' Fred Shipman had so impressed the other doctors at Abraham Ormerod that after just a just a few months in the job, they decided to make his temporary post permanent. It was good news for Fred, as his wife had already found a house to buy.

Sunnybank was part of a terrace of Victorian and 1930s houses known as Sunnyside that clung to the steep valley side to the west of the town. The name was appropriate as for the greater part of the year the sun is too low in the sky to reach the opposite side of the valley.

Shirley Horsfall, then a teenager, also lived in Sunnyside. 'I first got to know Fred and Primrose when they moved into the terrace. They moved into Sunnybank, which is just a few doors down from where we lived. We got to know them socially through getting together in people's houses. My first impression of the family was fairly down to earth, very jolly. Primrose was very bubbly and vivacious, very good company. She had two small children, Sara and Christopher, who were always playing out. I remember that Christopher was always falling out of trees.'

Shirley Horsfall may have found the 26-year-old Primrose Shipman good company but, according to Brian Whittle, some were less than impressed with the new GP's wife. 'Other doctor's wives I met have made the point that they are not being snobbish, but that she fell short of expectations. By the time she reached Todmorden she was plump although still pretty but she appeared not to care how she dressed. She was loud and slightly coarse. Apparently, when she was viewing prospective houses in Todmorden she was carrying Christopher and he had a piece of dirty old nappy pinned to his clothes as a comforter.'

In an echo of what police officers would say when they raided the Shipman family home in Mottram, Brian Whittle's research revealed that, when the Shipmans left Todmorden, the new owners of Sunnybank found it neglected and dirty. Shirley Horsfall simply remembers the house as untidy. 'The house they lived in was a sort of thirties semi, a very ordinary sort of house, a normal house, with a normal young family, with bits and pieces of toys and junk everywhere. But I did notice that Fred kept very close contact with his medical bag when he was in the house.'

If his young wife's lack of interest in cleanliness was a problem for the new GP he didn't show it and the couple appeared happy and comfortable in their new home. 'Fred was very down to earth, very easy to speak to. He was our family GP. He had a great, sarcastic sense of humour I remember really not liking him one day because I was desperate for a day off college. I told Fred I wasn't well, but he wasn't having the wool pulled over his eyes. He just laughed and I remember he did an impression of me not wanting to go to college but having to go,' Shirley Horsfall recalls. 'He was a good doctor; all the family went to see him if there was a problem and he'd come along to the house if anyone was ill. He'd just pop along or it would be "just pop and get Fred".'

It seemed that, for all his modernising ideas in the surgery, Fred Shipman was adopting an old-fashioned approach to his general practice. 'When I came to Todmorden in 1956, I was given a list of patients who were house-bound and I was expected to visit them on a fortnightly or monthly or what have you basis. This was the way in which individual doctors kept up their lists in the old days and it had carried on into the NHS,' Dr Grieve explained.

'There were masses of routine visits. You might well go and visit some-body just to see that they were still with us. In fact there was a certain number of people who were expected to die within the next year or two and you'd try to visit them before the time limit expired when you could do a death certificate, and they would understand this and they would expect this. Fred Shipman was a modern doctor – I think he would have liked to feel that he was at the forefront of innovation – but he had the traditional ideas of what made a good doctor, and this is why the older people would appreciate him, because this was the type of doctor they had been used to when they were younger.'

'The patents whom Shipman saw in his time in Todmorden hadn't got a bad word to say about him,' Detective Superintendent Chris Gregg of West Yorkshire Police told me. 'Just as when he practised in Hyde, he was consid-ered in Todmorden to be the perfect GP.'

In fact he was so perfect that Dr Grieve says he put his fellow partners to shame. 'He was very hands on. I didn't mind the nurse giving an injec-tion for me or a pathology technician taking blood samples at the weekly session but Fred would always do this himself. The trouble is that you look at this retrospectively and think that it was very suspicious, but at the time it made the patients feel that he was a much more obliging doctor than the rest of us.'

As well as immersing himself in his work, the new GP also got involved in the local community. 'He was very keen on local activities, in particular in reviving the Rochdale Canal. He became a member of the society and I spent time with him cleaning out these mucky locks. He didn't mind getting his hands dirty and he bought a little rubber boat for his own family to enjoy the canal. He obviously fitted into the place extremely well,' Dr Grieve explained.

Julian Boon believes that all this just reinforced and strengthened Shipman's blossoming egomania, that Shipman was creating himself as someone who was above everybody else in intellect and professional status and this meant an enormous amount to him.

It meant a lot because behind the perfection there was another Fred Shipman, struggling to control his innermost desires with the calming effects of pethidine. 'He had serious problems in respect of his addiction. He was using his position as a GP in Todmorden to mask the fact that he was a drug addict,' Chris Gregg explained.

'Fred Shipman got hold of pethidine in two ways,' Dr Grieve told me. 'Firstly, he prescribed it for patients. He could go and collect it for them, perhaps give them some of it and keep some for himself, or he could sign prescriptions in their names and so get all of it for himself. Secondly, he could get it perfectly legally from the chemist for the practice. It went into the practice drugs books and then, when he took it out of the practice, it would be entered into his own drug book, because we all carried out own little drug book for the drugs in our overnight cases. When you went out you would take drugs with you to give for emergencies and sometimes you would even provide pethidine for the midwife.'

By using the practice as a front to obtain the drug, he could get larger amounts than simply through the writing of a prescription and he could have a constant supply with him without arousing suspicion. But the drugs book was subject to scrutiny and this meant Shipman was risking eventual discovery. 'There was a yearly check on the dangerous drugs book by the Home Office and the police but he was only with us for about a year altogether. So you could say in a way that he was living on borrowed time – it wasn't sustainable, that amount of pethidine.'

According to the Public Inquiry Report, in February 1975, the Home Office Drugs Inspectorate and the West Yorkshire Police Drugs Squad did do a check and found that Shipman was obtaining abnormally large quantities of pethidine from local pharmacies. But when they contacted the pharmacists in Todmorden they were reassured that Dr Shipman was held in high esteem by them and was described as 'very efficient and confident'. The police report written at the time concluded:

It would seem from the enquiries made into this matter that there is no drug abuse by Dr Shipman. A watch will be maintained and should anything further come to light then a further report will be submitted.

But according to Brian Whittle, if they had actually examined Shipman they would have seen more than enough evidence of his drug abuse. He was taking the drug to such an extent that, when it was discovered, many of his veins had actually collapsed.

Shipman had then been taking the drug for at least five years and it was taking its toll. In giving evidence to the Public Inquiry several of Shipman's former partners recalled times when he suffered 'blackouts' or 'seizures'; one had occurred in the practice car park, and Dr Grieve recalled that Shipman suffered several blackouts in front of patients in the surgery waiting room.

'When we discovered that he'd been on pethidine we wondered whether he'd overdosed, because you can overdose with pethidine and knock yourself out, or was it that he was trying to withdraw from it and it had precipitated an epileptic type of seizure. We never found out.

'When he was having the blackouts, there were times when he wasn't there and we had to cover for him, but on the whole he seemed to be doing a man and half's work.'

Then in May 1975, an ambulance was called to Sunnybank. Shirley Horsfall remembers Primrose calling at their house one evening to say that Fred had collapsed in the bath. Primrose said he thought he'd had a heart attack and that an ambulance should be called to take him to hospital.

The distressed young mum had also called Dr Grieve. 'Primrose rang up because Fred had passed out and when we went to the house he was lying unconscious in the bath. He was transferred to hospital, Casualty, but at that point why it had happened wasn't discovered. When someone is found unconscious I would say that the commonest cause is acute diarrhoea. We got him a consultant, who advised us that he probably suffered from idiopathic epilepsy. It needn't stop him practising but he wouldn't be able to drive, so his wife would have to drive him everywhere.'

Faced with exposure, and by now a practised liar, Shipman used his medical knowledge to invent other symptoms, knowing that combined with the blackouts the diagnosis would be idiopathic epilepsy. He clearly also managed to avoid having a full examination. If he had, the needle marks on his thighs and genital area that were so prominent a few months later would have been clearly visible and the only possible conclusion would have been drug abuse.

Paul Britton believes that Shipman's deceit was pathological. 'He lies to other people, but he also lies to himself. He is able to picture himself as he would like to be and it's only at times of acute crisis, for example, when he was coming out of the police interview in Manchester towards the end, that he can't hold these things apart. Then he has to confront, even though for a short time, the terrible reality of who he might be.'

Shipman's lies had hidden his addiction from his fellow partners at the Abraham Ormerod Surgery, who never suspected anything at all. Back in the 1970s, drug abuse was not at the forefront of people's minds as it is now. So, safely diagnosed with epilepsy, Shipman carried on his day to day work, the only difference being that he now had to take his wife with him. Shirley Horsfall was roped in to look after Christopher and Sarah. 'I can remember I used to baby-sit for the children and sort of phone sit for when he was on call.'

'Primrose used to drive him everywhere. She was a formidable lady – imagine looking after small children and also driving your husband round to all his visits, looking after him and coping when he passes out. I have great admiration for her achievements. And he seemed to do just as much work as he ever did. By then he was quite indispensable and I couldn't imagine the practice running without him,' Dr Grieve told me.

Shipman's feeling of self-importance and superiority could only have been reinforced by this subterfuge. He started to show contempt for Dr Grieve, his older colleague.

'Fred didn't like me; he resented me. When I was a senior partner I tried to do things by consensus. Fred must have found this aggravating. I didn't exactly have rows with him, but I had the odd bust-up with his wife. When we had practice meetings to try to fix up holidays they were disrupted by Primrose. They didn't like me. They didn't like my style.'

But the young, arrogant doctor had made an enemy at the worst possible time. In early June 1975, it was noticed that a local pharmaceutical company was regularly supplying Boots the Chemists in Todmorden with abnormally large amounts of pethidine for injection. The amounts were accounted for by written orders on behalf of the practice and by prescriptions for the drug, both being issued by Dr Shipman.

When visited by two Home Office Drugs Inspectors and a detective constable from the West Yorkshire Police, the confident, almost cocky GP offered ready explanations for the amount of pethidine he had obtained and denied that he was abusing the drug. All doctors were required by law to keep a register of supplies to record the controlled drugs they used. It was one of the responsibilities Shipman had offered to take on when he arrived in Todmorden but conveniently he hadn't got round to it. Had there been a register the inspectors would have been able to see that some of the ampoules of pethidine obtained by Shipman were unaccounted for.

In early August 1975 the Home Office Drugs Inspector Donald McIntosh visited the Abraham Ormerod Practice. He saw all the partners, including Shipman, and told them he intended to keep the case under review. He requested from the police a further report in about six months' time, giving details of all controlled drugs obtained by Shipman over that period. The report was never prepared – events overtook it. In November 1975, he was in effect shopped by a pharmacist leaving a book open showing the amounts of pethidine he'd been prescribing.

Dr Grieve remembers, 'One of our receptionists went behind the counter at the chemists' where the dangerous drugs book was lying open and she said, "My word, who has been prescribing all this pethidine?" And the chemist said to her, "That's all Dr Shipman and we're rather worried about it." So she returned to the surgery and said to the first partner she met, "What's all this pethidine being prescribed by Dr Shipman?" He had then been investigated, but this was how the abuse of pethidine came to light because he had been prescribing pethidine for patients who had never received it.'

The partners looked at it over the weekend and confronted Shipman at the practice meeting on the Monday. He was asked what he was going to do about this and admitted that he himself had been taking the pethidine because he was addicted to it and had been for quite some time, before he even came to the practice.

Dr Grieve recalls that at first the partners seemed less concerned with the young doctor's addiction than with the fact that he had been caught and had compromised them. 'At the time we were more concerned with how we were going to cope without him. If Fred didn't wish to admit to being an addict when he had the blackouts, that was his business, not ours, wasn't it? It was remarkable how efficient he seemed when he was taking all this pethidine, but in retrospect there obviously were occasions when it was quite disastrous.'

Faced with this sort of reaction, Shipman asked his colleagues if they would give him a chance to get himself off the drug while they covered up for him.

It wasn't surprising. Julian Boon thinks that Shipman, like many doctors, saw the medical profession as being above everybody else, and that they would all stick together as some sort of elite. But he was in for a shock.

But Dr Grieve says that they refused to collude. 'We said no. I said: "We cannot conceal this, you must go and be treated in hospital and you will then have a future and a chance of living a normal life again. This must be fully investigated and everything must be open and above board." Initially he was very disappointed, but he saw the sense of what we were saying and said that he would go into hospital and be treated.'

Shipman would not have been able to comprehend why the other doctors would not protect him when they needed him. As Julian Boon told me: 'Given what we know about his grossly inflated opinion of himself in relation to other people's view of him, he can't take that, so he crashes like a stone. It is simply something he would not be able to countenance.'

His confusion was misinterpreted by Dr Grieve as compliance, but not for long. 'He came back very angry and said he wasn't going to go into hospital and, if we wouldn't cover up for him, too bad. No way was he going to resign or give up his keys or anything. We were used to a Fred who liked to be in control – he was very good but he did like to be in control. He was a better chief than an Indian.'

Paul Britton says Shipman's behaviour was simply true to type, the behaviour of a petulant, egocentric person who expects everyone to do things in his way. He would then re-categorise his colleagues as being 'just the same as the rest', people who didn't appreciate or support him. He was prepared to fight them all the way, as though he was back on the rugby pitch.

Faced with a fight, the other doctors sought legal advice. 'We didn't get any help from the GMC or the Medical Defence Union or anybody else because this was felt to be a matter between doctors, so we had to rely on the advice of our own private solicitor. I believe he also went and saw Fred before sending him a formal letter telling him that we could dismiss him and that, if he wished to appeal against that dismissal, he wouldn't get anywhere in court because, in being guilty of drugs offences, he'd broken the terms of the partnership.'

Brian Whittle says that at this stage even Shipman knew the game was up. 'He was always a control freak. He didn't like being criticised in any way and he came back in and slung in his medical bag and kicked it across the room and said, "Bugger this, I'm off now." He left in high dudgeon but he also left very quickly because the family up and left the town in forty-eight hours.'

Shipman now knew he would get no support from his colleagues. He needed to limit the damage to his career and that meant he had to find a way to rehabilitate himself in the eyes of the medical profession. He knew he needed to been seen to be cured of his addiction and so he immediately admitted himself to the Halifax Royal Infirmary. The hospital's consultant psychiatrist arranged for his voluntary admission to The Retreat, a private hospital just outside York that specialised in the treatment of psychiatric disorders.

According to Brian Whittle, while this was happening, Primrose had no choice but to go back home to Wetherby, taking the children back to live with her mother.

Obviously her mother knew what Shipman was accused of and that he was going to end up in court for serious drug abuse, and she remained convinced that he was a bad lot.'

Meanwhile Dr John Grieve had no choice but to call in the police. 'When Fred left and went into hospital, the police did a thorough investigation of everything in Todmorden and the Home Office doctors came and they went through all the drug registers in Todmorden, every chemist, every doctor. I think they traced pretty well all the pethidine that had been misappropriated by Fred over quite a long time, before he came to us as well as when he was with us. He was then charged by the police with drug offences, and he made a full statement of everything.'

Initially, when Donald McIntosh, the Home Office inspector, together with Detective Sergeant George McKeating from the West Yorkshire Police Drugs Squad, visited The Retreat Shipman he refused to see them. Then he apparently changed his mind and he them what appeared to be a full confession.

'It's interesting that his reaction when dealing with the doctors when they rumbled him about the pethidine was radically different to his reaction with the police,' Julian Boon muses. 'With the police it was this magnificent in-your-face bluster. He knows he has been rumbled but he is not about to be humbled by PC Plod, as he would look upon them.' Shipman's reaction to the police here is exactly the same as his treatment of the officers who first interviewed him in Hyde 20 years later.

DS McKeating was shocked at Shipman's condition. 'All the veins on his arms and legs had collapsed, something I would have expected to see on an addict of at least five years' standing, making me suspect that his habit was longer than he admitted.' But this did seem to support Shipman's claims that he obtained the pethidine entirely for his own use. He told McKeating that he had been taking 600 to 700 mg pethidine a day before he was detected. If this were true, his consumption could well have accounted for the amounts of the drug he is known to have obtained.

He admitted using a variety of deceptions to obtain the pethidine. He said his addiction had got worse since he had started taking pethidine about 18 months previously in May 1974 when he became depressed. He blamed his depression on the fact he did not get on with his partners, especially Dr John Grieve. This was revenge.

Dr Grieve says, 'He couldn't stand me. He thought I'd betrayed him in saying he must go. He blamed me for his addiction, saying that I had frustrated his desire to remodel the practice and do all sorts of wonderful things that he wanted to do.'

The withdrawal process had left Shipman suffering from depression. He was treated with antidepressants and finally discharged on December 30,

1975, with advice to continue under psychiatric supervision for several years. It appears he ignored this advice. Yet his time in The Retreat had taught him all about depression and psychiatric disorders.

Two months after his discharge, on the day before his daughter's ninth birthday, Dr Harold Frederick Shipman appeared at the Halifax Magistrates' Court. He pleaded guilty to eight specimen charges: three offences of obtaining ten ampoules of 100 mg pethidine by deception; three of unlawfully possessing pethidine; and two of forging prescriptions. He asked for 74 further offences to be taken into consideration. Unfortunately, no list of those further offences survives, but press reports of the case claim that 67 of the 74 offences concerned the obtaining of pethidine by deception.

Shirley Horsfall's father and a neighbour volunteered to be character witnesses. They were patients of Shipman's and could not believe that he could do anything like that, that he must have been under pressure at the surgery.

But Shipman didn't make mistakes when under pressure. When he was asked if he had anything to say in his defence he made a simple but carefully contrived statement to the magistrates: 'I have no future intention to return to general practice or work in a situation where I could obtain supplies of pethidine.'

His apparent cure and his promise not to work as a GP again saved him from a prison sentence. He was fined £75 on each charge, £600 in all, and ordered to pay compensation of £58.78 to the NHS Family Practitioners Committee.

Paul Britton comments, 'Remember you have a man who is a liar. He lies in his personal life; he lies in his professional life; he lies whenever necessary. So making a promise not to carry on in practice from his point of view is neither here nor there. It simply eases a difficulty for him.'

His former partners read about his conviction in the local paper. 'He was up in court in Halifax. We didn't know about it so we were not there. I only saw newspaper reports, but they did say that he wouldn't be practising or prescribing again, and he would be going on to do something academic up in Durham away from the hurly-burly.'

Shirley Horsfall admitted she was disappointed her friends were leaving Todmorden: 'After the court case, they moved to the north-east to join another practice where I think he wasn't prescribing drugs. I suppose I was pleased that he got another chance, but disappointed that they were moving away.'

Shipman's new job was at the Newton Aycliffe Health Centre where he worked in the Community Child Health Service, conducting health clinics and advising on child development in the Bishop Auckland, Crook and Willington areas of the county. One of the attractions of the job for the family was no doubt the fact that it came with subsidised rented accommodation.

But for Shipman this was just a stop-gap to allow him to appear rehabilitated. Eighteen months after they arrived in the north-east they were on the move again. They were heading off to Hyde where Dr Shipman was about to start practising as a GP again.

According to Paul Britton, Shipman would feel that the system owed him deference. He would take on health authorities and was unable in the main to tolerate other people's foolishness or resistance.

Dr Grieve explained his bemusement when he discovered, quite by accident, that his old colleague was working about 15 miles away, just across the pennines. 'When we heard that Fred was secretary of the local medical committee in Greater Manchester and was admonishing young doctors for their foolish behaviour, we were quite amazed, because we thought that he was up in Durham doing some pen and ink work, not dealing with patients. So, we gathered that he was fully rehabilitated and in fact he was, I understand, in a group practice for fourteen years, having made a full and frank admission of all his past. One felt very pleased that he had found his feet again and was as popular as he ever had been.'

But it wasn't just his old colleagues and friends in Todmorden that knew of the connection between the popular Hyde GP and the disgraced doctor from Todmorden.

Detective Superintendent Chris Gregg was in charge of the West Yorkshire Police investigation. 'We were approached by Greater Manchester Police at the time when Shipman had been arrested for the murders in their area. We were already watching closely as the case unfolded there because we were aware that this particular GP had gone on from his practice in Todmorden to become a GP in the Manchester area. We were also aware of why he had been dismissed from that practice in 1976 and we had looked into the background of pethidine conviction.'

Chris Gregg is a highly respected senior detective who has worked on a number of high-profile murder cases. He is a modern policeman, not afraid to use profilers and the media to help him with his investigations. He would have been well aware exactly where the investigation in Hyde was leading and that the court case would be just the start of a lengthy investigation.

'When Shipman was convicted of the 15 murders, we were certainly determined to try to unearth any evidence that we could, to see whether he'd been committing the same type of offences that he went on to commit in Manchester. The pattern that he went on to develop in Hyde could certainly have started while he was a GP in Todmorden. The signs were there – drug addiction, falsifying prescriptions, stealing the drugs that were meant for patients. These aren't the ordinary actions of an everyday GP. And that's what we set out to explore.'

Paul Britton pointed out that Shipman's move into general practice brought people to him so that the obvious solution to that growing need to kill actually came to his consulting room. All he had to do was decide who and when.

In 2001 it became the job of West Yorkshire Police to find out when and where. Chris Gregg and his team worked closely with Dame Janet Smith and the Public Inquiry and discovered that, during the 16 months Shipman worked as a GP at the Abraham Ormerod practice, he had certified 22 deaths. In the First Report of the Public Inquiry, Dame Janet Smith states:

> *I have examined the circumstances of nine deaths that occurred in 1974, with which Shipman had some connection. In five, he certified the cause of death. In the other four, the cause of death was certified by the coroner and I have found that the deaths were natural. Of the five for which Shipman certified the cause, I have found that four were natural deaths, although in two I have been unable to say that I am sure of my conclusion, not because there is any real cause for suspicion but because the evidence is scanty or vague. In the case of the remaining death, I have been unable to reach any conclusion, as there is so little information.*
>
> *I do not believe that Shipman began obtaining pethidine with the intention of using it to kill patients. Moreover, I do not even suspect that he killed any patient during his first nine or ten months in Todmorden.*

The first real evidence we have of anything untoward going on between Dr Shipman and his patients in Todmorden comes from August 1974 and it is very different from his later murders.

On August 21, 25-year-old Elaine Oswald went to the Abraham Ormerod Surgery to see Dr Shipman. She had a pain in her left side and he suggested she might have a kidney stone. He prescribed an opiate analgesic called Diconal and told her to take one or two of the tablets and to go home to bed. He promised to visit her at home after surgery to take a blood sample for testing purposes.

Dame Janet Smith in her Inquiry Report says she believes this was a 'spurious excuse to visit her, as the appropriate test would have been to analyse a urine sample. In any event, either type of sample could easily have been taken at the surgery'. Elaine Oswald was in bed and was feeling drowsy when Shipman arrived at her home in the late morning. It isn't clear whether or not he took a blood sample, but he did injected Elaine Oswald with a drug, which Dame Janet believes was probably pethidine. She rapidly became unconscious. Shipman did his utmost to revive her. He gave cardiac massage and the 'kiss of life'. Then he called an ambulance and she was taken to hospital. At the time Elaine Oswald was suspected of having taken a drug overdose.

Elaine – now Professor – Oswald believes that Shipman may have tried to kill her. Dame Janet is sure he did not, saying that if he had intended to kill her, he would not have gone to such lengths to revive her. She concludes:

Shipman had miscalculated the dose of pethidine he gave her or failed to take account of the Diconal she had already taken on his instruction. That leaves unanswered the question as to why he would have wished to give Mrs Oswald pethidine in the first place. He was already a regular user, if not an addict. I think it most likely that he wanted to involve the unwitting Mrs Oswald in taking pethidine, possibly because he hoped to involve her in some sexual activity.

Paul Britton believes the attack on Elaine Oswald may have been an early attempt by Shipman to control his desires through a sexual act rather than a murder: 'We really shouldn't ignore the very early use of pethidine. Having induced some form of unconsciousness or pliability in a victim, he went on then very vigorously to attempt to revive her and this was someone much younger than his later victims, someone who was sexually attractive.

'Remember that at this early stage, this attempt with its uncertain outcome and the sexual element is something that would give much more pleasure than later on. Unless he was finding this satisfaction within his marriage or perhaps in other relationships outside his marriage it would have been irresistible.'

It clearly didn't sate the desire that was growing stronger and stronger within Shipman 'This is one of the reasons why you see the escalation in the frequency of the killing. To begin with, he didn't, as far as we know, kill quite so frequently but that was the time when he was learning the craft, when he was refining the process.'

There is no evidence that he tried anything similar again. From then on he would seek only to kill his patients with the drugs he injected into them.

In February and March 1975, Shipman started to use his drug acquisition skills to gain morphine sulphate as well as pethidine. The records show that between January and November 1975 he obtained 70,000 mg of pethidine, but he had also acquired sufficient morphine sulphate to kill several people.

Morphine, despite its relationship with heroin, was still a drug that doctors could acquire in quite large amounts without arousing suspicion.

Dr Jeffery Moysey, of the Donneybrook practice in Hyde, told me that morphine is actually quite freely available to doctors. Most doctors until fairly recently would have carried some morphine in their bag to administer to patients who were in severe pain or who had had a heart attack.

West Yorkshire Police discovered that between January and November 1975 Dr Harold Frederick Shipman certified nine deaths. Normally, a doctor may be present at less than one per cent of patient deaths. Shipman had been present 41 per cent of the time. Of the 22 cases at Todmorden, he'd been there at nine, either at the time they'd died, or just before. Chris Gregg said that police thought this, at the least, extremely suspicious.

As Dr Grieve explained, Shipman's habit of visiting his patients at home would partly account for this statistical blip. 'If you practise modern medicine where everybody has to come to the surgery, it must be very unusual, but if you have the old-fashioned type of practice, where you're dropping in on people and not sending everybody off to hospital, every now and again you will be surprised by somebody dying in your presence, not all that often but once in a blue moon this does happen.'

For West Yorkshire Police the job in hand was to discover how many of these deaths were down to Shipman's old-fashioned doctoring and how many were suspicious. Chris Gregg says, 'We had to look very closely at the limited information that we had on these nine deaths and piece together the events as far as possible, to demonstrate what happened around the moments that the person died. Who was present? Was Shipman present? What was he doing? Did he inject any of the patients just before they died? If so, was there any evidence of the drug that was used to inject them?'

But this was going to be no easy task for the detectives assigned to the investigation. 'We knew it would be extremely difficult, and we had to act quickly because, again, there were no medical records. They were destroyed after 15 years so there was no chance of being able to piece together the medical background of any patients. So it was important that we gathered whatever evidence there was still remaining – the cremation records, death certificates, burial certificates – as quickly as we could.'

The police also knew that, because this had all happened nearly 30 years ago, they were going to have difficulties tracing witnesses, especially the next of kin of the patients who had died. 'The partners, the wives, the husbands, many of them had died themselves and we were now looking at grandchildren, nephews, nieces, who were very unlikely to have been there at the time that the person died.'

Ann Alexander, the solicitor for the Hyde relatives, now found herself being contacted by the relatives of some of patients who had died in Todmorden.

The evidence the police did find seemed to suggest that in one day alone, Shipman murdered three of his elderly patients.

On January 21, 1975 the signature of Dr H.F. Shipman appears on the death certificates for three of his patients. He attended all three shortly before they died. As Chris Gregg explained, the police looked very closely at these three cases. 'In one case, we unearthed evidence that he had injected them. With what, we don't know. But they passed away shortly afterwards. He may have killed one of these people, or all three, or none. But I believe that what happened that day is, at the very least, suspicious.'

Elizabeth Pearce was 84. She was probably frail and very short of breath. She was living with her daughter and a downstairs bedroom had been provided for her. Her surviving relatives told the Public Inquiry that she had been well over Christmas 1974 and had joined in family celebrations. Although Elizabeth Pearce seemed to have been well at lunchtime on the day of her death, she died during the afternoon, probably at about 4.10 pm. Her daughter and her daughter's partner were both present in the house, but have since died and so the Inquiry has no direct evidence to tell them anything about the actual circumstances of her the death.

On Elizabeth Pearce's cremation form Dr Shipman declares that he had seen the deceased alive on the day of her death. He said he also saw the body 20 minutes after death. That implies two separate visits, but could mean just one visit that spanned the death. Shipman gives the cause of death as a cerebrovascular accident and under mode of death he put 'collapse lasting 15 minutes'. He claims this information is based on his own observations and statements made by Mrs Pearce's daughter.

Dame Janet Smith believes that Shipman may have been present at the death. She suggests,

> He might have visited earlier in the day and been called back when Mrs Pearce suddenly collapsed and died in the afternoon. On the other hand, he might have been called out because Mrs Pearce was unwell and he might have then given her an injection, ostensibly to help her, but in fact ensuring that her death took place while he was there. As there is no witness evidence, I cannot reach a decision.
>
> 'However, I recognise that it is possible that Shipman killed Mrs Pearce. If he did, his modus operandi would be typical of many later killings. Later, Shipman often killed elderly people who were very ill, possibly facing a real risk of death. He would give an injection that ensured that the patient died, rather than treating his or her condition and giving a chance of survival and recovery.'

Paul Britton says the ambiguity of this death is to be expected. 'This was the time when he was refining the process. It's also a time when he would have been more apprehensive of being detected and would have expected more questions to be asked.

'He's beginning to kill people who are already vulnerable. He may very well have thought that they were going to die anyway and that serves two purposes. Firstly, it eases any uncertainty that he may have about the ethics. Secondly, it means that suspicion is likely to be that much easier deflected.'

That was certainly the case with the next one of his patients to die, on January 21. Robert Lingard, who was 62, was having trouble breathing and his son had been warned by Dr Grieve, who was actually his GP, that his father had not long to live. Robert Lingard died at about 7.30 pm. His wife had been with him all day. Unfortunately, she is also now dead and there is no evidence from anyone with direct knowledge of the circumstances of the death.

When the police interviewed Robert Lingard's son and daughter-in-law in 2002, they vaguely remembered being called to the house by Dr Shipman with news of the death. Shipman certified that the death was due to bronchiectasis with emphysema and it seems almost certain that Robert Lingard was suffering from these conditions. On his cremation form Dr Shipman stated that he had seen Mr Lingard alive on the day of the death. He also said that he had seen the body almost immediately after death.

'We were limited with detail,' Chris Gregg explained, 'but the fact that he'd been there, just before death, and this was evidenced on cremation records, and in some cases, he'd been there just before death and then again within five minutes of death – we think that this is certainly suspicious.'

Dame Janet Smith believes this probably means he was present at the death.

If he was, the suspicion arises that he might have been involved in it. I cannot say that he was but it is a real possibility. If Shipman did anything which hastened Mr Lingard's death, it would have been typical of later conduct.'

Paul Britton agrees: 'I think Shipman's selection of elderly people as his victim fulfils all the criteria necessary for him to get what he wants. They are the least troublesome group of patients, the most easily accessible, the least well supported, the ones whose dying is not likely to raise very much by way of questioning or surprise. They clearly give him the return that's necessary. Whatever it is that he gets from them, as and after they die, fulfils this need. He doesn't need to go to prostitutes; he doesn't need to seek out derelicts, and the risk in doing that is huge. He's in a situation where he has quite literally his own little factory; he really doesn't need to do anything else at all.'

The third of Shipman's patients to die suddenly on that same day was Lily Crossley. But here Chris Gregg had slightly more information to work with. 'She was being cared for at home by relatives. We know from information we have got from surviving relatives that the emergency doctor attended and gave Lily an injection, which appeared to calm her down. This was believed to have been Shipman. Lily passed away a short time later.'

Lily Crossley was suffering from terminal cancer. The relatives told the police that Dr Shipman visited her at about 7.30 pm and administered some sort of injection for pain relief. They did not know what the drug was but it may have been pethidine because, when Shipman was being interviewed by Donald McIntosh and George McKeating in November 1975, he admitted he had taken pethidine obtained through a prescription made out in Mrs Crossley's name.

Dame Janet thinks that Shipman may well have kept the pethidine for himself and used morphine on Lily Crossley. Whatever he used, she died about an hour after the injection was given.

A lethal dose, given intramuscularly, will cause death within about an hour. The fact that three deaths occurred on the same day gives rise to additional suspicion. Two of the deaths occurred in the evening. It would appear that Shipman must have been on duty that evening. His partners say that he was always willing to turn out after normal surgery hours. It seems a coincidence that three patients should die naturally within so short a time, all while under Shipman's care. On the other hand, I recognise that this was January and that old people with respiratory problems are particularly vulnerable at that time of year.

Chris Gregg has his view on the deaths of Lily Crossley, Robert Lingard and Elizabeth Pearce. 'It's certainly a coincidence of the highest degree if there is no involvement there of Shipman in any of those deaths, I would say.'

The criminal psychologists believe that by then Shipman may well have felt the overwhelming need to kill more than once in a day. 'There's a well-established pattern particularly where fantasy plays a big role in establishing the onset of crime. You initially have fantasies more and more regularly about committing whatever particular crime it is you want to do. Then you up the ante by increasing the number of crimes that you're committing more and more and more in order to feed the habit,' Julian Boon explains. 'As time goes on two things happen: the first is he becomes much more certain that nobody's going to know. So from that point of view he feels safe. But also the return, the emotional, the psychological return from the tableau, from the killing, diminishes. The period for which it endures shortens.'

In her Inquiry Report Dame Janet Smith concluded that in the cases of Elizabeth Pearce, Robert Lingard and Lily Crossley there was 'a suspicion of unlawful killing'.

With these three deaths the psychologists believe Shipman had begun to perfect his MO, his serial killing routine. The pattern he developed on January 21, 1975 he would continue to use for the next 23 years.

It's perfectly clear that he targeted the victims and that he tried to minimise any involvement, indeed, if anything, try and come out as the doctor of the hour who had done all he could to save and support.

Julian Boon, criminal and forensic psychologist

CHAPTER TEN

VICTIMS AND VIDEO TAPE

You learn from experience what worked, what didn't work, you don't make the same mistakes twice, you try to develop a proficient MO in order to pursue the commission of the crimes successfully.

Julian Boon, criminal and forensic psychologist

In March 1975, Dr Shipman paid an unexpected, late-night house call to the bungalow of one of his elderly and seriously ill patients. Seventy-year-old Eva Lyons was suffering from cancer of the oesophagus, and it was terminal. The unprompted visit seemed to be just another example of the caring, old-fashioned approach towards patients that the young GP, who had arrived in Todmorden the previous summer, was now known for.

Certainly Eva Lyons's husband, Dick, was extremely grateful to see the doctor since his wife was in a lot of discomfort and very poorly. Shipman went straight into the bedroom where Eva Lyons was sitting up in bed wearing her usual bed jacket. In the back of her emaciated hand was an intravenous drip that allowed painkillers to be injected quickly and directly into her bloodstream. By this stage, as with many cancer sufferers, finding a suitable vein in her arm would have been a laborious and often futile exercise. Shipman said he would give her 'something for the pain' and then, while the drug took effect, he stayed and chatted with Dick Lyons.

Eva Lyons had lived in Todmorden all her life. She had worked as a weaver at a cotton mill and at the age of 28 had met and married Dick, a shuttle-maker in another Todmorden factory. Her only child, Norma, recalls that her mother's illness started as an ulcer in her stomach, which doctors later discovered was cancer.

In 2004, Norma, told *The Guardian* newspaper, 'She had been trying new anti-cancer drugs at the Halifax Royal Infirmary. Her hair had grown back and she was eating properly. I had seen her just a couple of weeks before she died and she looked a lot better. The doctors never told us she was terminally ill, but we knew she was going to die.'

Norma remembers her father recalling the events of that night. 'Shipman simply took out a syringe from his medical bag and stuck it in the drip line. He then carried on chatting for five minutes to my father as if it was just another day. My mother was dying but my father was none the wiser. Then Shipman turned round and said she was dead. He didn't try to bring my mother back to life or call for an ambulance or the police. He even offered my father a sedative to help him sleep. Shipman signed the death certificate and left, as cool as you like.'

Chris Gregg is in no doubt her death was down to the injection given by Shipman. 'Eva Lyons was an exceptional case. She was very, very seriously ill. Her husband called the doctor out late at night and he arrived about half past eleven. He injected Eva into her hand, with what we don't know and her husband didn't know. But she passed away shortly afterwards. She was terminally ill and everything pointed to the fact that Shipman had helped the lady to die.'

Dick Lyons certainly told Norma that he thought Shipman had helped his wife on her way. 'I don't think my father quite understood what had happened. He just thought it was part of her treatment and there was nothing anyone could do.' According to Norma, her father trusted Shipman and thought his word was final. 'He was a good doctor,' she said. 'We never had any reason to question or doubt him.' The belief was that this was a mercy killing.

Dr John Grieve also believes his former colleague was probably helping Eva Lyons on her way. 'Fred Shipman was a very keen doctor, very caring for his patients, and I don't think he would willingly have seen any of them suffering. 'I saw the occasional person die at home with a great deal of suffering, and I did my best to relieve the suffering, but you do not try to hasten their end. Now perhaps Fred wasn't perhaps scrupulous enough about the sanctity of human life, but felt that he could not bear suffering, and he must finish it himself.'

I have already said I believe euthanasia or assisted suicide is practised by many GPs. Dr Hazel Biggs, director of medical law at the University of Kent and author of *Euthanasia: Death with Dignity and the Law*, calculates that at least 18,000 people a year are helped to die by doctors who are treating them for terminal illnesses.

Opinion polls show overwhelming public support for law changes that would make it easier for terminally ill patients in pain to request medical help to shorten their lives. In successive surveys, about 80 per cent of people support this. A recent survey found that 47 per cent of people said they were prepared to help a loved one to die, even if it meant breaking the law.

It is clear that many people feel that allowing a terminally ill patient in extreme pain to go a little before their allotted time is acceptable, but the law does not agree. If a doctor gives an overdose of an opiate drug with the intention of ending a patient's life, even though that patient made have died shortly afterwards anyway, that is murder.

As a High Court Judge, Dame Janet has no doubts that a mercy killing is illegal:

> *I recognise that it may be very difficult for a doctor to assess the dose of opiate necessary to relieve pain and that sometimes a doctor will unintentionally hasten the death of a terminally ill patient by giving pain relief. Provided that the dose is assessed in good faith, as being that which is necessary for pain relief, the doctor acts lawfully. In the case of Mrs Lyons, the close temporal association between the injection and the death persuaded me that there was a causal connection between the two. I had then to determine Shipman's intention. That he remained with Mr Lyons until the death occurred suggests that he knew that the death would occur within minutes. I infer that he intended that it would occur within minutes and must have given a lethal dose. The evidence of intent might appear slight but seems to me to justify my conclusion.*
>
> *I think he probably gave a dose of opiate, which was not assessed in good faith with the primary intention to relieve pain, but was intended to end life.*

An ageing population has meant that an increasing number of doctors are probably breaking this law, taking private decisions to aid the early demise of terminally ill patients, usually by increasing drug doses. But when it is left to the doctor to make the decision, there is always the risk of abuse. So, was Shipman carrying out a mercy killing or was he killing to satisfy his own needs?

Paul Britton is certain that this was no mercy killing because as a psychopath Shipman cannot feel compassion and therefore could only hasten a death for his own gratification, 'These are people that he doesn't particularly value, except as a source of victims. I think this man in some ways is rather like a child who is forever hungry. He has an appetite that cannot be properly filled.'

In her Inquiry Report, Dame Janet Smith concluded that Eva Lyons was the only Todmorden case where she could reach a positive decision because, under the letter of law, Shipman had murdered a patient. But she points out that there are six further cases that aroused her suspicion. As well as the three deaths that occurred on the same day in January, the Inquiry looked closely at three more cases where a patient of Dr Shipman had died suddenly.

Chris Gregg said that this was a very difficult job because the other cases weren't as clear as the Eva Lyons case. In the other cases, there was no suspicion around Shipman with the patients who had died.

Jane Rowland was also in the terminal stages of her respiratory illness and was in considerable distress. On February 15, 1975, roughly about the time the Home Office started investigating the abnormally large amounts of Pethidine Shipman appeared to be prescribing, the doctor visited 88-old Jane Rowland at home and gave her injection that he told her family would make her more comfortable and help her breathing. We will never know what the injection was and there are no witnesses left alive to say how it was administered. What we do know is that Shipman left and returned about two hours later, by which time Jane Rowland had died.

Her daughters thought that Shipman had hastened their mother's death but had done her a favour, as he had relieved her suffering. 'While the relatives were surprised at the sudden nature of the death, they had no doubt that the doctor had done the best he could,' Chris Gregg explained.

But Dame Janet is not so sure. In the Report she writes:

Suspicion arises because of the temporal association between the injection and the death. The death could have been completely natural but it might not have been. Such circumstances would not give rise to suspicion with other doctors, but with Shipman they do. All but one of the patients was very unwell and a natural death would have been entirely explicable. Of those five patients, three were terminally ill and death was probably imminent.

The other two were very unwell, although not expected to die imminently. Only Mrs Edith Roberts appears to have been in reasonable health at the time of her death.

Edith Roberts was found dead on March 21, 1975, three days after Dr Shipman's fatal visit to Eva Lyons. Sixty-seven-year-old Edith Roberts was a diabetic, who had had some history of chest pain, but she was described as living a fully independent life and her relatives remember her being in good health. Her death therefore seemed very sudden and wholly unexpected. She had spent the evening before with her two nieces, who thought she appeared to be perfectly normal and healthy, but the following day, she was found dead in bed.

The circumstances surrounding the death of Edith Roberts have an all too familiar feel to them. She was found lying back against the pillows, with the bedside light on and a book in front of her. It appeared that she had fallen asleep while reading. Dr Shipman was called. When he arrived, one of her nieces asked him if a post mortem would be required, because her aunt's death had been so sudden. Dr Shipman said that there would be no need because he had seen Mrs Roberts recently.

Dr John Grieve told me that most doctors would have referred such a sudden an unexpected death to the coroner, even though they had seen the patient a few days before. 'If there was any doubt at all the West Yorkshire coroner would have a post mortem. At that time we had a brilliant coroner who would have been absolutely determined that everybody could see what had happened and feel content with the conclusions that were reached.'

It seems Dr Shipman was determined not to inform this brilliant coroner. Could it be he knew what conclusions would be reached if he did? Julian Boon thinks it is likely that Shipman was trying to cover his tracks. Although there are aspects of a psychopathic personality that are impulsive, he was also intelligent enough when it came to that.

Dr Shipman certified that Edith Roberts's death was due to coronary thrombosis caused by ischaemic heart disease, and when he completed her cremation form, he made a number of entries that with hindsight are extremely suspicious. Edith Roberts's position and appearance in death, confirmed by Shipman on the form, are not typical of that usually seen following a fatal heart attack.

'In my practice I have never come across a situation like that,' Dr Jeremy Dirckze explained. 'Usually, if somebody has a heart attack they're in a lot of pain and they may reach out for something or at something and fall over. It's unusual for it to just happen and no signs of either a struggle or a fall or distress to be apparent.'

In the Inquiry Report, Dame Janet Smith concluded:

> *Usually, there is some sign that the patient has been aware that something dreadful is happening and has tried to seek help. Mrs Roberts' peaceful appearance, as if asleep, is the first chronologically of countless such descriptions I have received during the Inquiry. Her appearance was typical of what is seen following death by lethal opiate injection.*
>
> *The suspicious features of the case are not, however, enough to draw me to the conclusion that Shipman probably killed Mrs Roberts. However, if he did, it would appear that he must have been called out late the previous evening and must have given her an intramuscular injection of a lethal dose of opiate. He could not have given her an intravenous injection, as her front door was locked from within. If she had had an intravenous lethal injection, she would not have been able to let him out, lock the door and return to her bed. She would have been able to do all those things after an intramuscular injection.*

The final death that aroused Dame Janet's suspicions was the death of Albert Redvers Williams, who died on August 5, 1975. Primrose must have driven Shipman to see the 75-year-old as by now her husband had been diagnosed as having epilepsy. He had also had a second visit from the drugs inspectors and was aware that his pethidine addiction was close to being exposed.

Albert Williams was certainly quite unwell at the time, but was not thought to be close to death. Dame Janet concludes:

> *If Shipman killed him, he did so by the oral administration of a drug. This method was not typical of Shipman's later killings. Only in the case of Mrs Eva Lyons have I concluded that he was responsible for the death.*

In the cases of Jane Rowland, Edith Roberts and Albert Williams, just as with Elizabeth Pearce, Robert Lingard and Lily Crossley, Dame Janet concluded that there was 'suspicion of unlawful killing'. If that suspicion is added to the finding of one unlawful killing, then it seems possible that, during his short stay in Todmorden, Dr Shipman killed seven of his patients.

> *The remaining deaths investigated from this period were either plainly or probably natural or remain shrouded in uncertainty. The Inquiry's investigations into the Todmorden deaths were hampered by the passage of time and the fact that most of the witnesses with firsthand knowledge of the circumstances are now dead. Where cremation documents have survived, they provide an insight into Shipman's account of events and, in some cases, these accounts give rise to real suspicion that Shipman might have been involved.*
>
> *Where the circumstances do give rise to suspicion, they do not show the clear patterns of behaviour identifiable in later years. This could be because they were, in fact, natural deaths. Another possible explanation is that Shipman did kill some or all of these patients but had not yet established a preferred technique. It may be that he was experimenting with drugs and modes of administration. If any or all of these suspicious cases were killings, it would tend to suggest that Shipman's earliest killings were of patients who were in poor health and who were likely to die in the very near or not too distant future.*

The contents of the Public Inquiry's First Report shocked Todmorden. Even today, it is something the people there still find difficult to believe. The Inquiry has carried on much of its investigative work outside the glare of media publicity and the publishing of Dame Janet's First Report in 2002 was the first time many in Todmorden knew that their 'Doctor Fred' was the Harold Shipman who had murdered so many of his patients in Hyde.

Chris Gregg explained, 'We found that there was this disbelief at what he'd later gone on to do. So while we were rewinding the clock, back to 1974, 1975, there was an awareness that this doctor had gone on to kill. But it was certainly something that people found hard to come to terms with.'

Even those who knew it was the same GP could not believe he would have betrayed their trust. Shirley Horsfall was in a pub with a friend when her brother showed her the paper with Shipman's picture. They called him Harold Shipman, but it was Fred. 'I thought it was all nonsense. I couldn't quite believe it. I thought it was just a sales-boosting story for the tabloids. Up to the trial, talking to the family, talking to Primrose, writing to Fred, I really believed that a) it wasn't happening, and b) it would all work out well and they would realise that he hadn't done all these murders.'

Shirley Horsfall continued to write to her former GP and neighbour even after his conviction for 15 murders. 'I think that, later, when I read the transcript of the inquiry, there were a lot of things that really sowed the seeds of doubt in my mind that he perhaps had committed these murders.'

But there are some in Todmorden who still believe today that Shipman only started killing his patients after he had left the town. Even though Dr John Grieve admits that he and Fred Shipman were not close friends, he still doesn't believe that Shipman was killing people in Todmorden. He thinks that Shipman was doing a very good job until his drug habit caught up on him and he had to leave. He is also doubtful that it could happen: 'I don't see how he could have done it. I do know why Eva Lyons died, and I would have said death by natural causes. Our records weren't just available to the practice, they were available to trainees, to medical students – with safeguards – but it was all entirely open, not a little single-handed, closed shop. There were health visitors, nurses, doctors, working trainees, medical students, sharing your knowledge, everything – we hope everything was above board, but that's why it was so surprising when you discovered that somebody was abusing all this pethidine.

'When we heard that there was going to be a trial involving Fred for suspected murder, it was rather a shock because it did remind me immediately about the trial of Dr Bodkin Adams at the beginning of my medical career. He was completely exonerated and lived on to a happy old age and I hoped that something similar might be the case with Fred Shipman, that somebody had got hold of the wrong end of the stick and that this was all a mistake.'

John Bodkin Adams was a general practitioner in Eastbourne, who had been favoured over a hundred times in the wills of his patients, some of whom died under suspicious circumstances. In 1957 he was charged with the murder of two of these patients, Edith Morrell and Gertrude Hullett. In court, Bodkin Adams argued that Mrs Morrell had wanted to die – and that it was no crime to ease the suffering of the terminally ill. He further claimed the practitioner couldn't possibly be held guilty for such an action. He was acquitted unanimously by the all-male jury.

In reality Bodkin Adams was more than likely guilty of killing eight of his patients for financial gain but, rather like Dr Grieve today, back in the 1950s no one on the jury could conceive of a doctor killing his patients and so he walked free.

Paul Britton believes it was this misguided perception of Shipman as the caring and knowledgeable professional that allowed him to kill undetected. 'Again, you come back to the good doctor as being the central pivot. We now know it's not normal for apparently fit, healthy, elderly people to be found dead in their chairs, but the only linking factor is going to be Dr Shipman and Dr Shipman knows everything there is to know and everyone else turns the responsibility over to him. Remember that, for Shipman during that stage, he was doing the job of being Dr Shipman.'

Twenty-six years later, in April 2001, the recently convicted Harold Frederick Shipman, now stripped of his medical title by the GMC and serving life imprisonment for his crimes, would be questioned about doing the job of being Dr Shipman in Todmorden.

'After consultation with forensic psychiatrists, we thought bringing him back to the area, where we believed he possibly started his killing, would gain us an advantage and be the best way to try and unlock this person. So we brought him from prison to Halifax police station,' Chris Gregg explained.

'When we brought him from prison, he set still out from the outset to make it clear that he was certainly not going to be cooperative. He refused to speak, even when he was being booked through the normal routine process of custody. He refused any meals. He refused any books, he refused any radio. And he was being extremely unhelpful in any of the questions that we asked him. In fact, he never said one word. He was legally represented and had his solicitor with him throughout.

'We knew he'd be difficult and that it was extremely unlikely that he'd open up and start talking and explaining about the patients that we were going to ask him about. But we had to give it the best shot. We consulted with the forensic psychiatrist to try to work out the best strategy here.'

The psychologists suggested that the interviewing officers should use the details they had from the cremation records and death certificates, as well as some of the information they had got from next of kin. 'The idea was to let him know that we had evidence that was going to place him in the homes of these nine patients around the time they died.

'We had to take him back 25 years to Todmorden. So we decided that to help him, to jog his memory the best we could, we would try to get a photograph of the patients as they were shortly before their deaths. We had also taken photographs of the houses of those cases that we wanted to talk to him about, to try to take him back in time.'

This was the one and only time a police video was made during an interview with Shipman. When we started researching the ITV documentary we had heard various rumours concerning a police video tape. Originally, we were told it belonged to Greater Manchester Police and had been recorded when Shipman was taken to Longsight Police Station towards the end of his pre-trial interviews. Exhaustive enquiries, both through the official channels and via favours from research interviewees, came up blank. It seemed the video was just an urban myth.

Then we went to interview Chris Gregg. To this day I do not know whether I ambushed him into giving us excerpts from the tape or it was his plan all along to do so, but whichever is the case I am extremely grateful to Chris, to the Chief Constable of West Yorkshire Police and all those who worked so tirelessly to ensure we had a copy in time for filming.

The video makes extremely interesting viewing, not least because it is the first and the last time Britain's most prolific serial killer was seen since his trial – not that you see much of him, merely the back of his head.

'As soon as the interview started, he turned his back on the interviewing officers. His solicitor was facing the officers and Shipman was sitting beside him but he turned so that he was facing the corner. He'd clearly thought about how he was going to behave during this particular process.

'The detective inspector and detective sergeant wanted to take him through a process of systematic questioning about the nine cases. We'd discussed beforehand how this was going to be done – as each case was dealt with in turn, the photographs would be placed in front of him, to help remind him and refresh his memory. There was an audiotape running in the interview. When it came to showing the photographs, the detectives actually went and physically placed the photographs in front of Shipman and on the audio can be heard to say, "I am now showing Mr Shipman a photograph of –" then, "Mr Shipman is closing his eyes."

'They went through the process of asking the questions, facing his back, he refused to turn round and answer any of the questions.'

Undeterred, the officers carried on.

West Yorkshire Police Video Tape Interview with Harold Frederick Shipman

Police Officer: No replies are going to be given to any questions during the course of this interview and any subsequent interviews.

I think it is fair to say for the purposes of the tape that we are happy that we are interviewing Harold Shipman ...

(Officer gets up and walks round the table to place a picture in front of the face of Shipman, which is turned to the wall.)

To start with, if I can try and jog your memory by showing you a photograph ... that's Elizabeth Pearce. Of the three ladies there it's the elderly lady dressed in black. For the benefit of the tape Dr Shipman's eyes are closed ...

(Officer returns to desk and picks up two photographs.)

Unfortunately we don't have a photograph of Mr Lingard. To try and jog your memory here is a photograph of Eagle Street and there is a photograph of where Mr Lingard lived.

Just for the benefit of the tape, Dr Shipman's eyes are closed and he didn't look at all.

(Officer returns to desk and returns with another photograph which he places again in front of the face of Shipman.)

Just to try and jog your memory, Dr Shipman, I have here a photograph of Lily Crossley.

Just for the benefit of the tape Dr Shipman's eyes are closed and he didn't look at all.

Julian Boon watched the tape. 'The episode would have been comical were the context not so serious. Shipman goes into the interview room, turns the chair to present his back to the officers and gazes at the wall. This is the ultimate expression of his contempt for them, that he wouldn't even deign to look at them. He's not wanting to enter the waters, but I suspect it's more than that, it's a complete lack of willingness to even go there in terms of the discussion.

'So, when these officers have to go through the palaver of walking round in front of him saying, "This was such and such, do you recognise ...?" he would shut his eyes as a final way of indicating, "I will not go to discuss any of this."

'Of course, he can hear what they're saying but by giving no reaction he can switch it all off. He's not confronted with the reality that is so totally at variance with his personal preferred version of reality. It's also his way of expressing contempt and some form of power over the officers. Remember, power to a personality such as his is so important.'

Paul Britton watched the tape through with me. 'What I saw was a man who, without making a sound, without uttering a word, obtained and retained control of the interview situation. You had a person who came in, turned away, faced the wall, a variation of the old IRA "I'm not hearing you" approach and an interviewer who is faced with one of the situations that the police interviewer most fears, that's the silent – not even no comment – the silent interview. Naturally, that person is then quite stressed, even though they carry on manfully, and you can hear in his voice all the indicators that tell the interviewee that the game's over, he's won start to finish.'

'He was clearly determined that he was not going to assist in any way with any help or explanation, as to how any of the nine patients had died that we were questioning him about,' Chris Gregg told me. 'So he was wanting to control this to the bitter end. He knew what his strategy would be from the moment he arrived at Halifax police station until the moment he left. There was not one bit of cooperation to help explain what had happened to any of these patients. It came as no surprise to us. We knew that he was unlikely to start talking and giving us the fullest and frankest account of what had happened with each of these nine patients, but we thought we would make sure that he was given every opportunity to do so. We were giving him every help to remember – he chose not to.'

Shipman's reaction also came as no surprise to Julian Boon. He would not have expected Shipman to feel sufficient remorse to want to help the bereaved victims. Paul Britton believes it is not just his psychopathic nature that makes him lack remorse but that Shipman was likely simply to have forgotten how many people he had killed.

It may seem shocking to us at first that he cannot remember who or how many of his patients he has murdered but, as Paul Britton explains, it is the sheer volume of deaths that brings this memory loss about. 'He will know that it is more than a hundred. He may even think it's a couple of hundred. He may know that it's many, many more than we already know. But what is more likely is that there will be highlights in his recall, some experiences with people that he has killed that will stand out as being particularly valuable to him, particularly sustaining. But many will be just the same as tens of others.

'This is a terrible thing to say, but killing someone is rather like going to the theatre. A person who goes to the theatre often looks back at all the plays over the years and there are one or two or three or four that they remember as being particularly good and the others were OK. With the killing of these people, some will stand out and others will be, "Yeah it was OK, I'll do better next time."'

Shipman's behaviour in this interview provides Colonel Robert Ressler with a clear example of the reason why he had chosen to kill in the way he did. Ressler has come across it many times when he has attempted to interview serial killers for the FBI. He has found that psychopaths like power, control and authority over another human being and get their kicks from holding people's lives in their hands.

As the killings continued, Ressler believes that, as with other serial killers he has interviewed, there would be a dramatic change to Shipman's view of reality. 'Serial killers whom I have interviewed have told me directly that the first homicide and even the second is very frightening. It's exciting but also frightening because they surely believe that the next knock at the door will be the police and it'll be over.

'When that doesn't happen, perhaps on several occasions, they start feeling omnipotent – they have now stepped over the bounds of taking a human life and they've gotten away with it. And by the third and fourth homicide they're feeling like they are walking with the gods.'

But, at Todmorden, while Shipman the serial killer was still walking with the gods, Shipman the drug addict had been publicly exposed and humiliated. It was time to move on. He went first to a desk job in Newton Aycliffe, where he knew he must bide his time on best behaviour.

It does seem that during his time in County Durham he managed to control his urge to kill. The Public Inquiry certainly received no reports of concern about his conduct during his time at Newton Aycliffe and his work there would not have afforded him access to controlled drugs. Dame Janet concluded that there was no evidence that Shipman killed anyone while working in County Durham.

There is also no evidence that he killed anyone between working at Todmorden and going to court for his drug offences, during which time he had a short-term contract working for the coal board in Doncaster.

When two years passed after Shipman was confronted by his fellow doctors at the Abraham Ormerod Medical Practice, he felt he was fully rehabilitated in the eyes of the medical profession. It was time to move on to a new life and a new killing ground, in Hyde.

In 1977 one of the original seven doctors who had set up the Donneybrook Medical Practice in Hyde retired and the remaining doctors felt that they needed a new doctor to take over his list of patients. So, as is usual, an advertisement was placed in the medical journals such as the *British Medical Journal* and one of the applicants who answered that advertisement was Harold Shipman.

'At Donneybrook the seven doctors worked in true partnership and probably spent more time in each other's company than they did at home. This means that, if you don't get on with each other, it can cause major problems within a practice, particularly if you get factions one against the other,' practice GP Dr Jeffery Moysey explained. To make sure they got the right man for the job, there was an informal process where the applicant with his wife and family was shown around the practice. Shipman, like the other applicants, was also taken around the immediate area and shown the sort of demographics of the population and the housing and the town itself.

The following day, there was a formal interview with all of the other doctors in the practice, in which they explored the applicant's experience in medicine, their experience of general practice, their attitudes to controversial issues such as terminations of pregnancy and, of course, their own personal medical history.

When he was asked about his medical history Shipman made no attempt to hide the fact that he had convictions for drug misuse. In a matter-of-fact, almost nonchalant way, he told the panel that he had been through a rehabilitation process under the care of a psychiatrist in Yorkshire and that he had been passed fit to continue to practise.

Not confessing to his addiction wasn't really an option. His medical notes would have been sent to the practice and, if references had been taken from Todmorden, his former colleagues were bound to mention it. By stressing the cure more than the addiction he knew he was on to a winner.

'Misuse of drugs like this is not tremendously rare in medical practice. Most doctors who are found guilty of abusing drugs like this go through a period of rehabilitation and then re-enter practice quite safely and quite normally.' Dr Moysey explained that, as it costs several hundred thousand pounds to train a doctor, he and his colleagues did not think it unreasonable to make every effort to make sure that the National Health Service got productive use out of the people it trains.

Shipman must have been aware his drug abuse was not a massive stumbling block and he sounded almost as if he was boasting when he told the doctors that he had not been taking pethidine for some time. In a final flourish he invited them to monitor his behaviour during the six-month period of mutual assessment so as to leave no doubt that he was free of his addiction. It seemed that, in Shipman's eyes, the job was already his.

It was. He had put on a good performance and impressed the panel. 'He gelled with them as a group and appeared to have the same sort of outlook and the same sort of philosophy. He was obviously very approachable and very affable, and all the doctors seemed to feel that he deserved a second chance,' Dr Moysey said.

At the end of the six-month period it was felt that he was entirely suitable. He fitted in very well with them as a group, the patients liked him and they could find no reason to suspect the quality of his medical practice was lacking in any way.

Dr Harold Frederick Shipman's name replaced Dr John Bennett on the wall plaque that listed the seven GPs at the Donneybrook Surgery.

Paul Britton thinks that moving back into clinical practice did two things for Shipman: 'It puts him back in the driving seat. It means he's able to use his skills in a way that he thinks is appropriate to his vocation and I think that's entirely to be expected. It also happens of course to put him back in a situation where he can again begin to choose people to kill, to satisfy his growing powerful need.'

But Paul Britton believes that at this stage neither of these things would have had prominence over the other. Shipman did not see himself as a dark murderer, but as a saviour of some sort, an important community figure who happened to have this unfortunate peccadillo.

The way the practice was run certainly would allow Shipman to be reasonably confident that he could carry out his peccadillo without it arousing too much interest from the other doctors.

'Donneybrook Surgery was a group practice so what Dr Shipman did with his list of patients was very much up to him. We had little contact with any of his patients and would not have known what his visiting pattern was like. We would not have had access to his certification book for deaths. We wouldn't know how many patients on his list he cared for at home during terminal illness or how many of his patients were buried or cremated,' Dr Jeffery Moysey explained.

However, Dame Janet Smith thinks that, despite this apparent freedom, in the short term Shipman was aware that his admitted drug abuse and his offer to be monitored would put him under close scrutiny and so he acted accordingly.

In her Report she writes:

He would probably have been very cautious about the ways in which he obtained controlled drugs when he first arrived in Hyde. He had been caught out in Todmorden and must have realised that he had been lucky not to be disciplined by the GMC in 1976. He had had to admit to the members of his new practice that he had been convicted of drugs offences. He told them that he did not intend to keep a personal Controlled Drugs Register. That would mean that he was not allowed to carry controlled drugs in his medical bag. He would not have wished to do anything to arouse their suspicion, in the early days, until he had established a degree of trust and confidence. I think it unlikely therefore that he would have risked signing orders for controlled drugs at the pharmacies or prescribing for patients who were dead. It seems to me that, when Shipman wanted illicit supplies of controlled drugs, he would, at first, choose the method least vulnerable to detection, namely to take possession of the drugs left over after a cancer death. It would be easy for him to say to the family, and possibly to the district nurses, that he was taking the drugs away for destruction.

Certainly, Shipman did not start killing as soon as he arrived in Hyde. He started work at Donneybrook in October 1977 and during the three months to December he certified the causes of only four deaths. Two were almost definitely natural causes; almost nothing is known about the third and the investigation into the fourth death was closed. None of the four deaths were due to cancer neither was there any reason to suppose that opiate drugs might have been prescribed.

Dame Janet concludes that he did not kill in 1976. But there does, however, seem to be strong evidence that he started killing his patients the following year. Certainly, he very quickly re-established the routine he had developed in Todmorden, a routine that would help facilitate his murders.

As the relatives' solicitor, Ann Alexander represented many of the Donneybrook victims. She told me that the staff at Donneybrook had noticed that Shipman would go out and see patients who hadn't made appointments to see him. 'The patients, of course, thought that that was the sign of a caring doctor because no one these days expects their GP to call unannounced. But it was actually very much a feature of Shipman's killings that he would turn up unannounced.'

The death of Sarah Marsland in August 1978 is an early example of what was to become a typical Shipman killing. The 86-year-old widow lived alone and was in quite good health for her age. She was still mobile and independent, but had become depressed after the death of one of her daughters, Cicely.

On the day of Sarah Marsland's death, another daughter, Mrs Irene Chapman, who was later to become one of Shipman's victims herself, arrived at her mother's house. Sarah Marsland was lying on the bed with Shipman leaning over her. Shipman said that he had found her sitting in her chair and she had told him that she 'got an awful pain' when she thought of Cicely. Shipman claimed he had moved her onto the bed. She had collapsed and died. He said that he had tried unsuccessfully to resuscitate her. It seems unlikely that he would have attempted to resuscitate Sarah Marsland on her bed; normally such attempts are carried out on a hard surface.

In the Inquiry Report Dame Janet says:

> *It was the extraordinary coincidence that Mrs Marsland should die just at the time of Shipman's unsolicited visit which persuaded me that he had probably killed her. This case illustrates Shipman's ability to make up a story as an explanation for what had occurred and the willingness of shocked and grieving relatives to accept a most implausible account of the death.*

In late July 1978 Shipman collected the unused diamorphine from the homes of two cancer patients who had died. Those drugs were almost certainly used to kill Mrs Sarah Marsland on August 7 and Mrs Mary Jordan on August 30. He attributed both deaths to coronary thrombosis. Further cancer deaths occurred on September 25 and December 5. In both of those cases, the patient was receiving diamorphine for pain relief and it seems likely that Shipman hastened the deaths by giving an overdose. In either case, he might well have retained excess drugs.

On December 7, Shipman killed Harold Bramwell, who was suffering from cancer and had been prescribed opiates. From some or all of these deaths Shipman could have retained excess drugs and would then have had a supply with which to kill Mrs Annie Campbell on December 20. He also attributed these deaths to coronary thrombosis.

Julian Boon suggests, 'If the criteria were right – vulnerable, living alone, not in a position to answer back – so that he could call the shots afterwards and say what should and shouldn't happen, that's where he would go next. In his normal course of work, people presented who were appropriate to the criteria and then he would pounce. That would be the way I would see it, so it's random in one sense but also opportunity-based.'

Ann Alexander underlines that Shipman seems to have started off quite slowly, killing only a handful of patients in the first years that he was there, and then gradually the momentum built up so that he was killing more and more patients each year.

Dame Janet believes that Shipman didn't kill any patients in the early part of 1979. However, she suspects that Shipman hastened the death of Lavinia Wharmby, who died of cancer on July 18. She also suspects he acquired a supply of diamorphine at the time of her death. There was another cancer death on August 2, where again Diamorphine may have been available for collection by the GP, and on August 4 and 5, there were two deaths that Dame Janet found very suspicious but cannot reach positive conclusions about.

On August 9, 1979, Dr Shipman was due to make a routine visit to 76-year-old Alice Gorton who suffered from very severe psoriasis. The doctor was bringing supplies of creams and dressings she needed for her chronic condition. Although she had angina, Alice Gorton's general health was reasonable. Her daughter lived nearby and saw her every day. When she went home for lunch the doctor still hadn't arrived but her mother seemed in normal health.

About half an hour after she had reached home, Shipman appeared and told her that her mother had been taken ill and she must come with him immediately. Shipman left and she followed. When she arrived at her mother's home a few minutes later, Shipman was in her mother's front room. He told her that there would be no need for a post mortem examination. He did not tell her that her mother was dead, so the importance of what the doctor was saying was just dawning when she heard a loud groan coming from the bedroom. She rushed in to find her mother lying unconscious on the bed, fully clothed. Alice Gorton lay in a coma until she died the following afternoon. She was not admitted to hospital. Shipman certified that the death was due to a coronary thrombosis and it was not referred to the coroner.

Dame Janet believes that Shipman gave Alice Gorton a large dose of diamorphine. She also strongly suspected that Mrs Gorton's sudden collapse into unconsciousness had occurred in Shipman's presence and had been caused by him. The coincidence that she should have been taken ill in the short interval between her daughter's departure and Shipman's arrival was, in her opinion, too great to accept.

In the Report she states:

> *I was puzzled because, in the other killings that I had by this time considered, the deaths had all occurred very quickly. I had not come across a lingering death about which there was suspicion or concern. However, Dr Grenville explained that it was possible that Shipman had given a 'sublethal' dose of opiate, which was not quite enough to kill Mrs Gorton outright. The opiate could have depressed her respiration to such an extent that she had suffered permanent brain damage due to lack of oxygen. She could have then lingered until she died, either as the result of the brain damage or from bronchopneumonia (to which she would be vulnerable while lying unconscious) or possibly from a combination of the two. I concluded that that is what had happened. I infer that, for some reason, Shipman underestimated the amount of opiate needed.*

Three months later, Shipman was called out late one evening to the home of Jack Leslie Shelmerdine, who had chronic bronchitis and, in the few days before his death, was suffering from an episode of heart failure. Mr Shelmerdine was very breathless and Shipman gave him an intramuscular injection of diamorphine. Jack Shelmerdine went into a deep sleep from which he never awoke. He died from bronchopneumonia about 30 hours after the injection.

Shipman had promised to arrange a domiciliary visit by a geriatrician but he didn't turn up and so Jack Shelmerdine was moved to hospital and died not long after arrival. Mr Shelmerdine's son made a complaint to the Regional Health Authority and in a letter, written in response to the complaint, Shipman admitted that he had given 10 mg morphine at his late-night visit.

Dame Janet suspects he gave more but even 10 mg would have been excessive for a patient in Jack Shelmerdine's condition. Dame Janet believes that Shipman must have known that the likely effect would be to send the patient into a deep sleep and to depress his respiration and intended that he would die of respiratory failure during the hour following the injection.

I suspect that he intended to kill him outright but, as with Mrs Gorton, he underestimated the dose.

Shipman was clearly unnerved by these mistakes. He had failed to kill two victims outright. Shipman was probably also very worried by the complaint to the Regional Health Authority, even though he himself was not the subject of the complaint, and these two things together meant that he did not kill again for a while.

The exact time-scale is not clear. He may have killed Bethel Evans on January 3, 1980 and there are several deaths during this period about which Dame Janet has been unable to reach any conclusion due to the insufficiency of evidence, but if these deaths were not caused by Shipman then he left well over a year before killing again.

Ann Alexander also saw this pattern. 'There were interludes with Shipman with his killings when if there was a problem he would stop for a while. There were some occasions when he clearly thought he was going to be caught and so he would stop and it was noticeable when he started again that he tended to start on the patients who were terminally ill. I think Dame Janet described it as dipping his toe in the water in a swimming pool, because he probably thought he was less likely to get caught if a terminally ill patient died.

Between two homicides there is an emotional cooling down, an equilibrium if you will, where they come back to a normal state and there's a kind of constant but then that builds up again slowly to the point where emotion drives them to the next homicide. But these cooling-off periods would get shorter and shorter. Over time both the extent of the pleasure and the time that it lasted reduce, so in order to get that little bit of pleasure you've got to kill more and more frequently.

Col. Rob Ressler, senior FBI profiler

DEATHS AND DIAMORPHINE

In many cases when a person with cancer died the relative probably said there's a lot of morphine here, doctor and he would take it, probably telling them he would dispose of it legally. But of course he didn't, did he?

Len Fellows, patient and friend

The Donneybrook Practice was the first of its kind. When the architect-designed, purpose-built, red-brick building with its square tower offset to the side was opened in the early 1970s all of Hyde's GPs were under the same roof. This had never happened anywhere in the country before.

The practice, founded in the late 1960s, long before the days of fund holding, was already ahead of its time. The seven doctors who made up the Donneybrook Practice in Hyde had originally been split between three different practices. They had covered each other's out of hours services for years so it seemed a good idea to merge and share the costs.

When the other doctors in Hyde heard about the plan, they also wanted new premises, so in the end they found a site where the two large medical practices could be joined together by a central entrance, to the left the Donneybrook with its tower, to the right the Clarendon Practice, made up of the other doctors in the town.

Shipman was 31 when he arrived at Donneybrook. He had been a qualified GP for just three years, but had spent half that time in a non-prescribing desk job. Yet, as Dr Jeffery Moysey told me, he quickly established himself as a senior partner in the group.

'My first my first contact with Dr Shipman was when he actually showed me around the practice and the area when I joined the Donneybrook

Surgery in 1983. I found him, as his patients did, very approachable, very friendly, very open with his opinions. I found him an extremely affable colleague and he certainly seemed to be a very competent doctor. He fitted in very well with the other doctors in the group, but we were never a practice to mix very closely socially: we saw enough of each other during the working day, so we never had a great deal of social contact.'

Because Shipman was 'on trial' for his first six months, the family took a year's lease on a property in Gee Cross in Hyde, but a year later, in 1978, they moved to the house that would be their family home for 22 years. Mottram in Longdendale is a pretty, dark-stone village set back off the main A6018, a busy trunk route that has a constant stream of trans-Pennine, heavy-goods vehicles rattling along it. It seems strange that with two young children the Shipmans chose to buy a 1960s semi with a garden that backs on to this dangerous and noisy road.

However, it took him less than 15 minutes to get to work each day. He was always in early and often left late and it seemed he always had time for his patients. Carol O'Donnell worked as a receptionist at the practice and remembers Shipman as being very good with the patients. If anyone rang up to speak to him they had to be put through straight away and he made frequent home visits.

Dr Moysey agreed. 'His style of medical practice was to make himself available to his patients and he showed a willingness to be involved in all aspects of their lives, whether it was directly related to a medical condition or not. He was obviously very friendly with a lot of his patients; they found him very approachable and therefore very easy to talk to and explain their problems to. The fact that he was willing to help them with advice on issues that were not always strictly medically related also made him very attractive as a doctor and as a confidant.'

Within a few years it seemed that Shipman had re-established the reputation he had cultivated in Todmorden, that of the perfect GP. But Paul Britton thinks that this need to be the best would only bring him frustration.

'Being a good doctor was not enough. He knows that in the medical hierarchy the GP is not at the top of the list. In the hospital system it is the consultant in the particular specialities who is at the top of the list.

'He has already had a difficult time with most of his colleagues in both general practice and also in the hospital system. The structure of the system meant that there would always be people who would refuse to give him the recognition that he needed and the chances that he deserved so even with people around him thinking he was the most wonderful doctor in the world, it's not enough.

'Shipman is hugely arrogant; he has high self-esteem; he is a person who believes that he has struggled and is struggling successfully against the odds. He believes the main obstacle is all of those foolish people out there and around him, that grey mass, the people who really ultimately only have one value and that is to provide fuel for that fire that he has burning.'

Between 1981 and 1984, Shipman started fuelling this fire. To start with, he killed occasionally and sporadically. In the first three months of 1981 he attended two cancer deaths. Dr Jeffery Moysey can see how either or both of these could have provided him with diamorphine. Unused morphine from patients was, on occasions, used by doctors to replenish stocks from their own bags. The situation could often occur where a doctor visiting a terminally ill patient used the ampoule of morphine in his bag. Then a prescription would be issued to that patient for morphine and that ampoule was then replaced. Honest doctors would replace just the single ampoule used; this dishonest doctor simply accumulated any excess.

A month after he had accumulated the excess, Shipman was called to Bradley Green Old People's Centre as one of the residents, 84-year-old May Slater, was unwell. The centre provides sheltered accommodation and normally the warden, Doreen Laithwaite, would always accompany the doctor when he came to see one of the residents and stay during the consultation.

This time, it seems that Dr Shipman specifically asked the warden to go and meet May Slater's son James, who had also been called to see his sick mother, and prevent him from coming to Mrs Slater's bungalow. Shipman was left alone with his elderly patient. A while later, Shipman came out of the bungalow and told Doreen Laithwaite that May Slater had died. He also told her to tell James Slater the bad news. This gave additional support to his version of events and also meant he avoided having to explain the death to the relatives, something he knew did not always put him in a good light.

Ann Alexander says that the victims' families had commented that he could be quite rude and overbearing and one of the patterns that emerged was that, while he seemed to be very caring, as soon as somebody had died he developed quite a high-handed attitude and didn't really want to have anything to do with the family afterwards.

Shipman later certified that May Slater's death was due to congestive heart failure. It is impossible to say whether she had been suffering from heart problems as her medical records were destroyed after her death. Dame Janet Smith in her Public Inquiry Report assumes she had been, at least to some extent:

> I also assume that Mrs Slater was quite unwell that afternoon as the doctor was called out on a Saturday afternoon. It is possible that Mrs Slater died a natural death. However, as Shipman obviously contrived to be alone with

Mrs Slater, I think it likely that he killed her. Even if Mrs Slater was suffering from the effects of heart failure, it is typical that Shipman would take the opportunity to ensure that she did not survive.

In late August, another of Shipman's cancer patients died; the following day Elizabeth Ashworth was taken ill and Shipman was called. He gave her an injection and she died not long afterwards. She was living independently at home and was in reasonable health. She had also been fit enough to garden on the day of her death. The coincidence seems too great.

Then in September and October there were two deaths that raise the possibility that Shipman might have killed some of his patients using a freely prescribed sedative instead of a controlled painkilling opiate.

Ann Coulthard died on September 8, 1981. At the time her death seemed natural as she'd had a stroke and was plainly declining. Shipman visited her on the 7th and gave an injection in the buttock, after which she became very sleepy. Dame Janet believes that the injections might well have been a drug called Largactil, a strong sedative that induces the patient to sleep, but in larger doses can lead to unconsciousness and death by repressing the breathing.

The following morning, Shipman informed the family that she would die that day. He returned again in the early evening and gave another injection. Ann Coulthard died about an hour afterwards. It seems Shipman had kept Ann Coulthard very deeply sedated for something over 24 hours.

A month later, Shipman gave Elsie Scott a very large dose of Largactil on the day before her death. The dose appears to have been 100 mg, which could easily contribute to a patient's death – an appropriate dose would have been of the order of 25 mg. Here again, the suspicion arises that Shipman deliberately over-sedated this elderly patient for 18 hours before her death.

Using a sedative, rather than diamorphine, to kill his patients would have proved a very uncertain method for Shipman to use because the patient might not die. It would also prove slightly impractical because of the amounts of fluid needed and because it has to be given intramuscularly – Shipman preferred to inject into the hand or arm. Still, Dame Janet believes that it is not beyond the realms of possibility that at times Shipman might have found himself without a lethal dose of diamorphine. Largactil is not a controlled drug and Shipman would have been entitled to carry a supply in his medical bag.

Dame Janet concludes:

Largactil would have some advantages. It would be less likely to excite the suspicion of the care staff in a residential home than would an opiate, which, if given in a lethal dose, would cause death within the hour. Elderly patients who are over-sedated are at increased risk of developing bronchopneumonia, a common mechanism of death in the elderly. It is possible that Shipman deliberately over-sedated Mrs Coulthard and Miss Scott to ensure that they would not regain consciousness. There are other cases where a similar suspicion arises. Even where the factual evidence is clear (and in some cases it is not) I do not feel able to reach a positive decision ... In the light of these uncertainties, I cannot say whether Shipman ever deliberately killed a patient by over-sedation. I suspect that he might have done.

Julian Boon believes it is very likely that at about this stage in his killing, Shipman would want to try something different, that the same kind of death over and over would pall, so he was extending his repertoire. The main factor was power and the fact that he seemed to be able to get away with anything.

If Shipman did use Largactil to kill with then he clearly did not find it a satisfactory method. He did not kill again until 1983 and it appears that a large part of the reason was that there were very few cancer deaths in that period. Without a ready supply of his preferred drug, diamorphine, Shipman was prepared to wait.

In 1981, 14 of Shipman's patients died of natural causes. The following year it was 12. Nine died natural deaths in 1983, but two more were murdered by their GP. Still, as Dr Jeffery Moysey explained, an extra few deaths were unlikely to arouse suspicion. 'Death rates in general practice vary considerably year on year. The numbers are usually quite small and would not probably exceed seven to ten in a year. However a flu epidemic or a particular cluster of cancer cases would quickly raise the percentage quite high, so a few extra deaths wouldn't seem suspicious.'

In any case, Shipman's first murder that year was unlikely to arouse any suspicions. The doctor gave 90-year-old Percy Ward an injection, after which he died. His death was expected as he had a burst duodenal ulcer and was having great difficulty in breathing. He very ill indeed. Shipman was dipping his toe 'in the water' again with very little risk to himself.

Shipman did not kill a 'healthy' patient again until June 1983, when he killed Moira Fox. Not long before her death, Charles MacConnell died of lung cancer. It seems Shipman hastened his death by giving an overdose of diamorphine, but he had also made sure that he had prescribed more of the drug than was needed and kept the excess for his next murder.

The death of Moira Fox fits Shipman's MO perfectly. The 77-year-old lived in sheltered accommodation at Chartist House in Hyde. Miss Fox talked a great deal about her ailments; she had changed doctors more than once and it is likely that she was quite a demanding patient. On June 28, Ralph Unsworth, the caretaker, was approached by Dr Shipman, who claimed he had been summoned to see his patient via telephone. The doctor said that when he arrived he had found her door ajar and could see Miss Fox lying on the floor behind the door, preventing him from opening it. He had forced his way in, pushing her to one side. He had examined her and found that she was dead.

But, when the caretaker reached the flat, Moira Fox was lying on her back on the bed, looking as though she had been laid out by an undertaker. Ralph Unsworth was puzzled that Miss Fox's clothes did not appear at all disturbed. Shipman then behaved rather strangely and asked Ralph Unsworth to examine the body to ensure that Miss Fox was indeed dead and referred to her as a 'rum old devil' who had led people on a 'merry dance'. He certified that the cause of death was a coronary thrombosis.

Dame Janet Smith says that an entry in his own visits book the day before the death convinced her that Shipman had killed Miss Fox:

It is clear that Shipman went to see Miss Fox on 28th June, not because she had summoned him on account of feeling unwell, but because he had said that he wanted to take a blood sample. That Miss Fox should happen to collapse and die on the morning when Shipman was due to visit to take a blood sample is too much of a coincidence. I am satisfied that what really happened is that she let him in and he suggested that she should lie on the bed while he took the blood sample. That is why she did not look at all disturbed, as might have been expected if Shipman had had to pick her up off the floor and put her on the bed.

Although this was to become a regular excuse, it seems this was the first time Shipman used a blood sample as an opportunity to give an injection and kill his patient. I am sure that I'm not alone in looking away when a blood sample is being taken. Shipman seems to have played on this tendency and may even have suggested that the patient should turn his or her head away. They would have been totally unaware that, instead of taking blood, Shipman was killing them.

Shipman was now killing more and more frequently: in the next four years he would murder between eight and twelve patients a year and there were no long intervals between the deaths. Former FBI profiler Rob Ressler says that the interval is known as the cooling-off period. The concept of a cooling-off period is that, in serial homicide, the development of a plan or a fantasy that leads the killer to the eventual crime is an exciting process that they take great delight in. The crimes are committed in a higher state of emotion but then there is, after that, a cooling-off period. The act of homicide releases tremendous energy and calm follows. To start with, those cooling-off periods can be as long as two years; at the end they can be as short as two hours.

Paul Britton believes this is only to be expected, that over time both the extent of the pleasure and the time that it lasted would diminish, so that later on in his career in order to get that little bit of pleasure he's got to kill more and more frequently.

Dorothy Tucker was only 51 when she died in January 1984. She was overweight and suffered from leg ulcers. She could hardly walk and used a wheelchair out of doors. She was also another example of a patient who was probably rather demanding of Shipman's attention.

The surgery staff at Donneybrook had already started to notice that the caring GP seem annoyed by patients who constantly made appointments. Carole O'Donnell explained, 'If someone came in and they'd had an appointment the week before and they weren't happy with what he'd said or they didn't feel any better, then they'd book to come in the next day or the next week or whatever. He'd say, "Oh, she's here again, is she?" or "We'll get a permanent seat for her because she's in here every week" or "I don't know what she thinks, what she wants me to do" and things like that. I suppose he thought he was being funny in some ways but he wasn't.'

Paul Britton believes by this stage that would have been enough to single her out as a victim: 'If you have a person who becomes an irritation or an obstacle, who might in some way lead to difficulty, it's as easy, or easier, to kill them than it is to do anything else. What does it take? It only takes a few moments; it only takes the usual circumstances of unsupervised contact and whatever it is, the injection, and then your problem is gone, because you're going to sign the certificate, the person is going off to the crematorium and that's the end of the problem.'

Dorothy Tucker spoke to her cousin on the phone on the day of her death. She said she had called the doctor as she wasn't feeling well and that he had given her an injection and told her that she would 'feel better in a bit'. She said that she intended to have a sleep. She was found dead in the early evening. The lights were off; the gas fire was on high and the room was very hot. Dorothy Tucker was slumped in the corner of the settee, looking as if she were asleep.

Ann Alexander comments that the gas fire was to prove a regular feature of a Shipman murder. The patients were left in warm rooms, which would make it more difficult to establish what the time of death was. He would leave the gas fire on and that was particularly noticeable in the case of Mrs

Tucker in 1984 when one of the witnesses actually remarked on the warm temperature in the room when the relative went to visit.

'Dr Shipman would often quote body temperatures and estimate times of death from a body temperature,' Dr Jeremy Dirckze told me. 'I thought he must know a formula for working out a time of death from a body temperature. Now, logic would have it that, in a warm room, the temperature of the body wouldn't reduce quite as quickly and he could then suggest that the time of death was much later than it was, that is, after he had left the patient.'

Dame Janet concludes:

> It can be very difficult to find a vein in a very obese patient and Shipman might have decided to give an intramuscular injection. Alternatively, it is possible that he tried to give an intravenous injection but the needle slipped out of the vein and the drug entered Mrs Tucker's system subcutaneously. In either of those situations, the drug would act much more slowly and it would be quite feasible to suppose that, if Mrs Bennett had telephoned within about 15 minutes after the injection, Mrs Tucker would have been able to answer the telephone and speak sensibly. She might well have begun to feel a little sleepy, to plan a rest and then to settle on the settee. This is one of only a very few cases where I have found that Shipman killed an active patient by means of a slower-acting intramuscular or subcutaneous injection. The patient might survive and live to tell the tale. However, I think that Shipman may well have taken that risk in Mrs Tucker's case.

Shortly after the death of Dorothy Tucker two more of Shipman's patients died of cancer. The first was in a residential home where Shipman would have found it very difficult to steal any leftover diamorphine, but he clearly topped up his supply after the second death, because just a week later he killed Gladys Roberts. She was 78 and lived alone. As in a great many of his later murders Shipman claimed that he had called an ambulance and then had to cancel it as his patient had died suddenly.

Two months later, Joseph Bardsley was found dead, sitting upright in his usual place on the settee. He was a widower, aged 83, and lived alone in sheltered accommodation supervised by the same warden who had been present on the day of May Slater's death in 1981. Shipman told the warden he had been 'in the area' and wanted to take a blood sample. This is the first time he paid an unsolicited call on a patient, but this in itself would not have aroused suspicion.

Dr Jeffery Moysey explained, 'If you go back 15 or 20 years it was very common for doctors to visit patients unannounced. Most general practitioners would have a list of chronic visiting that they needed to do. They would call in and see elderly and sick people at home, often when they were in the neighbourhood, and unannounced. With better transport and a change in philosophy that has gone out of fashion and nowadays it is only common to visit patients who specifically request a visit.'

Shipman killed Mrs Winifred Arrowsmith in April 1984. She was a widow, aged 70, and lived alone in a flat in Chartist House, the sheltered accommodation. She was found sitting on her sofa, fully dressed, looking as though she was asleep. She was dead. When the family visited the flat the following day, they found signs that Mrs Arrowsmith had done all her usual chores and had eaten lunch on the day of her death. Shipman certified the death as due to coronary thrombosis.

In August, Shipman replenished his stock of opiate with the death of another cancer patient, Mary Haslam, and within a month Mary Winterbottom, a 76-year-old widow in good general health, was found dead lying on the bed, dressed in day clothes. The doctor had just arrived to see her. Oddly, Mary Winterbottom's dentures, which she never took out during the daytime, were not in her mouth. Shipman told her relatives he had removed them. Bizarrely, Shipman seems to have taken the dentures out of the mouths of a number of patients he killed, but not all of them. Dame Janet thinks she knows why:

> When a patient has been given a lethal dose of opiate and falls into a very deep sleep, the relaxation of the muscles might allow the dentures to become dislodged. If a denture were to slip into the throat, it might cause the patient to gag and begin to gasp and struggle. This might interfere with the smooth progress towards death that Shipman intended. He might, Dr Grenville suggests, have had a bad experience at some time, after which he thought it prudent to remove the dentures as the patient was falling asleep, if he thought there was a risk of them slipping into the throat.

Shipman was not removing the dentures to prevent the patient choking out of kindness: he was simply being practical. Choking or gagging might jolt them out of their unconscious state and he didn't want them to wake up.

Ada Ashworth's death in November 1984 was a typical Shipman killing. She was a widow who lived alone and was 87. Shipman went to her neighbours' home, claiming that he had arrived to visit Mrs Ashworth and had found her dead. When the neighbours went in with him, they saw Ada Ashworth sitting upright in her chair, looking as if she was asleep.

Shipman killed three patients over the Christmas period of 1984. Joseph Everall, who appeared to be recovering from cancer, died on December 17.

One day later, 76-year-old Edith Wibberley, who'd had a fall and broken her hip, was found dead. Eileen Cox was only 72 when she died on Christmas Eve. She was a widow and lived alone. All three deaths were typical of Shipman's MO.

The following year, eight of Shipman's patients died natural deaths; he killed 11 more. He started one day into the New Year and hastened the death of Peter Lewis, who was dying of cancer. He probably removed the remaining drugs from Mr Lewis's home after the death. Shipman obtained further supplies at the end of the month when a second cancer patient died of natural causes. Not long after these expected deaths, there were a number of sudden deaths among Shipman's patients.

May Brookes died during a routine visit from the doctor on February 1. She was 74, a widow, and lived alone. Shipman was also present at the death of Ellen Higson three days later. She was also a widow, slightly older at 84, and also lived alone. But on this occasion her home help was present when Shipman administered the lethal injection.

Margaret Conway was 69 and a widow living alone. She found dead in her chair on February15. On her cremation form Shipman lied about the time of his visit to distance himself from the death by pretending his patient was still alive after he had left her.

Miss Kathleen McDonald was 73 and lived alone in Carter Place in Hyde, where Shipman had several patients. Shipman made an unsolicited visit to Miss McDonald during the afternoon of February 22. He was later to tell her neighbour, Mrs Lucy Virgin (who in 1995 was herself to be one of Shipman's victims), that it was fortunate that he had called, as he had found Miss McDonald dying. He said that she had 'died in his arms'. He certified that her death was due to a cerebrovascular accident.

Four months later, Shipman killed two of his patients on the same day, Thomas Moult and Mildred Robinson. He even certified both deaths identically – coronary thrombosis with chronic bronchitis as a contributory cause. The next victim was 85-year-old Frances Turner. She was quite frail and had recently fractured her hip, but refused to go into a residential home and had been assessed for the provision of support at home. Dame Janet concludes:

> Her insistence on retaining her independence would have made her a likely target for Shipman.

Shipman killed three patients during the following Christmas period, Selina Mackenzie on December 17, Vera Bramwell on December 20 and Fred Kellett on New Year's Eve. Selina Mackenzie had also been determined to remain on her own, despite having had two strokes and being quite disabled. She was receiving considerable support from social services and it seems that patients who had this level of support were particularly at risk from Shipman.

Vera Bramwell was 79 and lived alone in sheltered accommodation. She had been shopping on the morning of the day of her death. Fred Kellett was 79 when he died. His wife was living in a nursing home in Denton. He was in quite good health and visited her regularly. He was found in his chair and looked very peaceful. Shipman certified that the death was due to coronary thrombosis.

By now the harvesting of leftover diamorphine from deceased cancer patients was not proving reliable or substantial enough for Shipman's escalating desires. In the last three months of 1985 he had only been involved in the care of one terminally ill cancer victim and she was actually a patient of Dr Moysey. He needed a regular supply and it was now he started to re-use an old trick he had developed during his pethidine addiction, prescribing drugs for patients who did not need them and would never use them.

When DS John Ashley accessed Shipman's computerised medical records in 1998, he was able to see how Shipman had done this. 'There was very little in the medical records that recorded diamorphine being actually administered to anybody who had a legitimate need. It should have been recorded for individual patients as x number of milligrams of diamorphine to patient A, for example. But, instead, the amounts on the prescriptions he submitted to the pharmacies did not match what he was administering. He was over-prescribing on the prescription and only using a small amount on the terminal ill patient, stockpiling the rest to enable him to kill other patients.'

It has been thought that many of Shipman's terminal ill patients went without their much-needed painkilling injections so he could use their drugs to kill. But the psychologists think it is unlikely that Shipman would have let them suffer in this way. 'This is a very complex human being. We tend to think of Shipman the serial killer as ruthless, emotionless and all the rest of it. This is true to an extent but this is also a man who believes that he is a great saviour, bringing health and community benefit. He's also likely at a very important fundamental level to try to hold away the meaning of this killing,' Paul Britton comments.

By collecting the prescriptions himself, he was also fulfilling this dual role. Doctors don't normally pick up prescriptions for drugs like morphine from a chemist, but it seems Shipman was the exception to this rule. Dr Moysey said that Shipman wanted to be involved with his patients, so that it would have been quite reasonable for him to tell them that he would collect their prescriptions. They would simply think that he was being kind.

In 1986, Shipman killed eight patients. The first was 81-year-old Deborah Middleton in January. In April, he murdered the 74-year-old dementia sufferer, Dorothy Fletcher, in Charnley House, a residential home for the elderly. In June, Thomas Fowden was his chosen victim. Despite being 81, Mr Fowden was quite independent and ran his house with the assistance of a home help, Joan Ralphs. Joan's mother, Lily Higgins, and mother-in-law, Anne Ralphs, would become victims of Shipman.

In September and October Dr Shipman had to deal with the intrusion of a couple of home helps, when he killed two of his patients who lived on the same road in Hyde.

Elizabeth Shawcross and Dorothy Foley were home helps who worked in that area. At about midday on September 15 they saw 63-year-old Mona White waiting for the doctor. A short time later, Elizabeth Shawcross popped in to see Miss White, as she had seen Dr Shipman who had told her he had given his patient a 'little injection for her pain'. Mona White was sitting in her chair, dead. Three weeks later, Mrs Shawcross and Mrs Foley found another of their clients, Mary Tomlin, in bed. She said she was not well and was expecting Shipman to visit. About an hour later, Shipman was seen going into the flat. Ten minutes later, Dorothy Foley arrived and was told by the doctor that Mrs Tomlin was 'going'.

In November, 59-year-old Beatrice Toft was found dead by one of her daughters. She was lying flat on her back in bed, a position that would have been most uncomfortable for her in life. She usually lay propped against pillows to ease her breathing. Her dentures were not in her mouth and, when one of her daughters mentioned this, Shipman suggested she might have swallowed them.

Only two of Shipman's patients died at Christmas in 1986, Lily Broadbent on December 16 and James Wood on the day before Christmas Eve. Both deaths fitted Shipman's MO. Lily Broadbent was found with her gas fire on very high; James Wood was not seen alive after he was visited by the doctor.

In 1987, Shipman killed eight patients. The first to die was in March. Frank Halliday was 76 and in poor health and on this occasion Shipman acknowledged he had given his patient an intravenous injection of 10 mg morphine – in fact, he gave him a much larger dose.

Diamorphine is twice as potent as morphine when given by intravenous injection. However, once in the body it quickly changes to morphine. Euphoria occurs very quickly but so does the suppression of breathing. The key in treatment is to find a balance, because if the patient stops breathing oxygen doesn't reach the brain and the patient quickly becomes unconscious and then brain-dead.

A standard adult dose of diamorphine would be 25 mg, slightly more if the patient was a regular user, as in the case of the terminally ill. Injected into a vein in the back of the hand or into the large vein in the crook of the elbow, it passes directly into the bloodstream and rapidly moves to the brain and the spinal cord. Again, to ensure this doesn't suppress the breathing, the injection should be delivered slowly, at 1 mg a minute.

Thirty mg of diamorphine delivered quickly would kill a fit adult, while 20 mg could easily kill an elderly, slightly frail, person. It is likely that Shipman used more than 30 mg on his victims and witness evidence shows he injected the drug extremely quickly.

Only two days later, on April Fools Day, Albert Cheetham was found dead. Shipman said that, as he 'happened to be in the area', he had called in to see Mr Cheetham. He claimed he had found him in a 'nervy' state and had promised to return the next day to give him a prescription. Shipman suggested that Mr Cheetham must have sat down to watch *Coronation Street* and died.

Shipman probably killed Albert Cheetham on his first visit when he was on out-of-hours duty. He left the body overnight, with the gas fire on full. It seems that, because he was unable to lock the door behind him, he went back the next morning to 'discover' the body. Sixteen days later, 83-year-old Alice Thomas died during a routine visit by Shipman. At the start of May Shipman killed 78-year-old Jane Rostron. Here, Shipman used what was to become one of his favourite explanations, blaming the death on the patient's refusal to go to hospital.

Seventy-one-year-old Nancy Brassington was Shipman's next victim in September 1987 and, once again, there was a cluster of killings around Christmas. Margaret Townsend was 80 and a rather demanding patient. She died on December 11, during a home visit by Shipman. Nellie Bardsley was only 69. She died suddenly on December 29. The following day, Shipman killed Elizabeth Rogers, who was 74 and was another resident of the Chartist House flats. Again, the warden was called to help Shipman 'discover' the body.

In 1988, four of Shipman's patients died naturally, 11 were murdered. Shipman killed 90-year-old Elizabeth Fletcher and partially sighted Alice Mary Jones in January. Then, within one week, he killed four patients. Ninety-year-old Dorothea Renwick died on February 9, shortly after a visit from her doctor who had brought her repeat prescriptions. Ann Cooper, who at 93, was Shipman's oldest victim, and Jane Jones, who had called the doctor out for an antibiotic for a cold, both died on the15th. The body of 83-year-old Lavinia Robinson was found the following day.

After this spate of killings, there was an interval of seven months.

Although there is no clear evidence as to why Shipman stopped killing for so long, Dame Janet Smith concludes:

It is quite possible that the occurrence of four sudden deaths within the week had caused comment, possibly from a doctor or member of staff at the Donneybrook practice. I think it likely that there was some such explanation for this temporary cessation.

While Dr Shipman's perfect doctor persona worked with his fellow GPs and with the relatives of the patients he had killed, it seemed the same could not be said of his surgery staff. According to Dr Moysey, there were times when Dr Shipman fell out with some of the practice staff, not the doctors and certainly not the nurses, but some of the reception and administrative staff. There were also times when he would not speak to the practice manager for a few days.

Carol O'Donnell, who had answered an advert for a full-time job receptionist at the Donneybrook Surgery, said, 'The second day I was there, he came in and was blustering around like he used to do. He said he had decided that week that we were all going to have injections for hepatitis and he told us we were all having them on the Friday. You could tell he was the boss of all the doctors.'

'The first week I was there he was fine with me, but into the second week, he started. I still don't know what I did, but I couldn't do anything right for him. He seemed to find fault in everything. Another lady who started the same time used to say to me that she was physically sick every morning before she went in to the surgery because of him and because of the way things were. I wasn't that bad but it does affect you when people around you are like that because they were walking on eggshells all the time with him. With the other doctors we were all part of the team, but Dr Shipman didn't want the receptionists to speak to him. You had to go through his practice manager if you wanted to speak to him.'

Neither Carol O'Donnell nor Dr Moysey recalls any suspicions being voiced but, if a member of his staff had been suspicious, Shipman would have felt threatened and stopped killing for a while. It is certainly true that, when he started up again, seven months later, he chose a soft target. Rose Adshead was already very ill when Shipman murdered her in September 1988.

In October and November he resumed killing patients who were not terminally ill. Alice Prestwich was 69 and awaiting an eye operation and Walter Tingle was 85 and lived in sheltered accommodation. He was also depressed about his health and almost certainly told Shipman that he 'had had enough'. Shipman may have contrived to send the warden away while he gave Mr Tingle an injection. Within a few minutes, Mr Tingle was dying.

Harry Stafford and Ethel Bennett were due to spend Christmas with their families but neither made it. Harry Stafford had a cold and called the doctor six days before Christmas. Shipman told the family that he arrived to find Mr Stafford having a massive heart attack and there was nothing he could do. Two days later, Ethel Bennett was discovered dead with the gas fire on full. Shipman claimed that, after examining Miss Bennett, he had diagnosed pleurisy and advised hospital admission but she had refused. He claimed that he had prescribed an antibiotic.

In 1989, three of Shipman's patients died natural deaths, 12 didn't. The first was Wilfred Leigh in January, then in March Shipman killed his first patient in his surgery. Julian Boon suggested that it was an element in Shipman's psychopathic personality that he would kill on impulse if an opportunity presented itself.

Mary Hamer was 81 and in good health. It is not clear why she had made a late morning appointment, but she looked quite normal when she went into the consulting room. A few minutes later, Shipman told the receptionist to send the next patient in as Mary Hamer was undressing in the examination room and would be some time.

He saw the final two or three patients waiting for appointments before telling the receptionist that Mary Hamer had died. She was on the bed, fully dressed. Shipman told her family that she had told him she had chest pain. He believed she was having a coronary, gave her a small dose of morphine for the pain and went to telephone the hospital. When he returned, she had died. He said that he had not attempted to resuscitate her, as he thought she had suffered brain damage.

Dr Moysey became aware of the death in the surgery on the following day. The Wednesday afternoon was his half-day so he wasn't present at the time, but it was commented upon when he came in the following morning.

'I don't think an explanation was ever given, it was just, "Oh, did you hear Mrs So and So died in surgery yesterday?" As a general rule, deaths in surgeries are very unusual. But it would not have been my position or my right to investigate the death of another doctor's patient.

'The whole basis of medical practice is mutual trust between fellow professionals. If Dr Shipman reported something there would have been no reason to doubt what he was saying. And if the patient who had died had been one of my patients, then he would have had no grounds to doubt me either.'

Shipman's reputation as a caring GP meant that he was perceived to be above suspicion even when the death of one of his patients happened in unusual circumstances. His reputation had gained him a large patient list, a high proportion of them elderly, but he had also come to the notice of researchers from Granada Television who were looking for an interviewee to talk about caring for the mentally ill in the community.

In the documentary called *Home Help*, Shipman was interviewed at his desk in the Donneybrook Surgery. In his thirties at the time, he is still easily recognisable as the fifty-something GP who held a press conference outside his surgery 20-odd years later. The beard is there but, like the hair on his head, it is dark brown instead of grey. The beard is also slightly less full. The glasses are thick-rimmed instead of the trendy metal frames he wore in the 1990s.

He comes across as confident and self-assured, but the lecturing tone I had heard so much about is already emerging:

> *Shipman:* In the past if a patient had got a mental illness that required admission to hospital the patient was formally admitted, undressed ... A consultant would come round often in a white coat and there was an invisible barrier between the patient and the doctor.

Shipman was championing a pioneering new approach to mental health: care in the community. But in reality his treatment of the mentally ill was very different. The case of his next victim, Josephine Hall, illustrates this. Josephine Hall lived in Garden Street in Hyde and she had a long psychiatric history. She suffered from agoraphobia, insomnia, depression and anxiety. She was in reasonably good health but the agoraphobia meant that she rarely went out.

But it seems that Shipman had no time for Josephine Hall's phobia and it distressed her. She didn't like him because he once told her that he would take her into the middle of Hyde and leave her there to find her own way home. Despite this, she remained a patient of his and appears to have made frequent demands on Shipman's time, making her a 'preferred target' as Dame Janet puts it.

Colonel Robert Ressler has an analogy that he believes sums up how Shipman viewed these murders. 'Some people have animals put to sleep because they annoy them and they're getting older and they're no longer fun to play with. They're causing problems just being alive so they're put to sleep and nobody thinks twice about it. So a doctor whose patients are annoying them can get rid of them with just a shot of morphine.'

A far cry from the caring approach he had championed in the documentary:

Shipman: If you've got a mental illness such as depression … if you can stay in the community, receive your treatment in the community with your family around you and your usual friends then this all adds to the speed of recovery from the illness.

The agoraphobic Josephine Hall clearly wasn't recovering quickly enough for Shipman. In April 1988, following a psychiatric referral, where the consultant reported that Mrs Hall was 'fed up with life', Shipman noted in her records: *No use, what do we do?*

It seems he had already found the perfect solution.

Her medical records report that Mrs Hall also took medication to control her blood pressure. During a routine visit, dated June 5, Shipman wrote that the patient had symptoms of a stroke or transient ischaemic attack. Her blood pressure was very high, which he attributed to her failure to take her medication. He was considering a domiciliary visit by a consultant, but he would review her the next day. The records were of course fabricated in the hours after Josephine Hall's death that very afternoon.

Ann Alexander discovered that she had been well on the day that she died. 'She'd spoken to her daughter in the morning and some time later on in the afternoon Elsie Cheetham, who was one of the neighbours in Garden Street, heard Mrs Hall's dog barking in the garden. It was Mrs Hall's choice to leave the dog outside when anyone came to visit but the dog had been barking for some time and Mrs Cheetham was concerned and went round to find out what was going on. She went into the house and Mrs Hall was there sitting in a chair – very much in line with the patterns that were emerging – dressed, with her cardigan sleeve rolled up, completely peaceful, and clearly she was dead.'

Josephine Hall was the first of five neighbours on Garden Street to be killed by their GP. Elsie Cheetham would also become a Shipman victim, as would her husband Thomas and their next-door neighbours Sidney and Kenneth Smith.

'There is clearly some suspicion that Mrs Cheetham perhaps didn't know what was going on, but was clearly concerned about it and Shipman killed her as a consequence of that,' Ann Alexander explained. From now on, those who witnessed his crimes would also enter his victim pool.

Shipman's next victim died in May. Beatrice Clee was frail and had poor eyesight but lived independently. Shipman fabricated entries in her medical records suggesting she had the symptoms of heart trouble. He did the same after he killed Hilda Fitton during an unsolicited visit in July. In August, Shipman killed Marion Carradice; in September he murdered two more of his patients, Elsie Harrop and Elizabeth Burke. In October, there were three killings within three days: Sarah Jane Williamson on the 15th, John Charlton on the 16th and George Vizor on the 18th.

Finally, for that year, in November Shipman killed the 85-year-old widower, Joseph Wilcockson. This one, however, would prove to be a very close call for Shipman; he only narrowly avoided being caught red-handed by the district nurse.

At midday when the district nurse arrived to dress Mr Wilcockson's ulcerated leg, she found him sitting in his usual chair, dead but still warm. She telephoned the surgery, but Shipman did not tell her that he had visited Mr Wilcockson that morning, probably to prevent the death being discussed in detail at the surgery. On his cremation form Shipman gave the time of death as 12.30 pm and said that he had seen Mr Wilcockson alive at 10.30 am. Both were lies.

Anne Alexander points out, 'The occasion in 1989 when he was almost caught red-handed probably gave Shipman a bad scare as he did not kill again for ten months.'

In fact, he waited until September 1990 before he risked killing again and then it was another terminally ill patient, Dorothy Rowarth. He would then wait another three months before killing Mary Dudley, a perfectly healthy patient of his.

Over 15 years, Shipman had killed 71 of his patients, of whom nine were under seventy and three were in their fifties. Of these, 56 were women and 17 were men. He did all this without being detected.

Dr Moysey has confessed that, since Dr Shipman's arrest and trial, the other members of the practice have gone back and wrestled with the question of whether they should have been suspicious, whether there were any clues that they could have picked up during that time. But, despite all their best efforts, they could find no way in which they could have realised what was happening or that he was doing anything out of the ordinary.

However, the reason why it was unlikely that the doctors would see anything wrong is probably exactly the reason why Shipman chose to work at Donneybrook. Up to 1994, the doctors in the practice had their own individual lists of patients and, provided they were there and not away on holiday or at a course or a conference, they would be responsible for the care of their own patients and not for anybody else's. This meant that Dr. Shipman would have been responsible for his list of patients only and anybody else's contact with them would have been very minimal indeed.

However, politics were about to put a stop to this medical anonymity. In 1990, the partners at Donneybrook had started talking about becoming fund holders, which meant they would act like the directors of a limited company, in charge of their own finances. By 1991 the doctors were actively engaged in gathering the necessary information to become a fund-holder practice and they were planning to enter the scheme as second wave just a year after it had been introduced nationally. It was good news for the practice and the doctors, but it was bad news for Shipman

'The practice was actively preparing for fund holding and this would have meant that there would be increasing use of computerisation, not only for the administration of the practice, but also for clinical day-to-day recording. This meant that the practice would have had to have worked much more like a partnership, where other doctors would be able to scrutinise medical notes made by their colleagues and behaviour and practice would have been much more open and much more transparent,' Dr Moysey explained.

Faced with the prospect of constant scrutiny, Shipman knew he couldn't continue to work there as a doctor and a killer.

Dr Moysey remembers the day that Shipman announced that he was leaving the Donneybrook Practice: 'Every Monday lunchtime we had a practice meeting where we all met together to discuss issues of mutual interest. Dr Shipman announced that for some time he had been looking around for a different practice, that he had attended a number of interviews but had not been successful in obtaining another partnership, so he had decided to leave the practice and set up in the town of Hyde with his list of patients as a single-handed practitioner.'

The speech was riddled with lies: there is no proof that Shipman ever looked elsewhere for a partnership. It seemed he had always planned to go it alone. As Ann Alexander points out, 'He could carry on his patterns of killing undetected. He was less likely to have people watching over him and as a single-handed practitioner he would not have other doctors in the surgery to pass any comment on how he was behaving.'

His excuse for leaving was ironic, to say the least. He said that he did not think that they were moving as quickly as he would like to embrace the scheme of fund holding.

Shipman didn't leave straight away. There was bound to be a lag period while he sorted out building work on his new premises. His former partners suggested that they should allow him to continue working from Donneybrook, seeing the patients on his list there, as they would need time to find a replacement. But, to allow him to start gaining new patients, they came to a financial agreement whereby Shipman paid rent for his room and contributed proportionately towards the running costs of the practice.

In most Practice Agreements there is a clause that prevents a partner from setting up in practice within a few miles of the original practice or taking his list of patients with him. The Partners were soon to realise that

Shipman had deliberately flouted both. His new surgery was within a hundred feet of the Donneybrook Practice and he had no intention of leaving any of his patients behind when he went. He even poached a few of the surgery staff as well.

Unfortunately for the Donneybrook doctors, these clauses are not enforceable legally and it would have been extremely costly to have fought a legal battle with every chance that they would have lost. 'At the time that Dr Shipman announced that he was leaving, several of the doctors who had been present at his original interview felt very let down. They felt that they had given him a second chance that had then been thrown back in their faces,' Dr Morrisey commented.

There was more bad feeling later on when it became quite clear that Shipman had chosen his time to leave very carefully. The preceding year had been an extremely good one for the practice financially, which meant that he walked away, leaving the remaining doctors to pick up a large tax bill on his behalf.

All this caused Dr Moysey to reassess his opinion of his former colleague. 'I would always describe Dr Shipman as a mercurial character. It was often quite difficult to predict what sort of mood he would be in from one day to the next. He was certainly a man with very strong opinions and he was never slow to let everybody know those opinions and that he felt that the way in which he practised medicine was the correct one and the one that everybody else should follow.'

The building work took much longer than expected and Shipman continued to practise from the Donneybrook for eight months. But his psychopathic nature meant that he wasn't the least bit bothered by the fact he was still working alongside people he had cheated. However, while he could still work there, the practice's more personal services were now no longer available to him.

Dr Shipman and his family had to look elsewhere for their own doctor and found Dr Wally Ashworth. 'At that time, my doctor, who was also in Hyde, had retired, so we did a swap. I and my family became his patients and he and his family became mine.' Dr Wally Ashworth would remain the Shipman family GP for the next eight years.

'He was a little overbearing and somewhat intolerant of people but, I say this without any reserve whatsoever, a damn good doctor – hard-working, never seemed to worry about the hours he worked. Let's be fair, if I'd thought it was an idiot practising, I wouldn't have been on his list myself. There was never, ever anything to suggest that he was either clinically or for that matter humanly incompetent or certainly my family wouldn't have gone on his list.'

It was a new beginning for Fred Shipman, a chance once and for all to be the perfect doctor he had always wanted to be. The past could no longer be allowed to haunt him. So, yet again, Dr Shipman would set about altering patients' medical notes, but this time they were his own.

'Naturally, being his doctor, I had access to his medical notes. There was only one note, one symbol that gave anything away at all that might possibly indicate that there had been evidence of addiction. Just the words "Pethidine Addict?". Nothing more. And this note had no date on it. There were no written notes from any hospital, no evidence whatsoever of him being addicted to pethidine,' Dr Ashworth told me.

From now on Shipman planned to be unstoppable.

Before he moved from Donneybrook the greatest number of patients it's believed that he killed was probably twelve in any one year but once he moved to Market Street the pattern changed and he was killing many more patients each year.

Ann Alexander, solicitor to the victims' families

CHAPTER TWELVE

ESCAPE AND ESCALATION

They were literally queuing up to be killed

John Shaw, Hyde taxi driver

Hyde is built on the slope of a Pennine foothill. From the top of Werneth Low you travel downhill, past the main Hyde Cemetery where the early morning exhumations were carried out, past street after street where victim after victim lived and died, down past the red-brick, terraced shops and pubs that flank Market Street to the town centre, where the indoor and outdoor markets face the imposing town hall, until, continuing over the crossroads, you reach a odd row of much more modern-looking shops.

In what can only be described as an ill-conceived attempt to create the impression of the elegance of a Georgian spa town, this functional block, sandwiched between old, three-storey Victorian buildings and the motorway junction, has been given an elaborate cast-iron portico that runs the entire length of the row. Here, towards the motorway end next to the Norwest Co-op Pharmacy is 21, Market Street.

Today, thick metal shutters cover the front of the premises, on which someone has scratched 'Justice' and another hand has used a black marker pen to scribble 'murderer'. But, back in 1992, 21 Market Street was about to become the home of Hyde's most popular GP.

From January 1, that year, a notice at the Donneybrook Surgery informed patients that Dr H.F. Shipman was now a sole practitioner working from rooms within Donneybrook House and he would be remaining there until his new premises in Market Street were ready. Shipman moved to his new premises on August 24. A large, shop-style sign above the whole frontage simple read: 'The Surgery'.

Paul Britton comments that the bareness of the practice name, implying that his was the only surgery, was not without significance.

There was certainly arrogance in his choice of location – directly behind 21, Market Street is the Donneybrook practice. It is so close that he and the doctors there could see directly into each other's consulting rooms. It seemed he was determined to rub the noses of his former colleagues in it.

He had poached a number of practice staff, including the senior receptionist from the Donneybrook, and he had also taken his entire patient list, nearly three thousand men, women and children, with him. To top it all, in the September Shipman held a grand ceremonial opening with a good deal of publicity. It looked as if he was touting for even more business.

To Shipman's patients this was the perfect surgery and he was the perfect physician. A locum who worked for Shipman in the early 1990s told the Public Inquiry that patients would often refuse to be seen by him and would prefer to wait until Shipman had returned to work.

Shipman's egotism relished this reputation and the adulation given to him by his patients. It seemed he saw himself as being more than worthy of the almost celebrity status accorded to him by so many of his patients. When he gave evidence at his trial he boasted about his achievements at the practice. When he was asked about a patient's blood pressure, which on a particular occasion was 140/80 and it was suggested to him that that was a perfectly acceptable level, Shipman replied that it might be for many doctors, but he aimed for 'perfection'.

According to Dr Wally Ashworth, one of his more frequent boasts was about his success in treating heart disease. He prescribed cholesterol-lowering drugs very freely and liked to impress upon his colleagues how successful his treatment was. The drugs are now widely championed as preventing heart disease and strokes. But this may not have been Shipman's reason for prescribing these very expensive drugs.

Ann Smith, who worked in the local pharmacy, certainly remembers Dr. Shipman's expensive tastes. He would prescribe the best-quality antibiotics. If there was one that wasn't any different but perhaps a lot cheaper, he would choose the one that was the more expensive.

Dr Shipman's insistence on using only expensive, brand-name drugs on his prescriptions instead of the cheaper NHS approved versions led to a long-running battle with the Health Authority. His prescribing habits were very, very expensive to the family practitioner committees, especially the cholesterol-lowering drugs, but he appeared to think that this was the right thing to do.

Ironically, while it was actually true that his patients did not tend to die from coronary thrombosis, his records of the number of deaths from coronary thrombosis among his patients was high. That was simply because it was his favourite 'cause of death' for his victims.

Although Shipman was generally admired, there were some people in Hyde who disliked him. Their usual criticism was that he appeared arrogant and conceited. Alan Royston's mother, Betty, was a patient of Dr. Shipman's. 'On occasions when I had met him, to arrange for him to visit my mother, I never liked him. From the first moment I met him, I found him arrogant and ignorant. His whole attitude to us seemed to be "Go away, who are you, don't question me".'

Betty Royston had mild dementia so her daughter-in-law, Susan, had to accompany her to the doctor. 'I never liked him at all. I thought he was very arrogant. One time, when I went with Betty, because she was so shy she wouldn't say anything, I spoke for her and he said, "Shut up, I'm not talking to you, I'm talking to your mother." So I really didn't like him.'

Shipman's habit of humiliating people was an unattractive trait. Carol O'Donnell, a former receptionist from Donneybrook, says that on one occasion a lady rep called on her very first day. Usually, the doctors were quite kind but he questioned everything about her and the drugs that she was telling him about.

'Unfortunately, understandably, she had not swotted up as much on her drugs as Shipman had,' Dr Wally Ashworth continued. 'Like many of these younger drug reps she was trying damned hard to earn a living. I felt so sorry for her. She had some sort of impediment in her speech. Shipman tore her to pieces and did the maximum to embarrass this girl.'

He challenged everything until he had the girl in tears. Carol O'Donnell describes him as having been 'a complete bastard to her'.

But, while a few saw glimpses of the darker side of Fred Shipman, most of his patients remained blissfully unaware. 'I think everybody else found him a very, very obliging and caring doctor. I liked him, but I didn't know he had two heads – when he had his Dr Shipman's hat on he was fine, a Dr Jekyll if you like, but I never met the Mr Hyde side of him,' Len Fellows explains.

Florence Lewis was so delighted when she was taken on to his list that she told her son it was 'almost as if she had won the lottery'. She had actually lost: she would become yet another victim of Dr. Shipman. She wasn't alone. Over the next six years over 140 of his patients would come face to face with the other side of their doctor. It would be the last thing they saw.

Serial killers seek out their victims from what the psychologists call a pool of vulnerable people. But as a doctor, Shipman didn't need to trawl the dregs of society for his murders, as Paul Britton explained. His move to a single-handed practice meant that all the victims he wants come to him and external scrutiny would be almost non-existent.

'Unlike the Yorkshire Ripper, he doesn't need to go to prostitutes; unlike Dennis Nilsen, he doesn't need to seek out derelicts. And don't forget the risk of exposure in doing that is huge. He's in a situation where he has quite literally his own little factory and he really doesn't need to do anything else at all.'

Only a few weeks after his grand opening, on October 7, Phyllis Holt was surprised when the doctor answered her sister-in-law's telephone. Monica Sparkes was 72 and lived alone. She had been 'bad on her feet' recently and had had a number of falls. Shipman explained that Mrs Sparkes had had a slight stroke. He said he had called for an ambulance but, as there was an emergency at Manchester Airport, there were no ambulances available. He was lying because, although there had been an incident at the airport that day, it would not have resulted in a lack of ambulances for other emergencies.

Shipman explained that he had told Monica Sparkes to lie on the bed and await his return. He said he had to go to the surgery. He returned about 3.30 pm and telephoned another sister-in-law to say that he had found Monica Sparkes dead. He certified that the death was due to a stroke.

Dame Janet Smith in her Inquiry reports says Shipman had resumed killing in much the same way as he had killed before:

Members of Mrs Sparkes' family then tried to contact her by telephone, but there was no reply. It is clear that Shipman had killed Mrs Sparkes during his (first) visit to her home.

Monica Sparkes was the first name on John Shaw's list and what follows now is, in its basic form, my catalogue of the murders of Britain's most prolific serial killer. Where relevant I've tried to explain either the significance of certain elements of the deaths, or facts that I believe provide an insight into Shipman's state of mind at this stage. I have made a point in this book of naming every victim: it is important for their relatives that there is a full and comprehensive list, but I warn you it is long. As well as the 15 women Shipman was convicted of murdering, Dame Janet Smith found he had unlawfully killed another 135 of his patients and she suspects he may have killed a further eight.

Monica Sparks was the only murder Shipman committed in 1992, but the following year, there is strong evidence to show he killed 16 of his patients and he was probably involved in the sudden deaths of another two. Dame Janet suspects he may have killed 83-year-old Harold Freeman at the start of February, but she is certain that at the end of the month he killed 86-year-old Olive Heginbotham and 92-year-old Hilda Couzins.

He visited both during the afternoon and on his return to the surgery he gave instructions for each to be visited by a consultant geriatrician. Hilda was found that evening, but the next day Shipman went to the house of Mrs Heginbotham and asked a neighbour for the key so he could discover the body. He then issued a prescription in her name to gain more diamorphine.

In March, among the many home visits requested by patients, Shipman was asked to see 82-year-old Amy Whitehead, who had a mild stomach upset. She could not have been very ill, as that morning she did all her usual household tasks, including putting the washing on the line and also making some lunch. Shipman arrived in the late morning and appears to have killed her in his lunch hour. He certainly told her daughter-in-law that he could not stay as he 'had to look after the living, not the dead'.

At this stage Shipman still seems concerned that he might have to face questions about the death so he fabricated an entry in his medical records to say she was suffering from a coronary attack and that he had given a modest dose of diamorphine for the pain. The admission in the notes gave him a ready explanation for the finding of morphine in the body. Also, it meant that, if the mark of an injection was spotted by the undertakers or members of the family, he could have explained it away.

During 1993, Shipman was using a 30 mg ampoule of diamorphine to kill each of his victims. Each time he killed, he replaced the ampoule ready for the next murder. But, after his drug conviction, Shipman had made a deal not to carry controlled drugs. He needed a regular source of supply that could not be linked directly back to him, so over a period of seven months he wrote 14 prescriptions, all for a single 30 mg ampoule of Diamorphine and all in the names of real patients. For two of the prescriptions he used the names of perfectly healthy patients.

Len Fellows ran the Patient Fund for Harold Shipman for six years, during which time he raised over £19,000, but Shipman had a unique way of rewarding one of his most loyal patients, as the former CID officer found out when the police rang him up shortly after Shipman's arrest. On going through the chemists' registers they had found that Shipman had taken out a prescription for morphine in August 1993 in Fellows's name. Fellows says that he felt betrayed.

Why Shipman chose to use Len Fellows's name is not known. Len cannot recall having a doctor's appointment around that time, so maybe Shipman just saw him in the street, or collecting the fund money in the surgery. It seems the choice of name was totally random.

The use of a perfectly healthy patient, whom Shipman had not earmarked as a victim, was unusual. The remaining 12 prescriptions were all in the names of patients he would kill or had killed. Four of the prescriptions were dispensed on the actual day of the death of the patient they were supposedly issued for, while six more were collected by Shipman a few days after the death.

Ann Smith explains that the usual way of getting a controlled drug prescription is for either the patient's relative to come in for it or a nurse or the Macmillan nurse or whoever was dealing with the patient. It was very rare for a doctor to come in himself for a controlled drug. But as mentioned earlier, Dr Shipman had great presence and he was quite reassuring in collecting the prescriptions and would by no means give any indication that they were for anything other than what they prescribed for.

The dose is an unusual amount to be prescribed, but such was the trust in Shipman's prescribing abilities that this was never questioned at the pharmacy. And he did know what he was doing: 30 mg would be lethal to anyone who was not a regular user of the opiate.

In April, Shipman killed cancer patient Mary Andrew, probably with a prescription in the name of his previous victim, then, just four days after Miss Andrew's death, Shipman wrote a prescription for 30 mg diamorphine in her name. It is clear that he was replacing the 30 mg ampoule that he had used on his now dead patient. He did the same with Sarah Ashworth. Her body was exhumed in 1998, but she had been buried too long for the forensic evidence to be clear.

Shipman killed two more of his female patients in April 1993, Fanny Nichols and Marjorie Parker, and used both their names to get more diamorphine. In May, Edna Llewellyn had an attack of angina. Shipman was called but, by the time he arrived, Mrs Llewellyn was much better. Shipman went into the bedroom with Mrs Llewellyn, while her daughter-in-law and a friend stayed in the living room. After a while, Shipman went to collect something from his car and returned to the bedroom. A few minutes later, he emerged and announced that Mrs Llewellyn had died of a massive heart attack. Three more of his patients died unexpectedly that month: Nellie Mullen, Emily Morgan and Violet Bird.

Two months later, Shipman was ready to kill again. He paid an unexpected house call on José Richards. Mrs Richards spoke to a friend at about 12.15 pm and seemed perfectly well, but when the friend called round about 90 minutes later she found Dr Shipman there. He had just made himself a cup of tea. José Richards was sitting in her chair; her dentures had been removed and her doctor simply announced that she had 'just gone'.

But, in a bizarre semi-admission of what had actually happened, he then told her family that he had given José Richards an injection for her pain. He explained that unfortunately he had not realised how frail she had become and that the injection had killed her. He was very matter-of-fact and his explanation was accepted, without further justification or suspicion.

In August, Shipman used his thirteenth diamorphine ampoule to kill Edith Calverley and then wrote one more prescription in her name. Dame

Janet believes that this, the fourteenth ampoule, was used in an attempt to kill Mary Smith at the end of August.

Shipman was disturbed during this visit when her step-daughters arrived unexpectedly at her flat. They found Shipman leaning over Mrs Smith, who was unconscious. Mary Smith slept deeply until the following morning, when she awoke with no apparent ill effects. Shipman had probably been interrupted by her step-daughters while he was administering the diamorphine, so she did not receive a lethal dose. It seems likely that Shipman felt that yet again he had nearly been caught.

It obviously scared him, as he didn't kill again for four months. But he made up for it in December, killing three patients in quick succession: 78-year-old Joseph Leigh, 54-year-old Eileen Robinson and 90-year-old Charles Brocklebent. But Shipman never again prescribed single 30 mg ampoules. For the first time he took advantage of a new and more prolific source of diamorphine

In November, one of Shipman's terminally ill cancer patients was provided with a new method of administering morphine – a syringe driver. The driver is a type of injection that feeds the patient a regular dose of diamorphine subcutaneously. The patient, David Jones, died shortly afterwards, his death probably hastened by Shipman, who took possession of two or three boxes each containing ten 100 mg ampoules of diamorphine.

He should have returned the unused diamorphine to the pharmacy for destruction but did not. From this time onwards Shipman always had a plentiful supply of the opiate and the frequency with which he killed patients increased accordingly.

The psychologist Julian Boon suggests that there was for Shipman a great expression of power in the act of deciding whether someone was going to live or die.

By 1994, Shipman had 3,124 patients on his list and killed 12 of them in this one year alone. In January, he killed Joan Harding in his surgery. It was her death that convinced taxi driver John Shaw to keep his list. But as John Shaw started to keep a record of the deaths, Shipman began to remove any evidence of them. From then on he destroyed his visits book, which recorded the times he visited his patients.

Shipman also killed Christine Hancock in January and at the beginning of February he killed Elsie Platt. Later the same month he had yet another close call.

He was called out to see 47-year-old Renate Overton, who was suffering from an asthma attack. Mrs Overton's daughter was with her but, once the asthma attack had been successfully treated, she went upstairs, leaving Shipman and her mother alone. Within minutes, the doctor called her back downstairs. Mrs Overton was unconscious on the floor. Shipman said that she had had gone into cardiac arrest. The daughter called an ambulance and was then asked to assist in resuscitation. The paramedics succeeded in starting Mrs Overton's heart. But she was deeply unconscious and had suffered irreversible brain damage. She lived in a persistent vegetative state for 14 months.

Shipman was in real danger of being exposed. He had told the paramedics and the hospital staff that Mrs Overton had suffered a heart attack at home and that he had given 10 mg diamorphine to relieve her pain. Staff at the hospital realised that, as Mrs Overton had just had asthma attack, Shipman had given far more opiate than he should have done. Dame Janet believes Shipman must have felt extremely vulnerable in the days and weeks following this incident:

> *If his apparent negligence were investigated, there must have been a danger that his possession of illicit supplies of opiate and his more sinister intentions would be uncovered. Shipman did not kill for three months after the episode involving Mrs Overton. It may be that he destroyed his cache of diamorphine, as he did not kill again until the day on which he next obtained a supply.*

By May, Shipman was desperate. He obviously needed to kill, but he also needed diamorphine. He wrote a prescription for a massive 1000 mg diamorphine, using the name of the patient he had tried to kill the previous August. He then paid another visit to Mary Smith, whom he had visited back in 1993 and had been disturbed while injecting her. This time she wasn't so lucky. Shipman used a small amount of the 1000 mg to kill Mrs Smith and kept the rest. He was clearly planning more deaths.

He killed again in May. Fifty-seven-year-old Ronnie Davenport died in her own home as did the two patients Cicely Sharples and Alice Kitchen whom he murdered in June. In July he visited Maria Thorton and killed her, but his 1000 mg supply of diamorphine must have been running out as he obtained 500 mg more before killing Henrietta Walker and Elizabeth Mellor in November. In December, after getting a further 1000 mg he killed John Bennett Molesdale. Eleven patients had been left dead and a twelfth was in a coma. The following year Shipman would more than double that total.

Alice Kennedy was 88 when she died suddenly in January 1995. She was the only patient he killed in the first month of this new year, but she was by no means the last. With a constant supply and a stockpile of diamorphine at his disposal, Shipman would kill 30 patients in 1995.

By then there was a change to his MO. He had been killing for over 20 years and it seemed he no longer needed to be there at the moment of death to enjoy his murders.

Paul Britton thinks that Shipman could picture the tableau, the room and the person he has just left. He would be able to visualise how they actually made the transition from being alive to being dead, and how they looked in death – because he had been there over and over and over again. Moreover, by not being there, Shipman was also distancing himself from the more distasteful elements of the murder. He could get the pleasure out of the death without any discomfort to himself.

From then on, in a number of cases Shipman probably injected his victim at a slightly slower rate. This would mean that the diamorphine would take slightly longer to work – normally it would take a couple of minutes. By protracting the length of time it took to inject the drug, Shipman had time to leave the victim and go back to work.

But he was taking a gamble. During this time, his victim, unaware they were about to die, might get up and fall over, or try to leave their home, or even just make a phone call.

'I had a phone call from my aunt who said that she'd had a visit from Dr Shipman.' Ann Smith's 70-year-old aunt Lucy Virgin lived on her own with her little dog for company. 'My aunt hadn't made an appointment; the doctor just made a visit. A few weeks before, she had had a bit of a chest infection. And when she phoned she just said that Dr Shipman had just come to check on how she was and he felt that she still had a little bit of a chest infection and would like to give her a course of antibiotics, which he did.'

But Dr Shipman had something else for his patient. 'She said he'd also given her an injection and told her not to move out of the house.' Lucy Virgin was Shipman's 143rd victim.

The day before her death Shipman had picked up ten 100 mg ampoules of morphine. He injected Lucy Virgin with diamorphine and left her to die. His arrogance was callous; he knew his advice not to leave the house would be followed. But, because he had left his patient to die, this is a case where we now know exactly what happened when the doctor came to call.

Lucy Virgin was obviously unaware that the injection was lethal and it is clear that the drug took some time to take effect and that during this time Shipman's victim felt fine. This must be some comfort for many relatives.

For Shipman, killing in this way was also an ideal way of avoiding suspicion. Paul Britton believes by this stage he had had too many close calls for comfort. 'I think that's why he introduced a killing method that interjected a gap between his delivery of the injection and the dying of the person. It is important to see that he needs to build in at least some safety devices. He needs to be in a position where it is known that Dr Shipman has been to the home; he has injected or whatever it happens to be, but he's not actually there when the person dies, he's got an alibi.'

But a watertight alibi meant someone else had to discover the body. Ann Smith's regular trip to the surgery was perfect. 'After lunch I went down to the surgery as I would normally do. Dr Shipman was there and he said, "Have you seen your aunt today?" I said, "No. Should I have done?" He said, "Oh, no," and toddled off back into the back of the room.

'So I didn't think anything untoward, but I thought perhaps she was really poorly. So I went back to the shop where I worked, and asked my pharmacist if I could phone my aunt. I phoned and there was no answer.

'I phoned again every ten minutes or so and by this time I was quite concerned, and I asked our driver to make my aunt's house his first call on his delivery. He did, and promptly phoned me to say, "I think you best come, I think your aunt has died."'

When Ann Smith got to her aunt's flat she found her sitting upright in her chair, slightly bent forward. She'd had a newspaper on her knee, which had fallen to the floor, and her spectacles had just come to the end of her nose

'She was just sitting as if she was just asleep. I phoned Dr Shipman. The driver had phoned the ambulance. Anyway, within ten minutes or so Dr Shipman arrived and he just walked into the living room where she was, came straight out and said, "I'm afraid she's died. What would you like me to write on the death certificate?" It took me aback. He was quite abrupt and just said, "We've no need to have a post mortem. Are you going to cremate?" I said yes, and he said, "The certificate will be ready for you tomorrow." And with that he left. It was very abrupt. Quite uncaring.'

Although Lucy Virgin had no history of heart trouble, Shipman listed ischaemic heart disease as the cause of death. It went unchallenged. Everything had gone exactly according to his plan. Ann Smith had provided him with a watertight alibi. She now realises that Dr Shipman alerted her to the fact that there was something wrong so that she would discover her aunt dead at her flat.

'I felt he showed no remorse at all about any of the people he killed and totally abused his position. She believed in everything he did. It stopped her moving into my aunt's house in Blackpool, because she continually said she would never find a doctor like Dr Shipman. My aunt looked on him as somebody she totally trusted and he took her trust and abused it.'

By then, Paul Britton believes that Shipman had gone through a significant transformation. He was no longer a doctor who wanted to save lives. Instead, killing had become a routine need.

The Public Inquiry certainly uncovered anecdotal evidence that Shipman had a morbid interest in death and derived some pleasure from the circumstances of death. Mrs Judith Page, a patient of Shipman, told the Inquiry that, during a consultation in his surgery, Shipman remarked to her that in the course of her work as a home help, she must sometimes find a client dead. She said she had and had found it very upsetting. Shipman seemed surprised and asked whether she did not find that it gave her 'a buzz'.

Clearly, by 1995 the 'buzz' Shipman got from his deaths was diminishing. His crimes were escalating and he killed nine patients in quick succession. He killed Joseph Shaw three days after Lucy Virgin and Maria West three days after that, but the following day he killed again, twice – Netta Ashcroft and Lily Bardsley. Killing two patients in one day seemed to sate him for a while as there was then a whole week's gap between the deaths of Marie Fernley, John Crompton, Frank Crompton and Vera Brocklehurst.

Renate Overton finally died on 21 April. It was a direct result of the injection that Shipman had given her in February. Shipman was questioned by the Coroner's Office about the circumstances surrounding her collapse. He said nothing about giving her diamorphine and merely told the same story as the paramedics. As a result the coroner decided not to hold an inquest and permitted the cremation of the body. With the publishing of the Public Inquiry Report, her death was added to the list of those murdered by their GP.

Three female patients, Angela Tierney, Edith Scott and Clara Hackney, were all killed in April. Shipman had also obtained another 1000 mg diamorphine in Clara Hackney's name, which meant he could kill 75-year-old Kate Sellors in May and four more patients in June. Clifford Heapey was first, followed by Brenda Ashworth, the cousin of Wally Ashworth.

'One afternoon, my wife got a phone call from the police asking me to go to such and such an address and did I know a Brenda? Brenda was dead at home, sitting up in a chair. I identified her and said to my wife that it was somewhat unusual for a person to be found dead in a chair sitting up. It happens, but not very often.

'Later, apparently uninvited, Dr Shipman turned up. At that point I didn't even know that Shipman was her doctor. He turned up and said, "Will you ask your wife to come round for a death certificate?", which she did.'

Perhaps if Dr Wally Ashworth had known that his cousin was the second of Dr Shipman's patients to have died in their own homes that month and that a third, Ernest Rudol, would be discovered shortly afterwards, he would have been more suspicious.

As it was, he simply thought it unusual, as was the death of the fourth patient that month, Bertha Moss, who died in Shipman's surgery. Later, in conversation with another daughter, Shipman suggested that it was all for the best that the 68-year-old Bertha Moss had died when she did, as she would have had to have her legs 'chopped off' on account of her diabetes and she would not have wanted to spend the rest of her life in a wheelchair and be a burden to her family.

In July Shipman killed two patients, Ada Hilton and Irene Aikten, and then in August another of his patients, Arthur Stopford, didn't answer his phone when his family made their daily call to his home. Arthur was 82, registered blind and partially deaf, and his granddaughter Barbara was worried.

'We used to ring to make sure he was okay. We rang and there was no answer. Now this had happened before, because he had been in the bathroom and he was a little bit deaf, so sometimes he didn't hear the phone. So I thought I'd go up and make sure, because we had a key to his flat just in case anything happened.

'He was just sitting in his armchair, with his hand against his head, leaning over. I thought he was asleep. It wasn't until I looked at him properly that I saw he was pale and he had what they call cyanosis, blue lips. So I knew something was wrong then. I picked the phone up. It was still ringing because my mum was still ringing. I told her to put my dad on and asked him to dial three nines and I was going to try and resuscitate my granddad.'

Barbara Eades is a registered first aider with the Red Cross, but she was fighting a battle she couldn't win. 'I got him on to the floor, did the checks to make sure there was nothing in his mouth, nothing – no obstruction – and I started CPR. And I carried on until the ambulance crew got there. They were about ten minutes. The ambulance crew took over and then pronounced him dead.' The diamorphine had caused brain death before Barbara arrived at her grandfather's home. She could not have saved him.

Two hundred and four of Shipman's patients had now died at home; 129 had been found in a chair or on the settee and they all looked as if they had fallen asleep. Arthur Stopford was one of the 129, but the family accepted his death as natural because they trusted their doctor.

It would be another seven years before they would find out the truth.

Even after Shipman was convicted of the murders of 15 of his patients, Arthur's family still thought they had been unaffected by the doctor's crimes. 'We did think, "My God, we could have been next on his list", because we were patients of his. But we never thought that he'd taken my grandfather's life, because the 15 were all women and, at the time, we didn't know that there were any male victims.'

*

The family wasn't alone. Most people believed that Shipman was a real-life lady-killer, preying on elderly women. It was a misconception that had been fostered by the trial and by press reports, before and after. The Public Inquiry discovered that many of Shipman's victims were male. Of the 215 confirmed unlawful killings, 41 were men and in 11 more cases where Dame Janet found suspicion of unlawful killing the victims were also male.

Paul Britton feels that the sex of his victim was not the most important criterion for Shipman. He was omnivorous as a killer and it was his relationship with death and the dead, rather than a dead man or a dead woman, that was important to him. His orientation was generally towards women and there was a sexual suggestion in the Inquiry Report, but he could get his pleasure from other possibilities as well.

Arthur Stopford's late wife Hetty had also been a patient of Shipman. 'We got a phone call saying that they'd what they called red-flagged both my nana and my granddad. It could have been Shipman who had killed them both,' Barbara Eades said.

Dame Janet Smith found that Hetty Stopford had died of natural causes. Arthur Stopford hadn't been so lucky: 'She believed that he murdered my granddad. Granddad was cremated, so we couldn't get any evidence other than the way it was, with Shipman turning up, and the way he was sitting in the armchair as if he was asleep. Some of the neighbours said they'd seen him go in and come out. That's how we knew that he'd been. He must have prepared for it because he put on Granddad's notes, "dying". He showed it to my mum.'

But it actually seemed that the medical notes refer to a completely different plan Shipman originally had for his patient. It started with the doctor telling Arthur Stopford's relatives that he was terminally ill.

'Dr Shipman came round to see him because he was a bit off colour the week before. There wasn't anything seriously wrong but after the visit he told my mum he thought it could be cancer. He showed her his record and he'd put on it "cancer dying" with three question marks.'

Arthur Stopford's medical records were falsified. There was no evidence of cancer – Shipman lied. It seems that Arthur Stopford was just another way for him to get diamorphine. Shipman planned to write out bogus prescriptions in his name to gain more of the drug. He needed to invent cancer victims as by now the diamorphine he was collecting from the terminally ill was not giving him enough of a supply. But he hadn't counted on Arthur's family becoming suspicious. They wondered why he hadn't booked a hospital appointment for their grandfather to have a check-up or a biopsy. Shipman therefore probably killed Arthur Stopford because he could no longer be of use to him as a regular supply of diamorphine.

*

In September Dora Ashton was found dead on the couch in Shipman's surgery, Shipman told her son that his mother had fallen to the floor as she was walking into his consulting room, having suffered a minor stroke. He had managed to sit her down, but she had had a second stroke and had died. Shipman had killed Geoffrey Bogle at his home a week before he killed in his surgery.

He only killed once in October, Muriel Ward, but in November he killed three times: Edith Brock, Charles Barlow and one of his youngest victims, 43-year-old Konrad Robinson. On December 14, Shipman killed the terminally ill cancer patient Kenneth Woodhead with an overdose of his diamorphine and then took the remaining 500 mg stock. Later than day, he killed Elizabeth Sigley. This brought the total number of murders committed by Shipman in 1995 to 30.

The Public Inquiry found that, by the beginning of 1996, Shipman had already unlawfully killed 130 of his patients, but that figure may be as high as 172, as there was a suspicion of unlawful killing in a further 42 cases.

Nineteen ninety-six was also a busy year. Dr Shipman killed another 30 patients in this 12 months. But by now he had learnt a lot of lessons and his methods of concealment were more sophisticated. His lies on the cremation forms became more elaborate. He always claimed that others were present at the time of death if he had been there, although normally he had been alone with the patient. He also began to claim far more frequently that someone had seen the deceased alive between his visit and the discovery of the body.

Rob Ressler believes that Shipman's psychopathy made him extremely cunning and that he was perfecting a scenario that would escape detection.

And despite the fact he was now killing several of his patients every month, he wasn't found out. He was their doctor and nobody for one minute thought that he would want to kill them. But he did. In the first two months of 1996 four of Shipman's patients were found dead in their own homes. Hilda Hilbert and Erica Copeland both died in January. In February he killed 80-year-old Jane Shelmerdine and 88-year-old John Greenhaigh. Minnie Galpin was his only victim in March.

In April he killed two patients. Marjorie Waller was killed and left on the bed. Shipman later said that a neighbour had seen her alive when she dropped a prescription in but this was a lie and she was not discovered until the following day. A week later, he killed John Stone. In May, he murdered four of his patients. A week after killing Elsie Godfrey in her own home, he killed Edith Brady in his surgery. Mrs Brady's son-in-law, Rodney Turner, a police officer, telephoned the surgery after he had received a message saying his mother-in-law had been taken ill. Shipman told him that Edith Brady had collapsed in the surgery. Mr Turner asked how serious it was. Shipman replied, 'How serious do you want it to be? The only way she's going to leave here is with the help of Robinson and Jordan.' They were a firm of Hyde undertakers.

Two weeks later, Len Fellows received some sad news about a good friend of his, Val Cuthbert. Her sister-in-law, a former colleague of Fellows at the police station at Mottram, told him that Val had died and that Shipman had found her. The next day he saw Shipman and asked what had happened. Shipman said that he had been called to see her and that he suspected that she had got heart trouble. He had recommended that she should go to hospital but she didn't want to, so he said that he would be back in the afternoon. He claimed that, when he returned, he knocked on the door, but got no reply. He then found that the door wasn't locked, went in and found her dead in the chair.

Fellows says, 'Two or three of Val's friends who I related this story to thought it odd that she didn't want to go to hospital. She didn't have a phobia about hospitals or anything like that. I thought it odd at the time, but obviously not knowing about all these other cases, I thought she must have had had some reason that I don't know about.'

Val Cuthbert was 54 and the former landlady of the Cheshire Cheese Pub in Market Street. She had been a patient of Shipman's but she and her husband had moved away to run another pub. When he died, she returned to Hyde but was upset to find Shipman had a queue of patients waiting to join his practice.

'She went to the surgery and tried to get back on Shipman's panel but the receptionist told her that they'd no vacancies. So she rang me to tell me.'

Val Cuthbert knew Len Fellows was good friends with her former doctor. 'She asked me if I could have a word with him. So the next day I went and saw Fred and I told him what she'd said. "No problem," he said. "Tell her to come in and tell the receptionist I've said OK."'

Len Fellows is the sort of person who will do anything for anyone. He raised thousands of pounds for Shipman's surgery. He still does huge amounts of charity work for the Masons and other local organisations. He even used to take Shipman's youngest son to rugby matches because he thought his father was too busy with his patients, but he will always regret the good deed he did for Val Cuthbert.

'It was the worst day's work I ever did, getting her back on Shipman's panel. And to make it worse I believe she left him about 250 quid in her will as a bequest.'

Paul Britton believes that by killing elderly patients he made more room on his list for younger patients. But also, as people fell off at one end, there was room at the other for new people to come on. This gave him a constantly developing population. From his point of view, the elderly or infirm would go first because they simply ceased to be as valuable as human beings and so there was no reason to keep them.

The day after he killed Val Cuthbert, Shipman killed 77-year-old Lilian Cullen. At the beginning of June, he wrote a prescription for 12,000 mg of diamorphine, enough to kill 360 people. He would kill 11 during the next two months.

His first victim of five in June was 63-year-old Rene Lacey. Four days later, Shipman killed 82-year-old Leah Fogg in her own home. His need to kill had now become an overwhelming force that seemed to engulf him as soon as he became aware of an available victim. On Friday, June 7, Leah Fogg's daughter went to see the doctor. She was concerned that her mother was depressed and still not coming to terms with the loss of her father some years before. She had noticed a sign in the waiting room that said counselling services were available and hoped Dr Shipman could arrange for her mother to receive some bereavement counselling. However, she didn't want her mother to know she had arranged it.

The doctor seemed more than happy to pay Leah Fogg a visit, unannounced. Three days later he did just that but when he left Leah Fogg she was dead. It would have been far less risky to wait a few weeks before killing her, but it seems he couldn't wait. However, Leah Fogg was extremely fit and well and her sudden death within a short time of his visit would have raised questions, so when Shipman was called to examine the body he didn't mention that he had visited her that afternoon, despite the fact that her daughter had asked him to. Leah Fogg lived on a busy road in an area where Shipman had few patients and he gambled on the fact that he hadn't been noticed.

Seven days later, he killed Gladys Saunders in her home and a week after that he killed two patients on the same day, Margaret Vickers and Nellie Bennett, both in their own homes. With Mrs Bennett he again claimed that a neighbour had seen her alive, which was untrue. In July, Shipman killed six of his patients: 77-year-old Tom Russell was the first; nine days later he killed Irene Turner. Her body would be later exhumed and he would be convicted of her murder. He killed Carrie Leigh, Marion Higham and Elise Hannible over a period of eight days, and at the very end of the month he killed Elise Barker

Shipman took a holiday from 3 to 19 August, so he didn't kill again until the 30th when he killed the second resident of Garden Street, Sidney

Smith. Sydney's brother Kenneth was in the kitchen at the time. Shipman believed he had witnessed the murder. Kenneth would be one of two more to die that year.

In September, Shipman killed Dorothy Andrew, who was 85, and Anne Ralphs, who was ten years younger, in their own homes, and in October he killed Millicent Garside.

But it was in September that he installed an improved version of his Micro-Doc computer software. From then on DS John Ashley would later be able to track every entry Shipman made in his patients' medical records, including all the false ones.

In November Shipman visited Mrs Irene Heathcote and killed her at about 4 pm in the afternoon. Friends tried to visit her in the evening but there was no reply and her body wasn't found until the following morning. The gas fire was on very high and, in a bizarre piece of theatre, when Shipman arrived, he placed a thermometer under her armpit and announced that she had died the previous evening at 8 pm. Three days later he killed 89-year-old Samuel Mills.

On December 4 Shipman arrived in Garden Street, where he had three elderly patients who lived next door to one another. There had been five, but seven years before, in June 1989, he had killed Josephine Hall, after growing tired of her agoraphobia-related problems, and, four months previous to this visit, he had killed 76-year-old Sydney Smith, while his 73-year-old brother Kenneth was just a few feet away in the kitchen.

Unfortunately for Kenneth Smith, he also happened to be with Shipman's intended victim this time. Thomas Cheetham was expecting the doctor to call. It was a routine visit: the 78-year-old had cancer although the illness was not terminal. The two elderly neighbours, who had been friends for years, had been watching the racing on television while keeping a look-out for Shipman. When he arrived, Thomas Cheetham went home.

Shortly afterwards, Elsie Cheetham came home from a shopping trip. Shipman was probably just leaving when he saw Mrs Cheetham but he waited outside, pretending that he had just arrived. She let him in and they found her husband dead, sitting in his usual chair, as if he had fallen asleep. Shipman pretended that he could estimate the time of Mr Cheetham's death, which he said had taken place between one and two hours earlier. He also pretended that he had not seen Mr Cheetham alive for twelve days before this.

But he had a problem. Kenneth Smith knew that the doctor had arrived much earlier and, if the neighbours talked, Shipman would be exposed as a liar. Worse still, Kenneth might remember the remarkably similar circumstances surrounding his brother's death just four months before.

Then there was Elsie Cheetham, who had discovered Josephine Hall's body in 1989, so she too could become suspicious. Shipman needed to do some damage limitation.

His first port of call was to Massey and Sons, Undertakers, where he asked for two cremation forms, because he had two seriously ill patients, so that he 'wouldn't have to trouble them over the holidays'.

Alan Massey's daughter Debbie thought the request somewhat odd, to say the least, but later that month she was shocked to discover that her GP appeared to be psychic. 'We'd shut the office up for Christmas and were having a drink when the phone went and it was to tell us that there had been a death and it was one of Shipman's patients. And we all looked at one another.'

Kenneth Smith, brother of Sydney, neighbour of Thomas Cheetham and unsuspecting witness to both murders, was dead. Shipman claimed he should have been in a residential home, but had refused to go.

Paul Britton believes that by now Shipman's patients meant nothing to him, but he still prided himself on being a good administrator. 'He knows himself. He knows that he needs to kill people. He recognises that there is an administrative aspect to it. He's simply keeping the books properly in order. He knows he's going to want to kill over a particular period, even if he hasn't selected a victim. So he wants to be prepared. The less prepared he is, the more there is an opportunity for other people to be involved after the killing and before the cremation. The chance of him being discovered increases and he simply wants to make sure that that is reduced.'

Shipman was clearly spiralling out of control. He now saw himself as a god with the power of life and death. He didn't believe anyone could doubt him. But he was wrong.

It's funny, as I talk about it, I still see it every day, you know, walking into my mother's flat and that arrogant look he gave me the first time he ever spoke to me. I see his face a lot.

Alan Royston, victim's son

THE LAST HURRAH

There was nothing left of all the things that were important to him, other than this last hurrah.

Julian Boon, criminal and forensic psychologist

It seems even serial killers reach a retirement age. The criminal psychologists and profilers are all agreed that, if undiscovered, over a period of about 30 years a serial killer will burn himself out and the murders will simply stop by the time the killer reaches his fifties.

Paul Britton explained that, in the early stages, there would probably be an escalation in the level of pleasure, but that would gradually decay. Later on, it's a return that can almost never be got back and at some point there is no return at all.

But Dr Harold Frederick Shipman was about to become the exception that proves the rule. On January 14, 1997 he celebrated his fifty-first birthday. His desire to kill should have been waning – instead, his killings were still escalating. During the next 12 months he would kill 37 of his patients. But, as Shipman celebrated his birthday with his family, he was unaware that this would be his last full year as a GP.

The desperate need to kill brought with it a reckless confidence and a volume of deaths that simply could not go unnoticed. And it was during 1997 that the first seeds of suspicion were at last sown in the minds of those around him. But Shipman seemed no longer to care if he risked exposure and at the beginning of 1997 he seems to have deliberately killed a patient in front of a witness.

He had mainly avoided killing patients living in residential or nursing homes. There were too many dangers involved, too many chances of being caught out. However, around lunchtime on January 2, 1997, Dr Shipman visited Charnley House residential home and injected 75-year-old Eileen

Crompton in front of the home's deputy manager. She was one of only three patients he was confident enough to kill in residential or nursing homes.

He obviously had not planned in advance of his visit to kill Eileen Crompton as he had to go to his car to get a syringe and ampoule. Shipman injected the contents of the ampoule into the back of Eileen Crompton's hand, and within a minute she was dead.

Eileen Crompton had quite severe Parkinson's disease and the doctor had been called out that morning because, in the words of her carers, Eileen Crompton had seemed 'very flushed' and may well have had a cold. But without even examining her, Shipman announced that his patient was in heart failure and that, unless he gave her an injection immediately, to 'kick-start' the heart, he was 'going to lose her'.

Despite the fact his murder had been witnessed and this must have given him some form of adrenalin rush, Shipman showed no emotion, but simply said, 'Oh, dear, this is what I feared would happen.' He certified that the cause of death was bronchopneumonia.

Once back in his surgery, Shipman wrote in Eileen Crompton's medical records that he had injected benzylpenicillin, an appropriate treatment if his patient had a very severe chest infection. But this antibiotic could not 'kick-start' the heart, neither would it have caused the patient's sudden death.

Paul Britton believes that by this stage even the added excitement of killing in front of someone wasn't enough for him. He simply had to kill more and more frequently. It would expose him to suspicion.

He killed 47-year-old David Harrison the day after he killed Eileen Crompton, and he killed on seven further occasions before the end of February. Elsie Dean was killed on January 8, 76-year-old Irene Brooder died 12 days later and seven days after that he gave a lethal injection to Charlotte Bennison.

His first victim in February was Charles Killan. The following day he visited dementia sufferer Betty Royston at her flat in Ogden Court at the request of her son Alan. 'I was concerned about my mother because she didn't appear to be looking after herself. She wasn't really unwell but she wasn't caring for herself. I went down to the surgery and asked if he would come up and pay her a visit.

'I'd just arrived home from work and he actually phoned there to say he'd visited my mother. He'd examined her and he thought she was going to be a problem. He said she might need residential care and that he'd done a blood test and that was it. That was the end of the phone call.'

Betty Royston did not like her doctor and Alan and Susan knew she would be upset that they had called him in. When she didn't ring they thought she'd probably fallen out with them because they hadn't told her.

'The next morning, when I went to work, I passed the flats and the curtains were shut which unusual because she was always sitting there in the window waiting for me to pass. I just thought she'd slept in,' Susan Royston explained.

'Then that morning in work I had a phone call from Christine, the warden at Odgen Court, to say that they'd found her and could I get in touch with Alan. We went down and Christine said, "Are you ready for this?" So I said yes, and we went in the flat and we saw her lying on the floor.'

Unlike most of Shipman's victims, Betty Royston certainly did not look as if she had just fallen asleep. Alan asked Christine if they had moved her but she said that all she'd done was cover her up. But he was immediately struck by the way she was laid out: it was almost as if she'd been placed there and did not look natural.

Susan Royston agreed with her husband. 'It was too perfect. Her cardigan and her glasses were on the settee; the skirt was down, it was just perfect. She was laid in the recovery position basically but everything was just straight. There was no mess.'

The husband and wife were more than a little suspicious. Susan Royston said that they had had time to think about it while waiting for the funeral director to come. 'We both sat there and kept saying it wasn't possible. She wouldn't have fallen in that position if she'd passed out. We just couldn't believe she was so perfect and then her glasses on the back of the chair, her cardigan over the arm of the chair. You couldn't get her clothes off her to wash them, because she'd be putting it back on as soon as you'd taken it off and she wouldn't ever go without her glasses.

'Then there were the two spots of mucus, as if she'd staggered around before she died, but we couldn't find anything disturbed or any sign that she'd fallen or she'd tripped over anything,' Susan Royston explained.

Her husband thought his mother's arrogant GP had simply been incompetent. His opinion of Shipman was that he was callous enough to have left her after she had died in his presence. One of his mother's sleeves was rolled up so it looked as though the doctor had taken a blood sample and then left her knowing the warden would find her the following morning.

Alan and Susan Royston had no chance to question Shipman that day. The warden had telephoned Dr Shipman as soon as she had discovered the body. He had arrived at Betty Royston's flat within minutes and left very quickly afterwards.

'We feel that maybe he was actually just round the corner waiting for the call,' Alan Royston explained. 'He told Christine, the warden, that there was no need to call the police because he'd visited her and then he left. So he'd actually gone when we got there. When I went down to the surgery next day for the death certificate I asked him what the actual cause of death was and he said, "Well, it's very difficult to ascertain that without a post mortem and you don't want your relative messed about with, do you?"

'He could see I was upset at the thought of a post mortem and, with hindsight, he was actually leading me away from saying I wanted one. He then said, "Shall we put it down as a stroke?" And I actually said to him, "Well, you are the doctor, I'm not." And that's how we left it.

'But walking back to my mother's flat, I thought what a strange conversation it was. It just seemed so odd and the more I thought about it the more I kept turning over in my mind and asking myself whether he'd killed her.'

The following day, at work, Alan decided to confide in a colleague: 'I said that I'd got this funny feeling that she either died in front of him and the callous so-and-so left her for the warden to find or that he'd killed her. And my colleague said, "You can't say that."'

Susan Royston got the same reaction when she told people of her fears.

Alan Royston is an ex-trade union shop steward. He led the infamous *Stockport Messenger* newspaper strike in the 1980s, so he is not afraid to stand up for what he believes in, but he knew that whatever he thought was now best kept to himself.

But Alan and Susan Royston were right. Dame Janet Smith found that Betty Royston was Shipman's 167th unlawful killing. 'Now I have a death certificate that reflects the true nature of her death. I've not had my day in court but now I have that piece of paper that tells me the truth and I've got to thank Dame Janet for that.

'I keep seeing my mother staggering about and I wonder if he actually injected her and then watched her stagger about. I just wonder what he thought it was like, that ultimate power over death.'

Alan and Susan Royston now believe that Shipman may well have underestimated the amount of diamorphine needed to kill Betty. 'They say that that's probably what happened because how long it takes for it to work depends upon how much food she had inside her stomach. It can be immediate or it can be a few minutes and it looked as if it was a few minutes. I have this picture in my head of her walking one way and then the other and possibly just collapsing and then him dragging her over and sorting her out. It's horrible.'

But Julian Boon believes that the elderly lady with slight dementia had simply seen a side of Shipman that his adoring patients couldn't. Those people who were 'normal' in terms of understanding the world would have been the ones who were especially vulnerable to the kindly old doctor who was trying to help them with an injection. They wouldn't dream of questioning him.

But someone suffering from dementia might not see the world like that.

They might be alarmed at the sight of a needle coming towards them and there might have been a struggle. So the crime would present a different appearance from the complete passive acceptance that what was being done was for the best.

Betty Royston had put up a struggle and, probably because Shipman feared he would be discovered by the warden, he had been forced to leave her on the floor. But, because he knew the warden logged the doctor's visits, he needed to make sure it would appear that she died much later in the evening. He left the heater on full in the flat, so it was 'like a sauna'.

Betty Royston's death clearly affected Shipman as he did not kill again for nearly three weeks. Once he started up again, he killed two patients in quick succession, Joyce Woodhead and Bill Catlow's ballroom dancing partner Lizzie Adams, who was one of the 15 patients he was convicted of murdering. But Lizzie Adams's death obviously exhausted his supply of diamorphine and it wasn't until the end of March, when he took 1000 mg from the home of a deceased cancer patient, that he was able to kill again.

Rose Garlick and May Lowe were his March victims and at the end of April he killed three more patients. After killing Mary Coutts, he told her son and daughter-in-law, who were in a state of grief and shock at the suddenness of her death, 'I don't believe in keeping them going.'

Just four days later, Shipman visited Jean Lilley. Like Lizzie Adams, 58-year-old Mrs Lilley was one of the 15 murder cases the police took to court. Shipman's final victim in April lived just a mile away from Jean Lilley, in Garden Street.

After murdering Jean Lilley, Shipman drove to Garden Street to deal with some unfinished business – Elsie Cheetham. It was she who had found both a neighbour and her husband after they had been killed by Shipman. He had also killed two more of her neighbours. She was a loose end that had to be tied up.

In May, after killing Lena Slater, Ethel Kellett and Doris Earls in their own homes, he killed the last of his patients in his surgery, Ivy Lomas. Another of the 15, her body was exhumed a year later and Shipman was convicted of her murder.

In June Shipman called in to see 69-year-old Vera Whittingslow, who was wheelchair-bound due to a rare neurological disorder. Shipman told her husband that her blood pressure was far too high and sent him to fetch a prescription. When he returned he found the doctor taking his bag back to his car. Shipman said his wife was fine and they had been having a chat.

Back inside the house, Vera Whittingslow appeared to be unconscious. Shipman feigned surprised and said she was dying. She was already dead. In either a moment of rare compassion or as part of some sick sense of orchestration, Shipman said he would wait in the living room while Mr Whittingslow 'said goodbye' to his wife. Julian Boon believes the latter is much more likely. 'It would be that sort of manipulative, contractual aspect rather than any genuine empathy or capacity for concern for anybody other than himself. It could also be again to do with power and expressing how he can get away with anything.'

In early July, the district nurses attending the cancer patient Maureen Jackson noted she had received 1500 mg of diamorphine. Shipman had written a prescription for 2300 mg. He kept back 800 mg for himself. After he hastened Maureen Jackson's death with an overdose from her own supply of diamorphine, he told the nurses to destroy what little stock of opiates were left in her home. Now if anyone did do the maths, Shipman could claim the extra ampoules were simply part of the amount destroyed by the nurses.

By the end of July, he had killed three more patients, Muriel Grimshaw, another of the 15 court case murders, as well as John Livesey and Lily Taylor. He killed Dorothy Hopkins just before he took his traditional August summer holiday. He returned to work on 26 August and killed Nancy Jackson a week later.

While he was away, another of his patients, Kenneth Pickup, died of a heart attack. His widow was devastated; they had been married for nearly fifty years. Shortly after his father's death, James Pickup went to see Dr Shipman to thank him for looking after his father. He was surprised by how brusque the doctor was about his father's death, but then Shipman did display great concern for his mother.

Shipman reassured the son that he 'would always be there for her' and suggested his help need not be limited to medical matters. Three weeks later, he killed Mavis Pickup after she telephoned the surgery, upset because children had been knocking on her door and running away.

Mavis Pickup's death also provides yet more evidence of Shipman's morbid interest in death. When he arrived to certify the cause of death, his 12-year-old son was with him, sitting outside in the car. Shipman went to get his son, to show him the body, but the boy refused to go into the house. Shipman appeared bemused and slightly angry at his son's attitude.

Later that month, and this time on his own, Shipman killed Bessie Swann. The 79-year-old had rung the surgery because she had felt dizzy after a bath. She just caught Shipman who was about to go on his rounds and he told her he would make her his first visit. A short while later, Bessie Swann's lodger Bill Avery walked in and found Shipman with his fingers down her throat. He told him that he was clearing the airway. Bill called Bessie Swann's son Barry.

Barry Swann arrived within five minutes. Shipman walked up to him and stood very close. He put his right hand on Barry's right shoulder and said, 'I'll just wait a few minutes in case she wakes up and frightens us all.'

Enid Otter was the fourth and last of his patients to be killed that month, by which time Shipman had clearly used up his supply of diamorphine, as there were no deaths in October. At the start of November, he replenished it with a prescription for 1000 mg, then killed Florence Lewis. There is a strong suspicion that a day later he killed Bertha Parr, but the evidence is much stronger in the sudden deaths of Mary Wells, Elizabeth Baddley and the last of his patients to die that month, Marie Quinn, one of the patients he was convicted of murdering.

Shipman killed five of his patients in December. Three died on three consecutive days. Elizabeth Battersby died on the 8th and on the 9th Shipman went in person to tell the daughter of his next victim that she was dead.

'He just said to me, quite bluntly, I think in retrospect, that he had just been with my mum and she had died.' But the grief-stricken Angela Wagstaff couldn't believe it when she arrived at her mother's house to find Ann Royle perfectly healthy and alive.

'I went to the door and knocked and opened the letterbox to see my mum walking down the passageway towards me. I phoned Peter, because he was on his way home, and I said, "I don't know what's happening and maybe he has got the mums mixed up."'

Peter's mother, Kathleen Wagstaff, was also a loyal patient of Dr Shipman.

'I phoned my mother's number and Shipman answered the phone and he half explained the fact he had made a bit of a mistake but then went on to tell me that my mother had become seriously ill and died. She was slumped in a chair and everybody was wondering what had happened. There was nothing wrong with my mother, she had not been ill and all of a sudden she just died in the chair.'

But how could Shipman, the caring doctor who knew both women extremely well, have mixed up his victims? Paul Britton thinks the answer is obviously that it was a mistake in the wake of him having been quite aroused and then coming back down and having his mind half somewhere else.

Shipman was killing so many people that it was possible that they got mixed up in his mind. There would be some that would be very clear but he would be just as likely as the rest of us to have what are know as cognitive failures. While his slip might be seen as sadism, Britton thinks that this unlikely. Shipman's track record suggests that he was not particularly interested in tormenting people or in drawing out the pain for the bereaved.

But his mistake over the victims didn't seem to throw Shipman at all. The day after, he murdered Bianka Pomfret. Both she and Kathleen Wagstaff would be among the 15 court case murders. Eight days later, he killed Alice Black and his final murder of 1997 was on Christmas Eve when he killed James King.

At the beginning of January 1998, Shipman wrote out another prescription for 1000 mg of diamorphine and, within the next three months, 18 of his patients would die. Only three died natural deaths and all but one would be cremated.

Towards the end of January he killed Mabel Shawcross and Norah Nutall, who was another of the 15 murder cases. At the beginning of February, the doctor lost two patients in one day. The first died of natural causes, but he then killed Cissie Davies. A week later, he killed Pamela Hillier, one of the 15, then Francis Linn and Irene Berry. Two days later, he killed Maureen Ward and made up medical notes about brain tumours within hours of her death. This was another of the murders for which he was convicted. At the very end of the month he killed 75-year-old Joan Dean.

At the beginning of March, he killed Harold Eddleston, who had been his patient for only about a week and whose wife had died of a heart attack in February. Harold Eddleston had cancer and when his son-in-law asked the doctor how long he was likely to live, Shipman replied, 'I wouldn't buy him any Easter eggs.' Three days later, Shipman prescribed ten 100 mg ampoules of diamorphine in Harold Eddleston's name and collected them from the pharmacy. He killed Eddleston the next day.

Two days later, he killed Margaret Walden and the day after he killed Irene Chapman, the mother of his own receptionist, Carol Chapman. He then killed four elderly female patients in three-day intervals – Dorothy Chapman, Lily Higgins, Ada Warburton and Martha Marley.

Shipman then did not kill for seven whole weeks. At this stage in his killing cycle such a long gap seems strange, but it was during March that Dr Linda Reynolds had gone to the coroner. The most plausible explanation is that somehow Shipman had discovered he was under investigation.

Dame Janet Smith concludes:

The Greater Manchester Police initiated a confidential investigation into Dr Reynolds' concerns. I think it likely that Shipman learned of that investigation in early April. However, that issue has been the subject of evidence during Stage One of Phase Two of the Inquiry and I have not yet reached a definite conclusion on the point. My provisional view is that he became aware of it in early April and it is likely that he knew that the source of the report about him was the Brooke Practice doctors who signed his cremation Forms C.

At the beginning of July, during a routine discussion about prescribing practices, Shipman told Dr Alan Banks, a West Pennine Health Authority medical adviser, that he'd had an unusually high number of deaths among his elderly patients during the first three months of that year. In fact, his death rates for the end of 1997 were just as high as the beginning of 1998. But it seems Shipman was aware that that was the period about which concern had been expressed.

Certainly, during the next few months, Shipman presented only two cremation forms to the Brooke practice doctors and they were for patients who had died naturally. This is hardly likely to have been mere coincidence.

At that point, Shipman must have been expecting that any death that came to the attention of the Brooke practice doctors would be referred to the coroner. So when he did kill again, in May, he chose Winifred Mellor, a devout Catholic who was bound to be buried. He didn't kill again until June and his victim, Joan Melia, was also a Catholic. His last victim was Kathleen Grundy.

Dame Janet Smith concluded that, between 1974 and 1998, Dr Harold Frederick Shipman had unlawfully killed 215 of his patients and she held a suspicion that he had killed a further 45, the total number of 260 deaths making him Britain's most prolific serial killer.

But it seems Shipman had not planned on Kathleen Grundy's death being his last murder. On July 6 he had taken 100 mg diamorphine from a cancer patient. It seems that he planned to resume killing once the suspicions had died down, but according to Paul Britton this killing was unlikely to have taken place in Hyde.

'Killing has become a routine need. His problem would have been finding enough to keep him going. It's quite an achievement to take 37 people from your practice in a year and kill them in a way that doesn't immediately give rise to suspicion. That takes some dedication, some planning, it consumes quite a lot of energy and it's something that was by then irresistible, and unstoppable.

'He has a very delicate choice to make. He will know that, regardless of how much the system has failed to see what he's doing, there has to come a point where people notice. He's already reached almost unimaginable proportions but even he knows you can't keep on for ever. So, he's going to have to do something about that. That's why he would have had to move.'

And Paul Britton believes that forging Kathleen Grundy's will was simply a way to fund this move to a new location, possibly even private practice. 'If he genuinely thought that things were closing in, not that he was in any immediate danger but because he couldn't continue at this level and not get caught, then three hundred odd thousand pounds is a possible way of taking himself to a different location.'

According to Julian Boon, the will was his downfall. He sees it as a chilling possibility that Shipman could have gone on undetected if he hadn't overreached himself and tried to extort money from the will.

Shipman believed in his own omnipotence. He had forged prescriptions successfully for 30 years, so why not forge a will? But the prescriptions themselves were not actual forgeries; he had even used the names of real patients. The will, however, was a complicated piece of forgery. Shipman had no idea how his elderly patient would have written her will and the result was amateurish. It made him the only likely forger, but also gave him a motive for the murder of Kathleen Grundy. Once the police looked at her death, they were bound to discover the others.

Shipman underestimated the police. Faced with this knowledge, he broke down during interview and only by regaining his belief in his own self-importance did he keep going through the trial. But once in prison, this would be taken from him.

'Control is a main engine of his sort of psychology. As soon as he loses control that sort of personality simply cannot cope, and where is the control over your life in jail? Absolutely none whatsoever,' Julian Boon explained

To start with, it seems Shipman tried to exert some control over his new life but quickly released this was impossible. Even when he was briefly difficult with staff, they had control over him. He had to wear prison uniform and his day was regimented. He realised there was no way he could win and, once that possibility was gone, so too was any desire to continue.

One of the things the psychologists covered was whether or not Shipman would want to commit suicide. They decided that there would be a very high risk indeed simply because the things that he wanted most in life were no longer available to him. All the edifice of self-importance built around being a doctor, being revered, was completely stripped away. He could no longer enact his power over life and death, which had been his *raison d'être*, and he found this lack of power and control intolerable.'

With no hope of release, Julian Boon believes that Shipman knew there was only one area where he could still be in control. 'He did everything he could to show that he wasn't going to commit suicide. So what we find in his letters is reference to the appeal and we see undue references to food. Why is he writing what he had to eat in jail last night to a friend? Well, as a GP he will know that people who are high suicide risks, who are depressed and so on like this, are uninterested in food, very uninterested in fighting life's fights. He knows full well that his letters will be read and he gives no evidence of a man who's going to commit suicide. So he gets himself de-categorised and then seizes his opportunity and takes the dishonourable way out, just as he lived life.'

On January 13 2004, shortly before 6 am, Harold Shipman tied his torn bed linen to the bars of his cell window and hanged himself. As a doctor he knew exactly how to make sure his strangulation was quick and painless. It was three years since he had been sentenced to life imprisonment and it was the day before his fifty-eighth birthday. That morning I, like many, woke up to the news that Britain's most prolific serial killer had taken his own life in Wakefield Jail.

The national newspapers ran banner headlines claiming that Shipman had killed himself for the financial benefit of his wife. A loophole in the pension law means that, because he killed himself before he was sixty, Primrose Shipman would receive a tax-free lump sum of almost £100,000, plus an annual widow's pension of £18,000.

They saw it as a loyalty payment for the wife who still believes in his innocence and who would visit him once a week in prison, when they would sit for an hour kissing and holding hands.

But the psychologists disagree. Julian Boon is very sceptical that he killed himself with the pension in mind and, if he was thinking about the pension, it would be more a matter of concern to him to make sure that money he had earned and paid out came back home rather than any genuine concern for his wife.

Paul Britton sees it as a response to Shipman's recognition that he is going to spend the rest of his life in prison supervised by what he would regard as cattle and that he would no longer be able to fulfil his need to kill people. He had seen so many people die and he knew that, even when it's uncomfortable, it can be quite brief. If it brought some financial gain to his family all the better, but it probably didn't matter to him at the end.

'I think that by the time Harold Shipman killed himself, he would have been only person in his world. Other people are there, but the only emotion, the only heart, is his,' Paul Britton says. 'He would've known that there was nothing left of all the things that were important to him other than this last hurrah, where he can use the one death show on earth left to him, his own life, and also stick two fingers up to the rest of the world.'

So Shipman's suicide was a final act of control by the man who had been able to enact the power of life and death over so many of his patients.

His death also closed off any hope the relatives had of gaining answers.

Angela Woodruff, whose initial investigation had exposed Shipman's crimes, let me in on a secret desire she had held in relation to her mother's death.

'I always had a little dream that I would, one day, go and see Shipman in prison at some stage and he would be well into his seventies and I would ask him why and he would actually confess. I did want him to confess.'

So had he lived, would he have talked? The psychologists believe not. They think that he would never have shared his experience with anybody at all. It was his private world, for him and him alone.

The long passage of time between the murders in Pontefract and Todmorden and Dame Janet's Inquiry Report has meant that the impact of his crimes has been less there, but in the close-knit community of Hyde there are few who have not been affected. Each time I interviewed a new relative I would be given a list of those they knew who had died.

I will let Alan and Susan Royston represent the others: 'So many people that we knew, nearly everybody I spoke to, knew somebody.'

'Friends, you know. Parents and people I knew because I used to work in Hyde in the market so I knew an awful lot of them. Every time you saw a picture you thought, "Oh, gosh, I know her, I know him."'

'Two people I worked with.'

'A girl I worked with, her mother-in-law was a victim.'

'Two chaps that I went to school with, you know, it's just everywhere. There's not a place in Hyde that doesn't seem to have been touched. Someone in Hyde has got a relative that Shipman has killed.'

'It's just horrendous; it's like a black mark over the town. And I can only hope it never, ever happens again.'

Shipman cast a long shadow that extended beyond his murdered patients and their families and friends. Many of those who Shipman used to discover the bodies have suffered breakdowns; one young mother has even suffered facial paralysis after a brain haemorrhage. His surgery staff were left to cope alone after his arrest, abandoned by the health authority and blamed by many for not spotting what was going on.

Meanwhile, the GMC, criticised for its inactivity throughout, finally launched its own investigations. The retired pathologist Dr David Lyle Bee was found guilty of professional misconduct in relation to a post mortem examination report on Renate Overton, who survived in a coma for a year after Shipman injected her with diamorphine.

Dr Peter Bennett, Dr Susan Booth, Dr Jeremy Dirckze, Dr Stephen Farrar, Dr Alistair MacGillivray and Dr Rajesh Patel have also been criticised. These doctors signed a total of 214 of the certificates – known as Form Cs – for Shipman's patients. The inquiry ruled that 124 of those patients were unlawfully killed and the GPs were criticised for failing to question the doctor's unusually high death rates, his presence at many deaths and his use of terms such as 'old age' and 'natural causes' under the cause of death section of the form.

One cannot help but think that yet more innocents are being punished for Shipman's crimes.

But lessons have been learnt. The Public Inquiry has now closed and its final report will be published in 2005. Dame Janet has recommended changes to the way in which doctors and deaths are monitored, how controlled drugs are prescribed and how cremation certificates are authorised. Time will tell whether any or all of her recommendations are implemented.

But for the relatives and friends of Shipman's victims, one question remains paramount.

Lucy Virgin's niece Ann Smith explained, 'I find it difficult to understand why he chose my aunt. I don't believe my aunt ever did anything to warrant being killed.'

'I can't understand why he would do something like that. Why he would kill somebody, take somebody's life? And it still baffles me now, even though he committed suicide, the fact that he could do something like that. My granddad was kind, he was gentle, he wouldn't hurt anybody. And yet he took him, and I cannot, for the life of me, understand why he would take somebody who was as loving as that.' Barbara Eades, who lost her grandfather Arthur Stopford, cannot contemplate what the answer would be.

'I dare say the same question has been asked by everybody in Hyde that has been touched by this. Most of the people were well. They'd not done any harm to anybody and along comes the man that you really trust, your GP, and he does this. It's just incredible,' Alan Royston added.

The psychologists have little comfort for the relatives. Julian Boon explains that the killings could be said to be random in the sense that if the opportunity arose and the criteria were right – vulnerable, living alone, not in a position to answer back – Shipman would kill.

No one is in any doubt that the reason this volume of murders went undetected was because Shipman was a doctor. He was in a position of trust that his patients simply could not conceive of him abusing.

As a young man Shipman had been so inspired by the medical treatment of his mother that he had become a doctor. But along the way he developed addictions to drugs and to murder. His old school friend Bob Studholme believes he may have an idea how and why it all went wrong.

'We were sixties kids. We were flower power, and all that sort of thing, and we were zealous. We really were. We were going to change the world. I went off into teaching and I wanted to change the face of teaching. I am sure Fred went scuttling off through his medical qualifications and couldn't wait to get started and be this sort of personable, affable doctor that people can rely on, and will turn to in difficulty, as indeed so many people would say about him.

'But on the way, it seems that the zealous ones always perhaps pick up too much. They try too much. They go a step too far. I almost believe that we have so much energy in life and that, once that energy is spent, we have a problem. I think Fred, as a doctor, made himself available and took on responsibilities that he perhaps should have waited to do.

'Fred wanted to be the best GP in the world, but gradually ground himself down, until his own thinking was so befuddled that he couldn't get it right. Rather than bring light, he's brought so much unhappiness to all those people and their families, who have lost people at his hands, that he's cast an incredibly dark shadow over so many people's lives.'

The psychologists told me that we are all capable of killing once, from rage, from fear, to protect ourselves and our loved ones; we can even kill twice, for the same reasons. But then we stop because we don't enjoy the experience. That's the line that serial killers step over.

Maybe Fred Shipman did start out with all the best of intentions, but what I have learnt is that both nature and nurture play very specific roles in a chain of events that create a human being capable of serial killing. Shipman was born with psychopathic tendencies, but that didn't make him a killer. His mother's illness and death fed on and expanded that psychopathy and linked it to a fascination with death. But that didn't make him a killer either. When all this was linked to his genuine desire to become a doctor, he was able to explore his fantasies about death to a level unreachable to those outside the medical profession. That made him a potential killer. His access to an almost inexhaustible supply of victims made him a potential serial killer and the level of trust vested in a doctor made him potentially Britain's *most* prolific serial killer.

But what actually ensured he gained that title was his ability to step over the line. Have no doubt about it – Shipman enjoyed what he did.

None of your victims realised that yours was not a healing touch. None of them knew that in truth you had brought her death, death which was disguised as the caring attention of a good doctor.

The Hon. Justice Forbes

APPENDIX

Inquiry decisions on Todmorden deaths investigated

Name	Date of death	Age	Place of death	Decision
Edith Annie Bill	22 Jun. 1974	67	Own home	Natural death
Alice Brown	11 Mar. 1975	72	Own home	Natural death
Sean Stuart Callaghan	9 Dec. 1974	18	Hospital	Natural death
Hena Cheetham	9 Oct. 1974	77	Ambulance	Natural death
Michael Connors	28 Apr. 1975	64	Own home	Insufficient evidence for decision
Lily Crossley	21 Jan. 1975	73	Own home	Suspicion of unlawful killing
William Earnshaw	9 Aug. 1975	88	Daughter's home	Natural death
Ruth Highley	10 May 1974	72	Own home	Natural death
Harold Edward Jackman	10 Nov. 1974	78	Hospital	Natural death
Moira Kelly	16 Dec. 1974	26	Hospital	Natural death
Robert Henry Lingard	21 Jan. 1975	62	Own home	Suspicion of unlawful killing
Jane Ellen Lord	8 Apr. 1975	86	Own home	Natural death
Eva Lyons	17 Mar. 1975	70	Own home	Unlawful killing
Wilbert Mitchell	1 Apr. 1975	87	Own home	Insufficient evidence for decision
Frances Elaine Oswald	This decision relates to the incident which took place on Aug. 21, 1974.			
Phyllis Oxley	26 May 1975	59	Own home	Natural death
Elizabeth Pearce	21 Jan. 1975	84	Own home	Suspicion of unlawful killing
Leah Pickering	4 Aug. 1975	86	Own home	Natural death
Edith Roberts	21 Mar. 1975	67	Own home	Suspicion of unlawful killing
Jane Isabella Rowland	15 Feb. 1975	80	Own home	Suspicion of unlawful killing
Lilian Shaw	27 Jul. 1975	54	Own home	Natural death
Winifred Isabel Smith	7 Apr. 1975	67	Own home	Insufficient evidence for decision
Joe Ainscow Stansfield	6 Apr. 1975	77	Own home	Natural death
Mary Ann Tempest	1 Sep. 1975	70	Own home	Natural death
Sarah Ann Thomas	29 Dec. 1974	86	Own home	Insufficient evidence for decision
Stanley Uttley	2 Aug. 1974	58	Surgery	Natural death
Edward Walker	25 Jan. 1975	70	Residential home	Insufficient evidence for decision
Colin Whitham	23 Jul. 1974	26	Own home	Natural death
Albert Redvers Williams	5 Aug. 1975	75	Own home	Suspicion of unlawful killing
Jack Wills	11 Mar. 1975	65	Own home	Natural death
Margaret Wilmore	27 Sep. 1975	38	Own home	Natural death

Inquiry decisions on Hyde deaths investigated

Name	Date of death	Age	Place of death	Decision
Lizzie Adams	28 Feb. 1997	77	Own home	Conviction
Rose Ann Adshead	18 Sep. 1988	80	Own home	Unlawful killing
Irene Aitken	31 Jul. 1995	65	Own home	Unlawful killing
Dorothy Mary Andrew	12 Sep. 1996	85	Own home	Unlawful killing
Mary Emma Andrew	8 Apr. 1993	86	Own home	Unlawful killing
Winifred Arrowsmith	24 Apr. 1984	70	Own home	Unlawful killing
Netta Ashcroft	7 Mar. 1995	71	Own home	Unlawful killing
Dora Elizabeth Ashton	26 Sep. 1995	87	Shipman's surgery	Unlawful killing
Ada Ashworth	27 Nov. 1984	87	Own home	Unlawful killing
Brenda Ashworth	17 Jun. 1995	63	Own home	Unlawful killing
Elizabeth Ashworth	26 Aug. 1981	81	Own home	Unlawful killing
James Ashworth	7 Jun. 1978	81	Own home	Insufficient evidence for decision
Sarah Ashworth	17 Apr. 1993	74	Own home	Unlawful killing
Elizabeth Mary Baddeley	21 Nov. 1997	83	Own home	Unlawful killing
Bertha Bagshaw	17 Nov. 1980	88	Own home	Insufficient evidence for decision
Joseph Bardsley	15 Apr. 1984	83	Own home	Unlawful killing
Lily Bardsley	7 Mar. 1995	88	Own home	Unlawful killing
Nellie Bardsley	29 Dec. 1987	69	Own home	Unlawful killing
Elsie Barker	29 Jul. 1996	84	Own home	Unlawful killing
Charles Henry Barlow	22 Nov. 1995	88	Own home	Unlawful killing
Elizabeth Battersby	8 Dec. 1997	70	Own home	Unlawful killing
William Baxter	4 Mar. 1982	70	Own home	Insufficient evidence for decision
Ethel Bennett	19 Dec. 1988	80	Own home	Unlawful killing
Nellie Bennett	25 Jun. 1996	86	Own home	Unlawful killing
Charlotte Bennison	27 Jan. 1997	89	Own home	Unlawful killing
Arthur Bent	22 May 1995	90	Own home	Suspicion of unlawful killing
Irene Berry	15 Feb. 1998	74	Own home	Unlawful killing
Violet May Bird	13 May 1993	60	Own home	Unlawful killing
Alice Black	18 Dec. 1997	73	Own home	Unlawful killing
Geoffrey Bogle	14 Sep. 1995	72	Own home	Unlawful killing
Miriam Bradshaw	13 Jan. 1984	88	Residential home	Insufficient evidence for decision
Edith Brady	13 May 1996	72	Shipman's surgery	Unlawful killing
Harold Bramwell	7 Dec. 1978	73	Own home	Unlawful killing
Vera Bramwell	20 Dec. 1985	79	Own home	Unlawful killing
Nancy Anne Brassington	14 Sep. 1987	71	Own home	Unlawful killing
Doris Bridge	26 Mar. 1984	83	Own home	Suspicion of unlawful killing
Jane Bridge	4 Jan. 1986	80	Own home	Insufficient evidence for decision
Albert Brierley	15 Feb. 1985	91	Own home	Insufficient evidence for decision
Lily Broadbent	16 Dec. 1986	75	Own home	Unlawful killing

Name	Date of death	Age	Place of death	Decision
Edith Brock	8 Nov. 1995	74	Own home	Unlawful killing
Charles Edward Brocklehurst	31 Dec. 1993	90	Own home	Unlawful killing
Vera Brocklehurst	31 Mar. 1995	70	Own home	Unlawful killing
Irene Brooder	20 Jan. 1997	76	Own home	Unlawful killing
May Brookes	1 Feb. 1985	74	Own home	Unlawful killing
Elizabeth Mary Burke	26 Sep. 1989	82	Own home	Unlawful killing
Ida Cains	17 Mar. 1995	84	Own home	Insufficient evidence for decision
Edith Calverley	16 Aug. 1993	77	Own home	Unlawful killing
Annie Campbell	20 Dec. 1978	88	Own home	Unlawful killing
Marion Carradice	14 Aug. 1989	80	Own home	Unlawful killing
Irene Chapman	7 Mar. 1998	74	Own home	Unlawful killing
Wilfred Chappell	31 Jan. 1989	80	Own home	Unlawful killing
John Charlton	16 Oct. 1989	81	Own home	Unlawful killing
Albert Cheetham	1 Apr. 1987	85	Own home	Unlawful killing
Alfred Cheetham	21 Mar. 1991	73	Own home	Insufficient evidence for decision
Elsie Cheetham	25 Apr. 1997	76	Own home	Unlawful killing
Thomas Cheetham	4 Dec. 1996	78	Own home	Unlawful killing
Fanny Clarke	18 May 1996	82	Own home	Suspicion of unlawful killing
Beatrice Helen Clee	12 May 1989	78	Own home	Unlawful killing
Thomas Condon	6 May 1984	73	Own home	Insufficient evidence for decision
Alice Hilda Connaughton	12 Mar. 1987	77	Residential home	Suspicion of unlawful killing
Margaret Ann Conway	15 Feb. 1985	69	Own home	Unlawful killing
Frederick Coomber	10 Feb. 1980	81	Residential home	Insufficient evidence for decision
Ann Cooper	15 Feb. 1988	93	Own home	Unlawful killing
Erla Copeland	11 Jan. 1996	79	Own home	Unlawful killing
Constance Anne Couldwell	5 Feb. 1988	88	Residential home	Insufficient evidence for decision
Ann Coulthard	8 Sep. 1981	75	Own home	Suspicion of unlawful killing
Mary Coutts	21 Apr. 1997	80	Own home	Unlawful killing
Hilda Mary Couzens	24 Feb. 1993	92	Own home	Unlawful killing
Eileen Theresa Cox	24 Dec. 1984	72	Own home	Unlawful killing
Eileen Daphne Crompton	2 Jan. 1997	75	Residential home	Unlawful killing
Frank Crompton	26 Mar. 1995	86	Own home	Unlawful killing
John Crompton	21 Mar. 1995	82	Own home	Unlawful killing
Lilian Cullen	30 May 1996	77	Own home	Unlawful killing
Valerie Cuthbert	29 May 1996	54	Own home	Unlawful killing
Cissie Davies	2 Feb. 1998	73	Own home	Unlawful killing
Fanny Dawson	4 Aug. 1979	68	Own home	Suspicion of unlawful killing
Elsie Lorna Dean	8 Jan. 1997	69	Own home	Unlawful killing
Joan Edwina Dean	27 Feb. 1998	75	Own home	Unlawful killing
Ronnie Devenport	25 May 1994	57	Own home	Unlawful killing
Mary Rose Dudley	30 Dec. 1990	69	Own home	Unlawful killing
Doris Earls	21 May 1997	79	Own home	Unlawful killing

Name	Date of death	Age	Place of death	Decision
Harold Eddleston	4 Mar. 1998	77	Own home	Unlawful killing
Bethel Anne Evans	3 Jan. 1980	92	Residential home	Suspicion of unlawful killing
Joseph Vincent Everall	17 Dec. 1984	80	Own home	Unlawful killing
Marie Antoinette Fernley	13 Mar. 1995	53	Own home	Unlawful killing
Hilda Fitton	6 Jul. 1989	75	Own home	Unlawful killing
Dorothy Fletcher	23 Apr. 1986	74	Residential Home	Unlawful killing
Elizabeth Fletcher	5 Jan. 1988	90	Own home	Unlawful killing
Leah Fogg	10 Jun. 1996	82	Own home	Unlawful killing
Edwin Foulkes	1 Jan. 1985	88	Own home	Suspicion of unlawful killing
Thomas Fowden	6 Jun. 1986	81	Own home	Unlawful killing
Moira Ashton Fox	28 Jun. 1983	77	Own home	Unlawful killing
Harold Freeman	20 Feb. 1993	83	Residential home	Suspicion of unlawful killing
Minnie Doris Irene Galpin	12 Mar. 1996	71	Own home	Unlawful killing
Rose Garlick	22 Mar. 1997	76	Own home	Unlawful killing
Millicent Garside	23 Oct. 1996	76	Own home	Unlawful killing
Mary Gaunt	26 Jul. 1987	76	Daughter's home	Insufficient evidence for decision
William Givens	28 Sep. 1981	77	Own home	Suspicion of unlawful killing
Elsie Godfrey	7 May 1996	85	Own home	Unlawful killing
Alice Maude Gorton	10 Aug. 1979	76	Own home	Unlawful killing
Edith Graham	18 Aug. 1979	72	Own home	Insufficient evidence for decision
Rebecca Gray	5 May 1993	84	Own home	Natural death
John Sheard Greenhalgh	27 Feb. 1996	88	Own home	Unlawful killing
Muriel Grimshaw	14 Jul. 1997	76	Own home	Conviction
Kathleen Grundy	24 Jun. 1998	81	Own home	Conviction
Clara Hackney	14 Apr. 1995	84	Own home	Unlawful killing
Violet Hadfield	24 May 1985	74	Own home	Suspicion of unlawful killing
Josephine Hall	5 Jun. 1989	69	Own home	Unlawful killing
Frank Halliday	30 Mar. 1987	76	Own home	Unlawful killing
Mary Emma Hamer	8 Mar. 1989	81	Shipman's surgery	Unlawful killing
Christine Hancock	13 Jan. 1994	53	Own home	Unlawful killing
Elsie Hannible	24 Jul. 1996	85	Own home	Unlawful killing
Joan Milray Harding	4 Jan. 1994	82	Shipman's surgery	Unlawful killing
Charles Harris	23 Nov. 1984	70	Own home	Suspicion of unlawful killing
David Alan Harrison	3 Jan. 1997	47	Own home	Unlawful killing
Samuel Harrison	9 Jan. 1982	87	Own home	Suspicion of unlawful killing
Elsie Harrop	22 Sep. 1989	82	Own home	Unlawful killing
Clifford Barnes Heapey	2 Jun. 1995	85	Nursing home	Unlawful killing
Gladys Heapey	27 Jan. 1984	69	Own home	Insufficient evidence for decision
Irene Heathcote	20 Nov. 1996	76	Own home	Unlawful killing
Olive Heginbotham	24 Feb. 1993	86	Own home	Unlawful killing
Florence Heywood	10 Nov. 1994	91	Nursing home	Suspicion of unlawful killing
Hilda Mary Hibbert	2 Jan. 1996	81	Own home	Unlawful killing
Robert Hickson	5 Dec. 1978	76	Own home	Suspicion of unlawful killing
George Eric Higginbottom	7 Mar. 1987	66	Own home	Insufficient evidence for decision

Name	Date of death	Age	Place of death	Decision
Lily Higgins	17 Mar. 1998	83	Own home	Unlawful killing
Marion Elizabeth Higham	19 Jul. 1996	84	Own home	Unlawful killing
Ellen Higson	4 Feb. 1985	84	Own home	Unlawful killing
Pamela Marguerite Hillier	9 Feb. 1998	68	Own home	Conviction
Ada Matley Hilton	12 Jul. 1995	88	Own home	Unlawful killing
John Hilton	4 Nov. 1994	64	Own home	Suspicion of unlawful killing
Alline Devolle Holland	3 Aug. 1981	84	Residential home	Insufficient evidence for decision
Alice Holt	23 Feb. 1982	75	Own home	Suspicion of unlawful killing
Dorothy Doretta Hopkins	10 Aug. 1997	72	Own home	Unlawful killing
John Howcroft	1 Jan. 1985	77	Own home	Suspicion of unlawful killing
Jozef Iwanina	16 May 1986	63	Own home	Suspicion of unlawful killing
Maureen Lamonnier Jackson	7 Jul. 1997	51	Own home	Unlawful killing
Nancy Jackson	1 Sep. 1997	81	Own home	Unlawful killing
Leah Johnston	11 Nov. 1979	80	Residential home	Suspicion of unlawful killing
Alice Mary Jones	15 Jan. 1988	83	Own home	Unlawful killing
David Jones	22 Dec. 1993	73	Own home	Suspicion of unlawful killing
Hannah Jones	10 Jul. 1985	84	Own home	Insufficient evidence for decision
Jane Jones	15 Feb. 1988	83	Own home	Unlawful killing
Mary Ellen Jordan	30 Aug. 1978	73	Own home	Unlawful killing
Ethel May Kellett	12 May 1997	74	Own home	Unlawful killing
Fred Kellett	31 Dec. 1985	79	Own home	Unlawful killing
Alice Kennedy	9 Jan. 1995	88	Own home	Unlawful killing
Charles Henry Killan	3 Feb. 1997	90	Own home	Unlawful killing
James Joseph King	24 Dec. 1997	83	Own home	Unlawful killing
Alice Christine Kitchen	17 Jun. 1994	70	Own home	Unlawful killing
Renee Lacey	6 Jun. 1996	63	Own home	Unlawful killing
Edith Leech	8 Mar. 1982	83	Residential home	Insufficient evidence for decision
Carrie Leigh	16 Jul. 1996	81	Own home	Unlawful killing
Joseph Leigh	16 Dec. 1993	78	Own home	Unlawful killing
Wilfred Leigh	30 Jun. 1982	74	Own home	Suspicion of unlawful killing
Florence Lewis	10 Nov. 1997	79	Own home	Unlawful killing
Peter Lewis	2 Jan. 1985	41	Own home	Unlawful killing
Jean Lilley	25 Apr. 1997	58	Own home	Conviction
Laura Frances Linn	13 Feb. 1998	83	Own home	Unlawful killing
John Louden Livesey	25 Jul. 1997	69	Own home	Unlawful killing
Edna May Llewellyn	4 May 1993	68	Own home	Unlawful killing
Harry Lomas	13 Aug. 1997	82	Nursing home	Natural death
Ivy Lomas	29 May 1997	63	Shipman's surgery	Conviction
Dorothy Long	13 Mar. 1998	84	Own home	Unlawful killing
Thomas Alfred Longmate	6 Sep. 1978	69	Own home	Suspicion of unlawful killing
Beatrice Lowe	17 Oct. 1984	88	Own home	Suspicion of unlawful killing
May Lowe	27 Mar. 1997	84	Own home	Unlawful killing
Charles MacConnell	24 May 1983	72	Own home	Suspicion of unlawful killing
Selina Mackenzie	17 Dec. 1985	77	Own home	Unlawful killing

Name	Date of death	Age	Place of death	Decision
Mary Ann Mansfield	23 Jun. 1980	84	Own home	Insufficient evidence for decision
Walter Mansfield	30 Mar. 1984	83	Daughter's home	Suspicion of unlawful killing
Martha Marley	24 Mar. 1998	88	Own home	Unlawful killing
Sarah Hannah Marsland	7 Aug. 1978	86	Own home	Unlawful killing
Kathleen McDonald	22 Feb. 1985	73	Own home	Unlawful killing
Joan May Melia	12 Jun. 1998	73	Own home	Conviction
Elizabeth Ellen Mellor	30 Nov. 1994	75	Own home	Unlawful killing
Winifred Mellor	11 May 1998	73	Own home	Conviction
Oscar Meredith	13 Nov. 1984	78	Own home	Insufficient evidence for decision
Margaret Metcalfe	13 May 1983	84	Residential home	Natural death
Deborah Middleton	7 Jan. 1986	81	Own home	Unlawful killing
Samuel Mills	23 Nov. 1996	89	Own home	Unlawful killing
Cyril Mitchell	4 May 1981	60	Own home	Insufficient evidence for decision
John Bennett Molesdale	29 Dec. 1994	81	Own home	Unlawful killing
Emily Morgan	12 May 1993	84	Own home	Unlawful killing
Bertha Moss	13 Jun. 1995	68	Shipman's surgery	Unlawful killing
Hannah Helena Mottram	5 Aug. 1979	69	Own home	Suspicion of unlawful killing
Thomas Moult	26 Jun. 1985	70	Own home	Unlawful killing
Nellie Mullen	2 May 1993	77	Own home	Unlawful killing
Miriam Rose Emily Mycock	3 Apr. 1980	91	Residential home	Insufficient evidence for decision
Fanny Nichols	26 Apr. 1993	84	Own home	Unlawful killing
Norah Nuttall	26 Jan. 1998	64	Own home	Conviction
Enid Otter	29 Sep. 1997	77	Own home	Unlawful killing
Konrad Peter Ovcar-Robinson	25 Nov. 1995	43	Own home	Unlawful killing
Renate Eldtraude Overton	21 Apr. 1995	47	Hospital	Unlawful killing
Marjorie Parker	27 Apr. 1993	74	Own home	Unlawful killing
Bertha Parr	11 Nov. 1997	77	Own home	Suspicion of unlawful killing
Mavis Mary Pickup	22 Sep. 1997	79	Own home	Unlawful killing
Elsie Platt	9 Feb. 1994	73	Own home	Unlawful killing
Bianka Pomfret	10 Dec. 1997	49	Own home	Conviction
Reginald Potts	29 Jul. 1978	83	Own home	Insufficient evidence for decision
Annie Alexandra Powers	10 Jan. 1992	89	Residential home	Suspicion of unlawful killing
Alice Prestwich	20 Oct. 1988	69	Own home	Unlawful killing
Marie Quinn	24 Nov. 1997	67	Own home	Conviction
Anne Lilian Ralphs	20 Sep. 1996	75	Own home	Unlawful killing
Dorothea Hill Renwick	9 Feb. 1988	90	Own home	Unlawful killing
Jose Kathleen Diana Richards	22 Jul. 1993	74	Own home	Unlawful killing
Gladys Roberts	8 Feb. 1984	78	Own home	Unlawful killing
Eileen Robinson	22 Dec. 1993	54	Own home	Unlawful killing

Name	Date of death	Age	Place of death	Decision
Eveline Robinson	21 Nov. 1977	77	Own home	Insufficient evidence for decision
Lavinia Robinson	16 Feb. 1988	84	Own home	Unlawful killing
Mildred Robinson	26 Jun. 1985	84	Own home	Unlawful killing
Elizabeth Ann Rogers	30 Dec. 1987	74	Own home	Unlawful killing
Jane Frances Rostron	8 May 1987	78	Own home	Unlawful killing
Dorothy Rowarth	18 Sep. 1990	56	Own home	Unlawful killing
Elsie Royles	23 Nov. 1978	70	Own home	Suspicion of unlawful killing
Betty Royston	4 Feb. 1997	70	Own home	Unlawful killing
Ernest Rudol	29 Jun. 1995	82	Own home	Unlawful killing
Tom Balfour Russell	2 Jul. 1996	77	Own home	Unlawful killing
Gladys Saunders	17 Jun. 1996	82	Own home	Unlawful killing
Edith Scott	13 Apr. 1995	85	Own home	Unlawful killing
Elsie Scott	6 Oct. 1981	86	Residential home	Suspicion of unlawful killing
Kate Maud Sellors	4 May 1995	75	Own home	Unlawful killing
Cicely Sharples	15 Jun. 1994	87	Own home	Unlawful killing
Joseph Shaw	3 Mar. 1995	88	Own home	Unlawful killing
Leonard Shaw	7 Jan. 1981	85	Own home	Insufficient evidence for decision
Mabel Shawcross	22 Jan. 1998	79	Own home	Unlawful killing
Jack Leslie Shelmerdine	28 Nov. 1979	77	Hospital	Unlawful killing
Jane Elizabeth Shelmerdine	21 Feb. 1996	80	Own home	Unlawful killing
Florence Sidebotham	29 Jun. 1981	83	Residential home	Insufficient evidence for decision
Elizabeth Teresa Sigley	14 Dec. 1995	67	Own home	Unlawful killing
Albert Slater	11 Jan. 1979	79	Own home	Insufficient evidence for decision
Lena Norah Slater	2 May 1997	68	Own home	Unlawful killing
May Slater	18 Apr. 1981	84	Own home	Unlawful killing
Kenneth Ernest Smith	17 Dec. 1996	73	Own home	Unlawful killing
Mary Alice Smith	17 May 1994	84	Own home	Unlawful killing
Sidney Arthur Smith	30 Aug. 1996	76	Own home	Unlawful killing
Monica Rene Sparkes	7 Oct. 1992	72	Own home	Unlawful killing
Harry Stafford	17 Dec. 1988	87	Own home	Unlawful killing
Louisa Stocks	29 Mar. 1982	80	Residential home	Suspicion of unlawful killing
John Stone	24 Apr. 1996	77	Own home	Unlawful killing
Arthur Henderson Stopford	29 Aug. 1995	82	Own home	Unlawful killing
Bessie Swann	26 Sep. 1997	79	Own home	Unlawful killing
Robert Swann	29 Sep. 1980	92	Own home	Insufficient evidence for decision
Florence Taylor	27 Jun. 1981	93	Own home	Suspicion of unlawful killing
Lily Newby Taylor	28 Jul. 1997	86	Own home	Unlawful killing
Alice Thomas	16 Apr. 1987	83	Own home	Unlawful killing
Maria Thornton	27 Jul. 1994	78	Own home	Unlawful killing
Angela Philomena Tierney	10 Apr. 1995	71	Own home	Unlawful killing

Name	Date of death	Age	Place of death	Decision
Walter Tingle	6 Nov. 1988	85	Own home	Unlawful killing
Beatrice Toft	17 Nov. 1986	59	Own home	Unlawful killing
Mary Tomlin	7 Oct. 1986	73	Own home	Unlawful killing
Margaret Townsend	11 Dec. 1987	80	Own home	Unlawful killing
Dorothy Tucker	7 Jan. 1984	51	Own home	Unlawful killing
Mary Tuff	21 Apr. 1997	76	Own home	Suspicion of unlawful killing
Frances Elizabeth Turner	23 Aug. 1985	85	Own home	Unlawful killing
Irene Turner	11 Jul. 1996	67	Own home	Conviction
Frederick Vickers	13 Aug. 1979	66	Own home	Suspicion of unlawful killing
Margaret Mary Vickers	25 Jun. 1996	81	Own home	Unlawful killing
Lucy Virgin	1 Mar. 1995	70	Own home	Unlawful killing
George Edgar Vizor	18 Oct. 1989	67	Own home	Unlawful killing
Jessie Irene Wagstaff	15 Apr. 1984	70	Own home	Insufficient evidence for decision
Laura Kathleen Wagstaff	9 Dec. 1997	81	Own home	Conviction
Margaret Anne Waldron	6 Mar. 1998	65	Own home	Unlawful killing
Henrietta Walker	25 Nov. 1994	87	Own home	Unlawful killing
Marjorie Hope Waller	18 Apr. 1996	79	Own home	Unlawful killing
Mary Walls	14 Nov. 1997	78	Own home	Unlawful killing
Sydney Walton	2 May 1979	57	Own home	Insufficient evidence for decision
Ada Warburton	20 Mar. 1998	77	Own home	Unlawful killing
Maureen Alice Ward	18 Feb. 1998	57	Own home	Conviction
Muriel Margaret Ward	24 Oct. 1995	87	Own home	Unlawful killing
Percy Ward	4 Jan. 1983	90	Own home	Unlawful killing
Eric Wardle	9 Jan. 1978	60	Own home	Suspicion of unlawful killing
Annie Watkins	17 Nov. 1986	81	Own home	Suspicion of unlawful killing
Maria West	6 Mar. 1995	81	Own home	Conviction
Ellen Frances Wharam	5 Jul. 1981	91	Residential home	Insufficient evidence for decision
Lavinia Wharmby	18 Jul. 1979	88	Own home	Suspicion of unlawful killing
Mona Ashton White	15 Sep. 1986	63	Own home	Unlawful killing
Amy Whitehead	22 Mar. 1993	82	Own home	Unlawful killing
Vera Whittingslow	24 Jun. 1997	69	Own home	Unlawful killing
Edith Wibberley	18 Dec. 1984	76	Own home	Unlawful killing
Joseph Frank Wilcockson	6 Nov. 1989	85	Own home	Unlawful killing
Emily Williams	25 Sep. 1978	75	Daughter's home	Suspicion of unlawful killing
Sarah Jane Williamson	15 Oct. 1989	82	Own home	Unlawful killing
Mark Wimpeney	6 Oct. 1981	86	Own home	Insufficient evidence for decision
Mary Winterbottom	21 Sep. 1984	76	Own home	Unlawful killing
Annie Wood	26 Mar. 1984	82	Residential home	Insufficient evidence for decision
James Wood	23 Dec. 1986	82	Own home	Unlawful killing
Joyce Woodhead	23 Feb. 1997	74	Own home	Unlawful killing
Kenneth Wharmby Woodhead	14 Dec. 1995	75	Own home	Unlawful killing

TIMELINE

1946   Harold Frederick Shipman born. The family live at 163 Longmead Drive.

1949   Primrose May Oxtoby is born in North Yorkshire.

1963   Shipman is in first year of sixth form at High Pavement Grammar School, Nottingham.

       Vera Shipman dies of lung cancer.

1965   Shipman enters University of Leeds School of Medicine.

       Meets Primrose on the Number 38 Wetherby to Leeds bus.

       Primrose gets pregnant.

1966   Shipman marries Primrose.

1970   Leaves University with MB ChB.

       Shipman's first job: pre-registration house officer at Pontefract General Infirmary.

1971   Shipman is fully registered with GMC.

       Primrose gives birth to Christopher.

       Shipman gains a diploma in child health.

       8 natural deaths + 3 suspected deaths here but not enough evidence.

1974   Shipman gains diploma in obstetrics and gynaecology.

       Answers an advert in a medical publication and goes for na interview at Abraham Ormerod Medical Practice in Todmorden.

       Does short probationary period as an assistant GP.

       Becomes a junior partner, undertakes disposal, restocking and ordering controlled drugs.

       Shipman attacks Elaine Oswald in her home after seeing her earlier in the day at his surgery.

1975   1 unlawful + 6 suspicious deaths. 10 natural deaths.

       Home office Drugs Inspectorate and West Yorks. Police Drug Squad become aware that Shipman is obtaining abnormally large quantities of pethidine.

       Shipman passes out and diagnosed as having epilepsy.

       Discovered by his partners obtaining controlled drugs for his own use. Admits it and resigns.

1976   Shipman appears at Halifax Magistrates' Court and pleads guilty.

       Starts work as clinical medical officer at Newton Aycliffe Health Centre, Durham.

1977   Moves to Hyde.

       Responds to an advert placed by the 7 doctors at the Donneybrook Practice in Hyde.

At the interview he confesses to his crimes. Joins the practice as a GP.
No killing in the first year in Hyde. 2 natural deaths.
1978   4 unlawful killings + 5 suspicious deaths. 14 natural deaths.
1979   2 unlawful killings + 4 suspicious deaths. 20 natural deaths.
Shipman starts his patient diaries.
After complaint to the Health Authority Shipman stops killing for a while.
1980   1 suspicious death. 12 natural deaths.
1981   2 unlawful killings + 4 suspicious deaths. 14 natural deaths.
1982   4 suspicious deaths. 12 natural deaths.
1983   2 unlawful killings + 1 suspicious deaths. 9 natural deaths.
1984   9 unlawful killings + 4 suspicious deaths. 11 natural deaths.
1985   11 unlawful killings + 4 suspicious deaths. 8 natural deaths.
1986   8 unlawful killings + 2 suspicious deaths. 4 natural deaths.
1987   8 unlawful killings + 1 suspicious death. 6 natural deaths.
1988   11 unlawful killings. 4 natural deaths.
7 month break in killing.
1989   12 unlawful killings. 3 natural deaths.
Kills for the first time in his surgery.
1990   2 unlawful killings. 6 natural deaths.
1991   Shipman announces he is leaving Donneybrook. No killings.
1992   Shipman working as sole practitioner at Donneybrook.
Moves to Market Street surgery.
1 unlawful killing + 1 suspicious death.
1993   16 unlawful killings+ one suspicious deaths. 10 natural deaths.
Starts to use computerised medical records as well as the Lloyd George
    manuscript notes.
1994   11 unlawful killings + 2 suspicious deaths. 4 natural deaths.
Shipman has maximum number of patients registered with him – 3124.
He stops maintaining/starts destroying his visits book.
1995   29 unlawful killings + I murder conviction + one suspicious death.
    8 natural deaths.
1996   27 unlawful killings + 3 murder convictions + 1 suspicious death. 13
    natural deaths.
Shipman's methods of concealment get more sophisticated, his lies on the
    cremation forms became more elaborate. He began to claim far more
    frequently that someone had seen the deceased alive between his visit and
    the discovery of the death. Shipman also made elaborate pretences to
    allow him to estimate the time of death with more and more accuracy.
1997   32 unlawful killings + 5 murder convictions + 2 suspicious deaths.
    8 natural deaths
1998   1I unlawful killings + 6 murder convictions. 6 natural deaths.
Shipman now perceived as the best doctor in Hyde. But he will now be
    investigated twice for the murders of his patients. The first inquiry will
    clear him.

3046 patients are registered with him.

Forges Kathleen Grundy's will.

Shipman is visited by West Pennine Health Authority. Angela Woodruff reports her suspicions to local police who contact Hyde.

Greater Manchester police begin investigation into death of Kathleen Grundy.

Police also search Shipman's surgery and home address.

Toxicology tests show morphine.

Police examine the 19 deaths brought to light in the March investigation.

Exhumations take place.

Shipman arrested, charged.

1999   Opening of trial at Preston Crown Court.

He pleads not guilty to the 15 counts of murder and the forging of the will.

2000   Shipman convicted on 15 counts of murder and forging the will.

Given 15 life sentences plus 4 years for the forgery.

DPP announces that no further criminal proceedings would be initiated because of the inability for him to have a fair trial.

Coroner now conducts 27 inquests. 25 unlawful killings and 2 open verdicts

2001   Inquiry established.

Coroner opens another 23 inquests.

West Yorkshire Police consider 81 deaths referred to the Coroner during Shipman's time in Todmorden. They carry out detailed investigations into 9 where there thought to be a real possibility of involvement by Shipman.

Police interview Shipman about Todmorden but he refuses to answer questions.

Coroner opens and ajourns inquests on a further 232 deaths.

Public Inquiry holds an opening meeting.

Shipman written to and asked to take part – he declines.

Oral evidence for phase one begins.

2004   Final stages of Inquiry Public forums held.

Shipman commits suicide.

Inquiry has to re-investigate Pontefract.

2005   Final Report published.

SOURCES

To Kill and Kill Again – Dr Shipman
A Brook Lapping Production for ITV 1
Programme script. Compiled by Author
Interview Transcripts. All interviews
carried out by author.
Research Interviews. Undertaken Anna
Shelmerdine (Assistant Producer) and
Beth Salt (Researcher).
Copyright Brook Lapping

The Shipman Inquiry
Chairman Dame Janet Smith DBE
First Report July 2002
Volume One. 'A Death Disguised'
Volume Two. 'Todmorden Decisions'
Volumes Three 'Six. Hyde Decisions'
Second Report July 2003 'The Police
Investigations of March 1998'
Fifth Report 'Pontefract'
Crown Copyright

Greater Manchester Police PACE Audio
Tapes September/October 1998
Recordings of interviews with Harold
Frederick Shipman
Copyright GMP

West Yorkshire Police Video Tape
Interview with Harold Frederick Shipman.
Copyright WYP

Additional Sources

To Kill and Kill Again
A Brook Lapping Production for ITV. 2001
Copyright Brook Lapping
*Prescription for Murder: The True Story of
Dr. Harold Shipman*
Brian Whittle and Jean Ritchie
Copyright Brian Whittle and Jean Ritchie
*Addicted to Murder. The True Story of
Dr. Harold Shipman*
Mikaela Sitford
Copyright Manchester Evening News

Manchester Evening News
(various articles)

Daily Telegraph
20.08.98
26.02.04 Prison was too good for him.
Adam Lusher

Sun
20.08.98

The Times
20.08.98

European Journal for Health
September, 2004

The Observer
19.10.04

INDEX